Set for a King

200 YEARS OF GARDENING AT THE ROYAL PAVILION

Set for a King

200 YEARS OF GARDENING
AT THE ROYAL PAVILION

MIKE JONES

Published in the United Kingdom by
The Royal Pavilion, Museums and Libraries
Brighton, East Sussex

ISBN 0 948723 62 9

Set in Bembo 11.5pt

Printed in the United Kingdom by
B A S Printers, Salisbury

Brighton & Hove

Rosa pimpinellifolia

CONTENTS

The Royal Pavilion Garden Chronology

Aucuba japonica (Spotted Laurel) introduced into England in 1783. The male and female flowers are born on separate plants (the shrub is dioecious). To begin with only the female plant is introduced. In 1861 the male shrub was acquired so that the shiny red berries now brighten dull autumnal corners of our gardens.

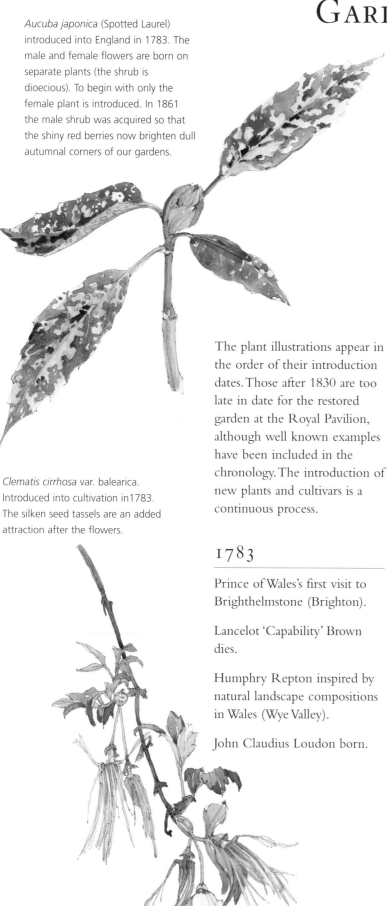

Clematis cirrhosa var. balearica. Introduced into cultivation in1783. The silken seed tassels are an added attraction after the flowers.

The plant illustrations appear in the order of their introduction dates. Those after 1830 are too late in date for the restored garden at the Royal Pavilion, although well known examples have been included in the chronology. The introduction of new plants and cultivars is a continuous process.

1783

Prince of Wales's first visit to Brighthelmstone (Brighton).

Lancelot 'Capability' Brown dies.

Humphry Repton inspired by natural landscape compositions in Wales (Wye Valley).

John Claudius Loudon born.

1786

'Cottage' at Brighton leased on Prince's behalf by Louis Weltje.

Work suspended on Henry Holland's alterations to the Prince's London home, Carlton House, because of mounting debts. Prince uses the rented 'cottage' at Brighton as a refuge.

Holland proposes a formal garden at Althorp for Lord Spencer.

1787

Weltje leases land and property for his own house and the stables for the future Marine Pavilion at Brighton.

Henry Holland summoned from Althorp to design the Marine Pavilion.

Paeonia suffruticosa (Tree peony). First arrives in England in 1787

1788

Symmetrical planting on either side of the lawn separates and frames the new Marine Pavilion. Sundial by John van Nost moved from Hampton Court to Brighton.

Repton sets up as a landscape gardener.

1789

Paris; the Bastille is stormed and the French Revolution begins. Many French flee across the Channel to Brighton. Foreign travel is suspended resulting in more tourists travelling around Britain's beauty spots.

Phormium tenax 1789

1790

Holland proposes chinoiserie designs for Carlton House.

1791

The Rev William Gilpin publishes *Remarks on Forest Scenery and Other Woodland Views*.

Macleaya cordata (Plume poppy) 1792

1792

French Republic declared.

The Prince pays for the draining of the Steine in return for extra land for his garden.

1793-1802

Britain at war with France.

At Brighton the Promenade Grove pleasure garden opened on land opposite the Marine Pavilion.

1795

Holland proposes to extend the Marine Pavilion with a formal garden replacing Weltje's house.

Holland's alterations at Woburn for the Duke of Bedford include a Chinese Dairy.

Lord Foley introduces Repton to John Nash.

1795-1808

Thomas and William Daniell's *Oriental Scenery* published.

1800

Weltje dies. His property becomes part of the Marine Pavilion.

Repton's use of straight lines in garden design approved of by the Prince.

Allium cernuum (Wild onion) 1800

1801-1803

Holland enlarges Marine Pavilion. Angled wings are projected into the new garden.

Samuel Lapidge plants the garden.

Holland proposes a Chinese courtyard garden and purchases land to expand the garden at Brighton. In London he builds a Chinese covered way in Piccadilly.

Liverpool Botanic Garden founded, the first to be opened to the public.

Newly-arrived Chinese plants successfully propagated at Kew.

William Porden (Holland's successor at Brighton) purchases land and property to build the new Stables.

1804-1815

The Napoleonic Wars between France and Britain.

Porden levels and plants the new ground.

1804

The Horticultural Society founded in London.

1805

Repton summoned to transform the Marine Pavilion and its gardens.

Achillea filipendulina (Yarrow) 1803

Kerria japonica (Jew's mantle) 1804

Lilium lancifolium
(Tiger Lily) 1804

Yucca glauca 1817

Olearia paniculata
(Daisy bush) 1816

Mahonia aquifolium
(Oregon grape) 1821-3

1806

Repton presents the Pavilion's Red Book.

1807

Repton designs the garden at Carlton House.

1808

Repton's plans come to nothing, but his designs for the Pavilion published.

1811

Prince of Wales becomes Prince Regent. John Nash appointed architect to his personal residences.

In London Regent Street links Regent's Park to Carlton House.

1812

Marlborough House purchased and incorporated into the Marine Pavilion.

1813

William Townsend Aiton plants garden at Carlton House.

1815

Napoleon defeated at the Battle of Waterloo. Nash designs a tented rotunda in the garden at Carlton House for the victory celebrations.

Nash and Aiton design and plant the 'cottage' in Windsor Great Park (Royal Lodge).

The Prince Regent at Liverpool Botanic Gardens, given poplar trees for the garden at Brighton.

John Furner, the Brighton gardener, summoned to London to meet Nash and Aiton to discuss the new layout and planting of the garden.

Nash's first recorded visit to Brighton.

The first trees and shrubs arrive for the new garden.

A greenhouse built on the former Promenade Grove.

1815–1818

Nash enlarges and transforms the Marine Pavilion.

The first named plants arrive in 1816.

1820

George III dies.

Prince Regent becomes King George IV.

1821

The Horticultural Society leases land from the Duke of Devonshire at Chiswick for their showground.

1823

Sylva Florifera published by Henry Phillips.

1824

Flora Historica published by Henry Phillips.

1826

George IV commissions Nash to prepare a record of the completed building. Nash's *Views* published, including proposed garden plan.

Eschscholtzia californica 1825

Clematis montana 1826

1827

King George IV's last visit to Brighton. John van Nost sundial presented to the Earl of Egmont.

George IV remodels Windsor Castle, Aiton designs a formal garden.

Garrya elliptica
1828

1829

'Wardian' case (a portable miniature greenhouse) invented.

Bougainvillea spectabilis 1829

1830

George IV dies.

Duke of Clarence becomes William IV.

1831

William IV builds the North and South Gates with a straight carriage drive between them separating the garden from the Pavilion.

Wisteria floribunda 1830

1837

William IV dies.

Victoria becomes Queen.

Fatsia japonica 1838

1845

Queen Victoria buys private estate on the Isle of Wight where Prince Albert designs Osborne House.

The tax on glass abolished, making greenhouses popular.

1847

The Pavilion emptied with a view to sale. The garden plants sold at auction.

The Queen commissions watercolours to record the Pavilion and its garden before she leaves.

Clematis 'Victoria' 1850

1850

The Royal Pavilion bought by the Brighton Town Commissioners for £50,000

1851

The grounds opened to the public for the first time.

The Great Exhibition held at the Crystal Palace, designed by Joseph Paxton.

1854-1856

Crimean War.

1858

Japan and China open to European trade. Government of India transferred from East India Company to the British Crown.

Akebia quinata
(Chocolate vine) 1845

Abelia chinensis 1844

Clematis x jackmanni 1858

x Cupressocyparis leylandii
(Leyland Cypress) 1888

1861

The Horticultural Society becomes the 'Royal' Horticultural Society after Prince Albert visits their Chiswick grounds.

1861–1865

American Civil War.

1864

Hillier's Nursery founded at Chichester.

1875

James Shrives, head gardener at Brighton, makes shaped beds for colourful bedding.

A greenhouse was built near the North Gate.

1877

William Morris founds Society for the Protection of Ancient Buildings.

Rosa 'Madame Alfred Carrière' 1878

1878

Exotic tropical plants displayed in the Pavilion's grounds.

1880–1881

First Boer War.

1893

Winter Garden proposed for Pavilion lawns.

1895

Octavia Hill founds the National Trust.

1897

Forsythia. Genus honouring William Forsyth 1737–1804, Curator of the Chelsea Physic Garden. The only European species, *F. europaea*, was not found until 1897.

Clematis armandii 1900

1899–1902

Second Boer War.

1901

Queen Victoria dies.

Edward VII crowned King.

1912

The Royal Horticultural Society holds first show at Chelsea.

Meconopsis delavayi 1913

1914–1918

First World War.

1921

Indian Memorial Gateway presented to Brighton.

1922

Road widening reduces size of garden.

1927

Proposals to extend the Pavilion for banquets.

1939-1945

Second World War.

Rosa 'Peace' 1947

1950

Permanent tea chalet built in the grounds.

Pavilion painted 'duck-egg' blue.

1955

Threat to build Conference Centre and to use grounds as a car park.

Chusan palms arrive from Guernsey.

Rosa 'The Queen Elizabeth' 1954

1955-1980

Bedding schemes continue to add seasonal colour to the East Front and the entrance to the grounds.

1965

Fibreglass minarets used as a restoration solution.

The Garden History Society founded.

1974

Town and Country Amenities Act (first reference to historic gardens in legislation).

1977

Queen Elizabeth II's Silver Jubilee celebrated with a bedding display in the Pavilion Garden.

1979

National Council for the Conservation of Plants and Gardens founded.

1980

Research collated on Regency gardens. Pavilion undergoes full structural restoration.

1981-1982

First shrubberies recreated on the East Front.

1987

Hurricane causes devastation.

1989

First Hampton Court International Flower Show.

1992

Road in front of the Pavilion removed and the turning circle reinstated.

The fibreglass minarets replaced by stone.

1995

First paths and planting established on the West Front.

Visit by HRH The Prince of Wales.

1996

Garden listed by English Heritage.

Fargesia dracocephala (Bamboo) 1979

INTRODUCTION

'A garden is the purest of human pleasures; it is the greatest refreshment to the spirits of man, without which buildings and palaces are but gross handy-works … men come to build stately, sooner than to garden finely; as if gardening were the greater perfection.'

– FRANCIS BACON, *Of Gardens*, 1625.[1]

THE ROYAL PAVILION is one of the top tourist attractions in Britain. It represents a lasting monument to the Regency era in the popular imagination. Stories of indulgence, extravagance and decadence that fuelled the 'pleasure domes of Brighton' are legion: from whoring to boring. For those of us charged with its care the building is simply a work of art. As with exceptional people or ideas this building has the power to lift the spirits; it is that extraordinary. After years of familiarity it can still transform everyday life to a more magical level. What is less obvious are the difficulties which had to be overcome to create the building and the setting that we know today. What was the sequence of events that had taken place? What happened to its garden and how and why was it restored?

This account of the gardens at the Royal Pavilion includes the development of the site, with its buildings. They are interdependent. Each phase of the enlargement of the building was accompanied by a new garden. It began as a tiny circular rented lawn fronting the Steine and became an enclosed space of over seven acres. The changes to the gardens would reflect the stages in the life and fortunes of the heir to the throne, from Prince, to Prince Regent, to King. Each phase adapted the latest trends in gardening and architecture. The site continued to respond to changing fashions and uses long after the King's death.

The exquisite neo-classical building that first replaced the rented house in 1787 was a foretaste of what was to come. The Marine Pavilion was an innovative building for England, let alone the fashionable resort of Brighton. It announced the independence of the twenty-five year old Prince of Wales, his individual sense of style and his sophisticated personality to the town. This building was set on a simple geometric lawn. There was no attempt at privacy; the view of the South Downs from the lawn was then part of the setting.

When extensions were proposed eight years later, they incorporated a formal garden. At this time the siting of a formal garden next to the house was a new idea. The formal style of gardening had not been fashionable in England since the end of the seventeenth century. The Landscape Movement of the eighteenth century had swept them away to create acres of 'stylised' countryside.

By 1802 the Pavilion would reflect the changes in the way that houses were designed and used. It would be less formal with an irregular lawn. The house was extended into the garden with verandahs, canopies, trellis and a conservatory. The earlier formality was softened by disguising the Marine Pavilion as a garden building. This transformed the former eighteenth century building into the nineteenth century resulting in a long, low 'Regency' villa, a decade before the Regency period. Its garden would be designed to form a circuit walk surrounded by trees to provide privacy from the Steine and the encroaching crowds.

Brighton had become the most fashionable seaside resort in England. A building boom and the resultant increase in land prices were due, in part, to the presence of the heir to the throne. At this period a glimpse of the Prince and his Pavilion was more prized than a sea view. In front of the building was an open space, known as the Steine, which became the main focus of the town for fashionable visitors. Society appeared here, rather than on the seafront, using it as an open-air stage set on which to parade, display and meet.

Even for a Prince the difficulties of extending a house and garden in a booming town are obvious. Nearby land and buildings would need to be purchased and roads would have to be diverted. By the time he was Regent, in 1811, all these obstacles had been brilliantly overcome and a grand plan was in place. This remarkable achievement involved complicated negotiations for land, the purchase and demolition of two rows of nearby houses, and the diversion of the main road. Once the difficulties of the site had been overcome, it is easy to imagine the impatience and determination of the Prince to put them into effect. From the outset it would take him over forty years before the final scheme was realised.

The resulting final garden, large for a town centre, was an outstanding example of contemporary ideas on the setting for a house. The composition of the garden took ideas from natural landscape and planting seen in the countryside, adapting them to make irregular shrubberies that projected into the lawns, forming a series of changing pictures or views as one approached the building. The planting combined native and well-known varieties with plants newly introduced into England. The garden included a revolutionary element that we now take for granted; a combination of trees, shrubs and plants, arranged together to provide year-round interest.

The garden would change and develop after the Pavilion Estate was purchased by the Town Commissioners in 1850. The road, which ran in front of the building, having been closed as a town thoroughfare for forty-eight years was reinstated. The grounds were used as a green open space, for concerts, lawn tennis and relaxation, a welcome retreat from the busy town centre. The garden survived proposals to build over parts of the grounds to provide new amenities such as a large Winter Garden and a conference centre. The Victorian fashion for colourful bedding would result in spectacular seasonal displays in these gardens up to the 1980s. Brighton was famous for its annual flower displays and designs for bedding out were exchanged with other towns. Local government reorganisation of parks and gardens departments brought dramatic changes; areas that had been beautifully planted and looked after were flattened and simplified in the move to balance maintenance costs with diminishing resources. The Pavilion's garden became mostly lawns overshadowed by large trees. The relationship of the building to its setting was lost and the tarmac areas were used as a car park.

The garden has now been remade. It was the first major restoration of a Regency garden in Britain. It will be the main focus of this account and was the inspiration for it. After two decades the garden has matured and can now be appreciated in all its seasonal aspects, from the arrangement of evergreens and flowering shrubs in the winter to the floriferous height of summer. The plants (only those available before 1830 have been used) have become sought after and visitors often take more photographs of the garden than of the Pavilion itself. The garden has been listed by English Heritage. This large central space is planted with such variety and complexity that it requires constant attention and care if the principles behind it are to be maintained. A small team of volunteers tend the garden under the professional guidance of the Head Gardener. The restored garden is a haven for wildlife as well as a green space enjoyed by residents and visitors alike. The demands of the twenty-first century must be taken into account. Few historic gardens cater for hundreds of people lunching on the grass, or staging public music performances whilst maintaining access for fire engines, or managing the threat of increasing vandalism and anti-social behaviour. It is an enormous challenge.

The garden is no longer a private space or a Royal retreat. A rare shrub to a gardener can all too easily become an obstacle to those using it as a recreational space. The garden has been through 200 years of change. As it continues to evolve its future will depend on the attitude of those who use it and the determination of those who care for it. The removal of the road in front of the building and the reinstatement of the original layout of the garden has reunited the Royal Pavilion with its intended setting to delight future generations of Brightonians and our visitors.

The Prince of Wales first visited Brighton in 1783. As his carriage pulled up in front of Grove House he faced the land that would become this unique garden. The sequence of events that would lead to its creation forms an extraordinary story.

LEFT A queue for seeds from the restored garden, 2004.

A New Era for
Gardening and Brighton

IN SEPTEMBER 1783 the Prince of Wales's uncle, the Duke of Cumberland, was staying at Grove House in Brighton. He had leased the large, newly built house. Owing to the success of the fashionable seaside resort the Season would extend until Christmas. Grove House was to play an important role in the future of the Pavilion and its garden. Looking across the road from its entrance front was a grove of elm trees, which gave the house its name. Its position on the site can be seen in the drawing on page 21. Grove House was on the edge of the town, in an enviable position with open views over the surrounding Downs. These formed a kind of arena, centred on the Steine, the flat open space in front. To the Duke and his friends, besides the attractions of the town, Brighton offered good riding and hunting country. His hunting parties would often meet and set off from the Steine with his own pack of hounds. His royal nephew was also a keen sportsman.

The Steine was the main promenading area. It was the place to see and be seen, the hub of the town. The *Morning Herald* of 26 September 1782 sets the scene. 'This place is, at last, as full as an egg, but the company is a motley group, I assure you … The Duke of Cumberland is at the head of the whole … and associates with all, from the Baron down to the Blackleg! Play runs high, particularly at Whist … We have every kind of amusement that fancy can desire for the train of folly and dissipation; and all are crowded beyond measure! … few people think of stirring from hence.'

Such reports would have reached the Prince and his father. In deciding to visit his uncle, the Prince had gone against the wishes of his parents, who thoroughly disapproved of the Duke of Cumberland's profligate lifestyle. Now, at the age of twenty-one, he wasted no time. Mrs Lybbe Powys, a regular on the society circuit, wrote in her diary after seeing the Prince at a ball, 'with such ease and grace he dances that he was sure to be known by his manner, tho' without star or other signature of his birth … what a pity that such an accomplish'd young man, knowing so well how to make himself admired and beloved, can be wanting in duty to such parents as his'.[2]

On Sunday, 7 September 1783, the young Prince made his first visit to Brighton. He stayed with his uncle at Grove House. That evening they appeared on the nearby Steine. It was the height of the season and the place was packed with visitors. There were gun salutes, fireworks, bells rang and the town was specially lit up for the occasion.

It was a new era for the town; changes were in the air, which would also affect the countryside. Society was undergoing a period of great change. The countryside had been opened up, becoming more accessible and easier to visit. Roads and transport had improved so that touring the countryside, visiting country houses and towns such as Brighton became quicker and more comfortable for those with the means and leisure time. There were new light sprung coaches and carriages. The Prince of Wales had his own phaeton, the sports car of the eighteenth century. The ease of travel was a boon to architects and gardeners. A celebrity such as 'Capability' Brown had not only changed the face of England, but had travelled it! In gardening there was an increased

interest in natural countryside. Garden design would reflect the new enthusiasm for looking at Nature unimproved by man.

At this key date, 1783, the principal influences on the future development of gardening ideas were already in place. They would all eventually be represented in the garden at Brighton. 'Capability' Brown, the most famous landscape maker in England died in 1783. His successor, Humphry Repton, was already influenced by the new fashion for looking at 'natural' landscape, untouched by man. Repton later modified Brown's parks and separated the garden from the park. 1783 was also the year in which John Claudius Loudon was born. He would adapt and build on Repton's ideas to suit the growing urban mass market as gardens became smaller.

Lancelot 'Capability' Brown had changed the look of thousands of acres of countryside that belonged to his influential and wealthy clients. He earned his nickname from his ability to realise the capabilities of the landscape that he was commissioned to improve. His fame was perhaps linked to the fact that he was creating a national style of gardening. The reputation of England as a nation of gardeners dates from the eighteenth century; until then there was no native English garden style. Gardens had been modified versions of Italian, French or Dutch styles. Now Britain would lead Europe in gardening ideas. The influence of the English Landscape Movement would spread as far as Russia and America.

Brown created idealised landscaped parks. His way of laying out grounds became the accepted fashion. Naturalism in garden design was a completely new idea at the beginning of the eighteenth century. To make the new landscapes existing formal gardens and geometric avenues were removed. The new parks were easier to maintain than formal gardens and had the added benefit of producing valuable timber.[3] Vast acres were transformed and composed as a picture using as many as 100,000 oak trees to create a beautiful landscape setting. That investment was also a source of future income for the family.

To contemporaries, this style was seen as the triumph of Nature over Art. Mrs Lybbe Powys, commenting on the garden at Holkham Hall in Norfolk, thought the changes towards naturalism had not gone far enough. She thought it boasted more 'art than nature's charms, and to me the reverse is so much more pleasing'.[4] This very telling comment sums up the way that 'Nature's charms' had won the day. The new 'natural' landscapes were, in fact, completely artificial as no natural landscape ever looked like these designed spaces. At Croome Court in Worcestershire, Brown's first architectural commission (1751), he had positioned the house in open parkland. He drained and transformed the waterlogged marshland into a landscape that forty years later the *Gentleman's Magazine*, 1792, commented that, 'If there be a spot to make a death bed terrible, it is Lord Coventry's at Croome'. George III visited Croome in July 1788, when he was nearby at Cheltenham, taking the waters. It makes a telling contrast that in the same year the Prince of Wales was at Brighton enjoying his new house and freedom. Nature had been reduced to a simple, grand formula of gently rolling acres of grass, trees and an irregular reflecting lake. The success of these artificial landscaped parks depended on unlimited acres of land. At Brighton, as elsewhere, Brown's formula would not adapt well to small plots although it was tried as a temporary solution. Also at Brighton the desirability of a lake would be proposed several times. Jane Austen's popular novels made landscape design a potent symbol of genteel aspirations and social acceptability. The quiet serenity and the softly rounded forms of the landscaped parks related to the philosopher Edmund Burke's idea of Beauty as being feminine. Beauty was sensual as 'nothing very suddenly varied can be beautiful … most people must have observed the sort of sense they have had, of being swiftly drawn in an easy coach on a smooth turf, with gradual ascents and declivities'.[5] This smooth perfection would soon be thought of as bland and boring. These artificial domains encircled by trees had shut out the world with Nature tamed to a formulaic sameness. The parks had many limitations and critics. Such landscapes lacked excitement, variety, surprise and interesting plants. Above all they were criticised for not representing the attributes of 'real' landscape.

Landscape paintings, brought back from the obligatory Grand Tour by the eighteenth-century grandees, were an important influence on the way that landscape was viewed, appreciated and recreated in the landscaped parks. The seventeenth-century paintings and drawings of Claude Lorraine, that were based on observed landscape and plant groupings selected and sketched in the Roman countryside, were so popular that the 'Claude Glass' had been invented. The Claude glass was a slightly convex mirror backed with black foil. It reflected views of a landscape, formed as *pittoresco* (from a picture). Travellers could now create their own 'Italian' landscapes at home.[6] The glass became part of the standard tourist or artist's equipment and enabled the traveller to see their edited views of the countryside transformed immediately into a Claudian picture, reflected in a tinted mirror.[7]

Perhaps inevitably after Brown's death a reaction set in against his stylised landscapes. Nature as it was found, rather than as created by a 'Capability' Brown, became a new craze.

By 1783, Humphry Repton was already sketching the celebrated natural landscape at Welsh beauty spots.[8] Repton, in separating the garden from the park, would later reintroduce formality to garden design. The new fashion would be for the house to be linked by terraces and conservatories to the garden. This was a perfect response to the influx of new and exotic plants, which were arriving from abroad through the expanding nursery trade. Repton described a formal terrace as 'an additional room or gallery, [in] which when there is much company, [it is a] delight to saunter on such an esplanade'.[9] At

BELOW Thomas Gainsborough, *Study of a Man Sketching Using a Claude Glass*, c.1755, pencil sketch.
© The Trustees of The British Museum. The idea was to scan the view through the convex mirror glass, as if looking through a camera lens, with your back to the landscape and the face of the glass screened from the sun. Several different types were produced, some with filters or silvered mirrors for overcast days. The image could be simply enjoyed or sketched since it was already composed and framed.

LEFT *Koelreuteria paniculata* (Pride of India). The 6th Earl of Coventry, the owner of Croome, is credited with the introduction of many plants from abroad, including this tree from China. It was sent to him in 1763. The Pavilion garden has a specimen positioned near the path at the side of the Dome. As well as the pyramidal panicles of flowers, the leaves turn butter-yellow in Autumn with spectacular pink seed pods, especially after a hot summer.

Sheringham in Norfolk Repton's embellishments blurred the divide between outside and inside, giving ample opportunity for the new craze for horticulture. Repton in calling himself a landscape gardener, had differentiated himself from the former 'place makers' of the Brown school. His view that 'Gardens are works of art rather than of nature', was used on the frontispiece to his *Designs for the Pavillon* [sic] *at Brighton*, 1808. Repton had brought back a welcome note of colour and scent as flowers would again become an important element in the composition of a garden seen from the house. The flower garden returned to centre stage; formerly flowers were hidden in separate enclosures within landscaped parks.[10] Repton had sensed this new market for landscape garden–ing (he was the first to use the term): 'Within the last 40 years the property & even the characters of individuals have undergone more change than in any other period of the English History'.[11]

BELOW Vase from Loudon's *The Suburban Gardener and Villa Companion*, 1838. Mass-produced garden ornaments became fashionable. The Pavilion would have many examples decorating the later grounds.

ABOVE Sheringham, Norfolk, 1812, Humphry Repton. He was particularly pleased with this commission. It shows the way that houses were now integrated into their setting. Unlike Croome, the house is linked to the wider landscape with a terrace, used as a platform to extend the house into the garden and gives views over the surrounding countryside. The garden is seen as an artificial setting next to the artificial house. The artificial aspects of a garden would be developed by Loudon. The right-hand side garden at Sheringham was a precursor to many suburban aspirations.

RIGHT Flower garden, Hoole House, near Chester, 1850. Loudon praised this garden in his *Villa Gardener*. The uniformity of the circular beds contrasted with the irregularity of the rock work, which was taken from a model of the mountains of Savoy. Circular edged beds had been proposed at Brighton and used by Repton in the garden at Sheringham. At both they were to be scattered over the lawn. At Hoole House they have become a regimented formal garden motif.

In Repton's proposals for Brighton the garden would be linked to the house with long glazed corridors filled with seasonal flowers. He called it 'a perpetual garden … it will be necessary to provide for a regular succession of plants; and the means of removing and transplanting'.[12] This return to formality was perfectly suited to the smaller gardens of the new villa owners and also the industrial tycoons who would want different ideas as power and influence moved down the social scale. Loudon, through his many publications, would distil gardening fashions and bring them to an increasingly enthusiastic gardening public. He was one of the first gardening 'professionals'. Loudon and his wife provided encouragement, education and practical help to gardeners. Over time the garden at Brighton would reflect changing gardening styles, from a green landscape of trees and grass to ornamental shrubberies with flowers, to blazing shows of carpet bedding.

ABOVE Repton's flower corridor from his *Designs for the Pavillon* [sic], 1808. The long glazed areas linked to the house would have provided a delightful perimeter walk, especially in winter. The staging of the plants was a precursor to later bedding-out displays. The gentleman in top hat and cane could represent Repton, the two gardeners, with their aprons tucked in, the local Furner brothers, who were employed by the Prince at Brighton.

2

SETTING THE SCENE

'a pretty and picturesque little fabric … where a few shrubs and roses shut out the road, and the eye looked unobstructed over the ocean'.

– GEORGE CROLY, *The Personal History of George IV*, 1841.

BELOW Johann Sebastian Müller, after Samuel Wale (detail), *General Prospect of Vauxhall Gardens*, 1751. © The Trustees of the British Museum. The Promenade Grove in Brighton had conforming avenues of trees, gateways and constructions. Both had a structure called The Saloon. The central space was used for entertainments, music and refreshments. At Brighton, the houses in the foreground would be fronting North Street and on the area above the enclosure the stables would be built.

BELOW-RIGHT T. Rowlandson, *Vauxhall Gardens* (detail), 1779. © The Trustees of the British Museum. The Promenade Grove would have been a similar, though smaller enclosure. It also attracted large crowds, including the Prince of Wales, who is seen here at the front on the extreme right-hand side, accompanied by the actress 'Perdita' Robinson. The gardens at Brighton were illuminated and as at Vauxhall there were spectacular firework displays.

AFTER THE SUCCESS of his first visit in September 1783 the Prince of Wales rented Grove House for the following two seasons. By the 1780s Brighton was already well established as a fashionable health resort, on a par with Bath or Tunbridge Wells. The Prince's decision to return to the town and build himself a residence ensured its social status and future prosperity. The improvements in road travel enabled the members of fashionable society (and Royal hangers-on) who surrounded the young Prince to follow him to the coast after the London season finished at the end of June. The Prince of Wales was the principal arbiter of style and fashion. This would soon be seen in his plans for a house at Brighton.

Brighton had considerable advantages over other resorts. It had all the attractions required by fashionable visitors: assembly rooms, inns, circulating libraries, shops, a race course and a theatre. In addition it had the Steine and the Downs, sea bathing, medicinal sea-water cures, spas and was now favoured by the heir to the throne. It was a short journey from London and the Channel crossing from Brighton was one of the most popular routes to the Continent. It was a winning combination; Brighton was no longer provincial.

Visiting society also required the provision of a pleasure garden as part of the attractions. A garden called the Promenade Grove opened in Brighton in 1793. It was on the opposite side of the main road to Grove House (opposite). Although it was smaller than the Vauxhall Pleasure Gardens in London (a noted outdoor venue for amusement and popular entertainments), there were similarities, as described in a contemporary guidebook, 'These beautiful gardens surrounded with large

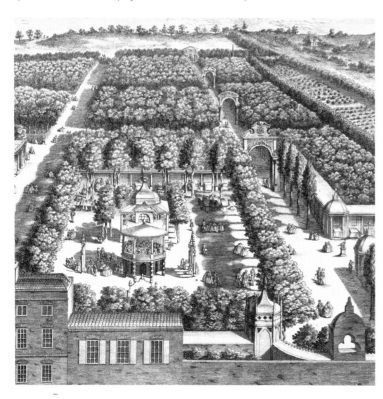

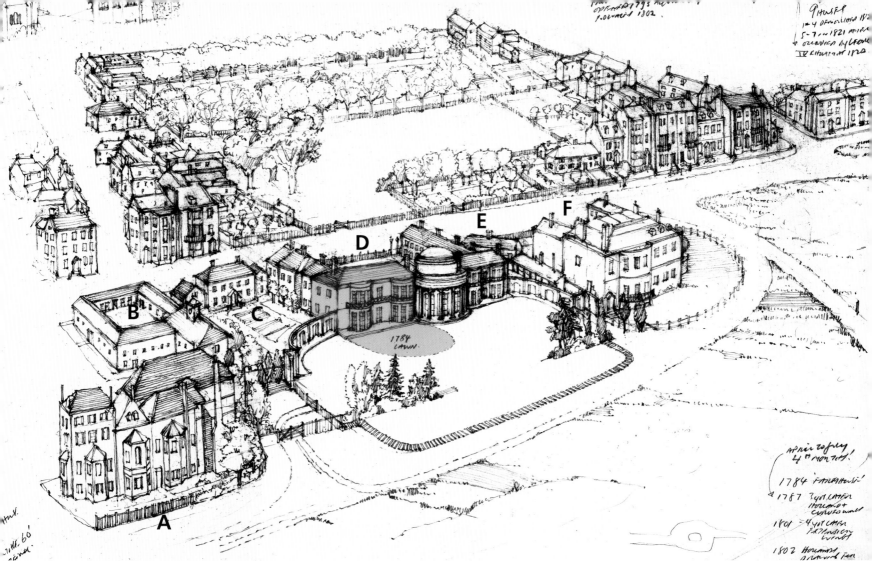

overspreading trees … are supported by subscription, and are open every day … Parties … come here to breakfast, drink tea, take refreshments … read the papers … The saloon, which is fitted up in a style of neatness is expressibly elegant. The orchestra is an Octagonal building adjoining … although the gardens are quite in their infancy, they promise to be one of the most fashionable places of amusement in Brighton'.[13] The place would be packed with visitors, more so if there was a special evening event or if the Prince of Wales put in an appearance.

ABOVE Reconstruction of the site at Brighton, c.1794. Great East Street runs straight through the site, cutting off the Marine Pavilion from the land opposite. The Promenade Grove, at the top of the sketch, has avenues of shady elm trees. From the left (A) represents the Castle Tavern and ballroom, (B) the stables, (C) Weltje's house and garden, (D) the Marine Pavilion with its entrance court facing the street and the garden front, extended with a ha-ha facing the recently drained Steine, (E) represents the kitchen and outside court built against the large blank wall of (F) Grove House. The balanced curved walls either side of the Marine Pavilion hid the kitchen area on one side and Weltje's house and garden on the other. The shaded area represents the first rented house and circular lawn as shown on Yeakell and Gardner's map (p.24).

LEFT The Promenade Grove drawn by Repton. *Designs for the Pavillon* (sic) *at Brighton* 1808.

The idea of using a garden as an outside room for entertaining was later taken up by the Prince, when Regent, at his house in London. Promenade Grove was a commercial venture that provided an outdoor garden area surrounded by avenues of elm trees. At Brighton they were the only trees in the town centre, which must have made it a popular alternative to the Steine for promenading.

By this time the use of avenues in garden design was old fashioned; they had been swept away by the fashion for naturalistic parkland: 'in the ancient style of gardening, these kinds of walks were considered as great ornaments; no country seat was without them, many still permit the old ones to stand....but modern planters rarely admit any such thing as a regular Avenue in their designs; even often demolishing entirely the old ones of a century or two standing'.[14] In the late eighteenth century avenues became one of the first conservation issues to affect gardens. Brown was accused of destroying them and Henry Holland, the first architect commissioned by the Prince of Wales, advised that they be kept. Promenade Grove was later purchased by the Prince of Wales and incorporated into his garden. Repton, the landscape gardener, when he was summoned to advise on improvements to the grounds in 1805, would propose that one of the avenues be cut down. Within twenty years of the Prince's first visit magnificent stables and a riding house were built, centred on the main avenue of Promenade Grove. Grove House itself and its garden would become part of the Pavilion. The house was eventually demolished to allow for the completion of the Music Room and the erection of the north front of the Royal Pavilion.

The area of land between Grove House and the Castle Tavern facing the Steine was to be the site of his first house. The only visual record we have of what the area looked like is Lambert's view of 1765. This clearly shows a large barn and rickyards on the site a decade earlier. The land was developed by Thomas Kemp whose family had owned parcels of this land since 1775. The exact details of the transactions are complex, but we do know that the barn is still shown in Donowell's view of 1778. The land must have been developed immediately afterwards since by the following year, Yeakell and Gardner's map (p.24) shows a house on the site of the barn.[15]

The property was leased from Kemp by Louis Weltje the Prince's cook and factotum, who in turn, rented it to the Prince. The *Sussex Weekly Advertiser* of 6 November 1786, announced the news, 'we are well assured that the Prince of Wales has taken Mr Kemp's house ... on a lease of three

LEFT John Donowell, *A Perspective View of the Steyne at Brighthelm-stone*, 1778 (detail). A view from the sea end of the flat open Steine and surrounding Downs. The building on the right is a library and orchestra tower. Facing it, on the opposite side, is the Castle Tavern. Within nine years the area just beyond the tavern would become the first garden of the Marine Pavilion.

years, a convincing proof of his … partiality to that place'. We do not know what this first house looked like. Humphry Repton, on his visit in 1805, drew an impression of the existing view from the front door of the Marine Pavilion. It gives an idea of the general atmosphere of the place and included part of the property before it was redesigned. It resembles a corner of a typical rural Sussex village (p.60).

For the Prince this first house became a modest refuge where he could distance himself from the enormous debts he had run up at Carlton House, his London residence, which was being re-modelled by the fashionable young architect Henry Holland. Work was suspended in 1786 and he returned to Brighton for the season, based in his new house. The only description we have of this first house was written many years later when it was described as a 'a pretty and picturesque little fabric … in a small piece of ground where a few shrubs and roses shut out the road (Great East Street), and the eye looked unobstructed over the ocean … yet the happiest hours of the Prince's life were spent in this cottage'.[16]

The Prince's ostentatious display of economy portraying himself as a cottage dweller struck a chord. The ideal of a simple life, not too far from London became a fashion, from which the *cottage orné*, or decorated cottage was to develop. Jane Austen's character, Robert Ferras, in *Sense and Sensibility* describes their appeal: 'For my own part … I am excessively fond of a cottage; there is always so much comfort, so much elegance about them. And I protest, if I had any money to spare, I should … build one myself, within a short distance of London, where I might drive myself down at any time, and collect a few friends about me, and be happy. I advise everybody who is going to build, to build a cottage'.[17]

Unintentionally the Prince of Wales was ahead of the fashion, although he did not remain a cottage dweller for long. He was able to enjoy the best of both worlds in that his 'cottage' was on the edge of the most fashionable town in the country. Ironically he began his architectural pro-jects with a modest house and he later remodelled a cottage in Windsor Great Park. Royal Lodge, as it would be called, became an enormous secluded *cottage orné*. In both instances John Nash would be called in to make dramatic changes to the existing buildings. Both would reflect stages in the Prince's life. At Brighton as a young Prince he wanted to be near to and part of society. Later at Windsor, as King, he wanted to be as far away from it as possible. The gardens at both properties would reinforce his changing attitude to public visibility.

The 1779 map of Brighton by Yeakell and Gardner, shows the house, garden and adjoining areas. The location on the map has been shaded. From the angled bay windows of the house, overlooking the lawn, the Steine and the sea can be clearly seen. The curved lawn in front of the building is shown fenced round. The entrance to the property was through the formal, stylised garden which faced Great East Street. The only description of the garden was 'a few shrubs and roses to shut out the road'. It was probably typical of many small gardens. As the building was new it would have been recently planted. At this date urban gardens were usually laid out with simple areas of grass or beds with paths between and shrubs or fruit trees around the edge. The varieties of roses that could have been seen in this small front garden were later to be incorporated in the planting of the Regency garden at Brighton.

On the map is a fenced circular clump of trees in front of the curved lawn. A sketch of the park at Warwick Castle (opposite) shows a similar group of trees. In eighteenth-century parks, clumps of trees were used to break up the expanse of grass and provide massed effect. The fencing protected them from animals until they were established and could be thinned out. Repton objected to the look of clumps of trees. To him they demonstrated a lack of tree management, 'small plantations of trees, surrounded by a fence, are the best expedients to form groups, because trees

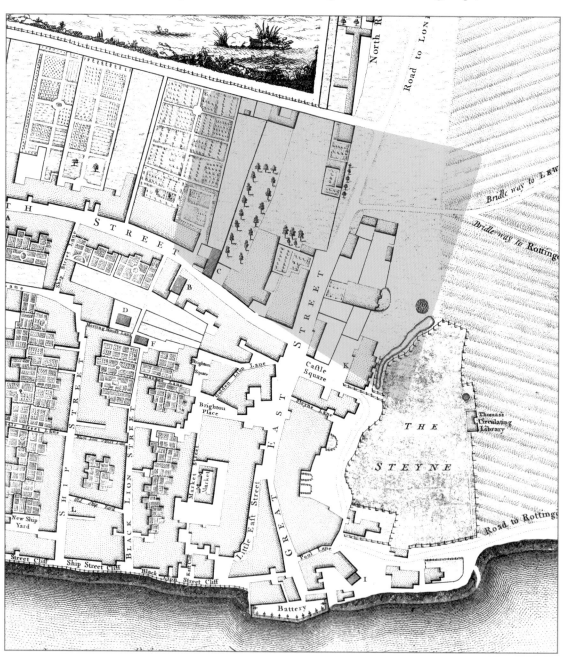

planted singly seldom grow well; neglect of thinning and of removing the fence, has produced that ugly deformity called a "Clump"'.[18] Clumps of trees, which had been a feature of eighteenth-century parks would later be ridiculed. There is an amusing reference to round clumps in Thomas Love Peacock's *Headlong Hall*, written in 1815. One of his characters is taking a swipe at this kind of landscape: 'I never saw one of your improved places, as you call them, and which are nothing but big bowling-greens, like sheets of green paper, with a parcel of round clumps scattered over them, like so many spots of ink, flicked at random out of a pen'.[19]

The rectangles of market gardens in the top left area of the map belonged to the Furner family who made their living from them. They played a major role in the development of the Pavilion's grounds. John Furner and his brother were employed as gardeners by the Prince. Their long strip of market gardens were

purchased and a road was built over part of them. The thin meandering shape between the Steine and the round clump of trees was a strip of water. It often flooded as it was fed by a spring further up the valley and this explained why the Steine had not been developed. The area was later drained by the Prince and in return he was allowed to take in some of the land to extend his garden.

Throughout the negotiations the Prince used Weltje, first as a go-between and then as the Prince's landlord. This minimised and hid any apparent expense. Predictably the Prince was soon anxious to enlarge his cottage and Weltje's next role was to finance the building of the Marine Pavilion.

In May 1787 Weltje leased additional property,[20] which became Weltje's own house and the new stables for the Marine Pavilion. The frequent use of Weltje as an intermediary led to complications when he died three years later. Ownership should have reverted to the lord of the manor, but Weltje had sublet it to the Prince of Wales. The property was seized and granted to his wife and brother as his heirs. The Prince eventually had to purchase it from them in 1807 for £17,000, which, ironically, was loaned to him by Christopher Weltje, the brother.[21]

Also in May 1787 the *Sussex Weekly Advertiser* announced: 'The Prince of Wales is expected today to view the improvements being made to his Royal Highness's House there … it is to be finished … by beginning of July next. For the accomplishment of which there are upwards of 150 workmen employed on it'. They were building the Marine Pavilion, designed by Henry Holland, whose work for the Prince at Carlton House had been temporarily suspended the year before. In the intervening period Holland had redesigned Althorp in Northamptonshire and had drawn up proposals to transform its garden. He would later make similar innovative proposals for the garden of the Marine Pavilion after Weltje had died.

The new Holland building was called the Marine Pavilion for the first time in Weltje's lease to the Prince, dated 1 March 1788. It comprised 'messuage [house] or Tenement with the Court Yard, Stables, Coach Houses, Gardens and Appurtenances … and also an Ice House and a Room over the same, for the term of Twenty-one years from Christmas One Thousand seven hundred and Eighty seven … and also the House, Coach House and Stables which were then building by the said Louis Weltje, and which were afterwards in his Occupation …'[22]

Weltje's own house and the Stables were the last part of this first phase to be constructed. They were not complete by March 1788 and his large garden had been left blank on the Holland plan.

The next phase of the development of the site would begin in seven years. In total, four of the most fashionable architects of the day would be involved at the site. Three of the four would be involved in the garden. Six gardeners, including the Royal gardener, would be called upon to make the grounds.

3

THE FIRST GARDEN

'his new house is very handsome ... and a good deal of ground before with a Ha! Ha!'

— ANON., *a letter from Brighton,* 1787.

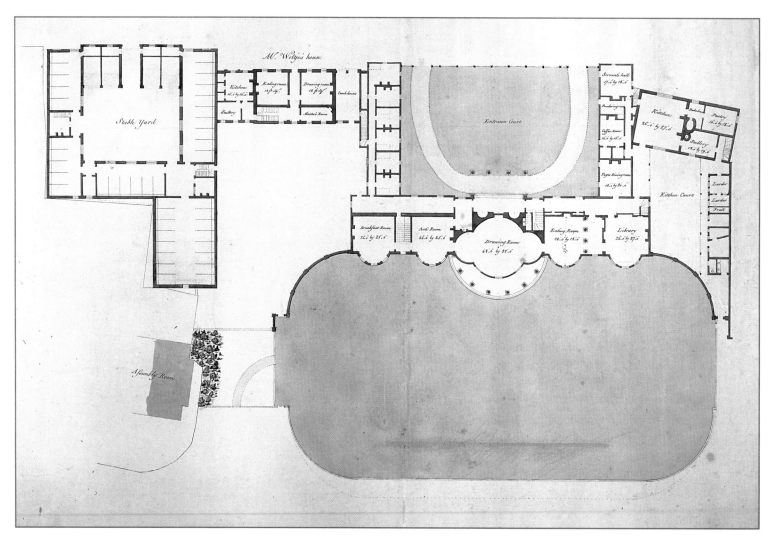

ABOVE Henry Holland's 1787 plan. The only planting indicated is a group of trees to hide the Assembly Rooms of the Castle Tavern. The area from Weltje's house to the curved wall is blank. The outline of the lawn mirrors the plan of the building.

IN HOLLAND'S 1787 plan for the first Marine Pavilion the area adjoining Weltje's house was left blank. Contemporary sketches show vestiges of planting in the space as the building work was taking place. S. H. Grimm's watercolour shows the building under construction and also Weltje's own house, which had just been purchased. It was later remodelled by Holland, made taller, with larger windows and the same shutters as the Marine Pavilion. This house was rebuilt last so that Weltje could be on site during the construction of the Marine Pavilion. Some of the building materials for the Marine Pavilion were reused from Carlton House.[23] This apparent cost-saving measure would later lead to disagreements over Weltje's estimates for the building costs. Grimm's sketch shows huge mounds of earth in front of the building. As there were limited foundations for Holland's building they related to work in the garden. Nash later criticised Holland for his lack of preparatory work. His buildings 'were of the slightest kind being constructed with timber placed on a few courses of brick upon the damp soil without cellars or excavation under the floor so that they were subject to the rot, generated by stagnant exhalations from the ground'.[24]

The Saloon windows were to be of plate glass. They had not arrived at the time of Grimm's sketch and the stone platform, apart from the section under the Saloon columns, was incomplete. The mounds of earth must relate to the levelling and preparation of the ground. As can be seen, the ground was then below the French windows. They could be heaps of soil and marle, a kind of manure.[25] We know from the garden accounts that many cartloads of marle were used as a fertiliser in the Pavilion gardens. Weltje's house and garden area can be seen on the left, although they were to be hidden by the curved side walls, then being built. The building of the Marine Pavilion was completed in four months, from April to July 1787. The advantage of the building methods criticised by Nash was the speed with which the building could be transformed.

Edye's watercolour gives an impression of the completed Marine Pavilion, Weltje's new house and the curved side walls. Weltje's garden is now planted, and trees including a poplar mask the bulk of the Castle Tavern. Poplar trees would be used in the garden of the Royal Pavilion later. They were the quickest growing trees. In this view the Saloon windows, all the shutters and the stone platform are in place. The trees behind the chimney pots were in Dairy Field, across the road from the Marine Pavilion. They would later be incorporated into the garden. The lawn is awaiting it sunken fence and the window balconies their decorative railings. The curved side walls are shown planted, but the lawn is at an early stage.

Middleton's view, one of the most accurate and detailed, depicts the building a year after its completion. Now we see a balanced composition of trees and shrubs at either side of the building appearing as theatrical 'flats' in the manner of stage scenery (one can imagine pushing on the wings of greenery). The planting was an attempt to prevent the eye from seeing just a group of disparate buildings; the ballroom of the Castle Tavern on the left, the Marine Pavilion and Grove House. The curved lawn is surrounded with a wide ha-ha, or sunken ditch, in this case with flat rails on the top to prevent people from falling in (hence the name). The ha-ha provided a barrier, but did not interrupt the views from the windows. The flat railed ha-ha was described by Loudon as an invisible fence 'With the advantage that it remained unseen from every point of view. An excavation is formed eighteen to twenty inches deep and six or eight feet wide; a railing made of larch wood is placed horizontally above it; the bottom … is sown with grass seeds, which will grow about as high as the rail, and, covering it, will render the hole invisible. Should it grow much higher, it can easily be topped with a scythe. This will be a sufficient barrier for sheep, cattle etc. … the objection that in winter it may be covered with snow could be easily remedied, by fixing it upright at that season'.[26]

A letter written from Brighton on 22 August 1787 gives a glimpse of the Prince at Brighton and of his new house, a month after its completion, 'We have frequent views of His Royal Highness and Mrs Fitzherbert, the Duke and Duchess of Cumberland … last night they were all walking on the Steine, the P- between the Duchess and Mrs F-. Each had hold of an arm, and in that manner went tugging him along; his new house is very handsome, a grand Dome in the Centre, with Wings, and a good deal of ground before with a Ha! Ha! and behind is a noble square, with Pillars and Lamps between, the stables are not yet finished'.[27]

The pillars (of the portico) and the lamps can be seen in a watercolour of c.1787 showing the entrance front facing Great East Street (opposite). The indistinct silhouette in the centre represents a sundial. It had initially been placed on the entrance front to William III's new Privy Garden at Hampton Court. That famously elaborate formal garden (recently restored) incorporated statuary as focal points in the design. The sundial was supported by a painted lead figure of a 'blackamoor' by John van Nost, a celebrated sculptor who had installed it at Hampton Court in 1701.[28] The figure must have

contrasted with the numerous other classical marble sculptures in that garden. It was removed from Hampton Court and positioned directly outside the Marine Pavilion, yet near the road, for all visitors to see. According to a contemporary guide book, 'In the court is an handsome dial, supported by the figure of a Negro, which is much admired for its beauty and accuracy, as is the figure for its elegance and justness of sculpture'.[29]

ABOVE *The West Front of the Pavilion*, 1787, watercolour from Holland's office. The elegant lamps, topped with the Prince of Wales's feathers swung within their supporting brackets. The 'comings' and 'goings' at the Entrance Portico were disguised with large shrubs. The sundial in the centre, directly behind the fence, provided a good time-check for visitors, or even coaches on the busy road in front.

The planting depicted in Middleton's view from the Steine would have suited a gentleman's residence. It was a 'tough' composition of evergreens. The landscape gardener and surveyor William Marshall, describes 'Masculine' planting as 'the box, the Holly and Laurustinus'. He thought that 'the species of shrub should vary with the intention. If the principle intention be a winter retreat, evergreens, and the early blowing [flowering] shrubs should predominate, but in a place to be frequented in summer and autumn, the deciduous trees ought chiefly to be planted'.[30]

This comment is apt for Brighton where the season for visiting was to extend to the winter. Evergreens would look good all the time. The Marine Pavilion would challenge any garden designer: its hard, sophisticated elegance would not allow for any fuss. It demanded a strong handsome setting, the 'star of the show' would always be the building itself. The planting seems ahead of its time. It is almost a Regency ornamental shrubbery twenty-five years before the Regency. All that was needed was a more irregular, relaxed and natural outline with the introduction of flowers and more mixed-height planting for the idea of the Regency shrubbery to be realised. J. C. Loudon, one of the most prolific writers on gardening, advised in 1806 on the grouping of trees for ornamental effect. He selects evergreens, 'Scotch fir – first from its uncommon picturesqueness and ease with which it may be grown in almost any situation. It mixes beautifully with exotic evergreens, as Laurel, Box, Privet, Holly and Arbutus'.[31] The use of evergreens was appropriate to the site as Loudon remarked that the 'best exposure for a garden is the south east … trees of the fir kind make the best shelter'.

The scale of the trees suggests that they must have been planted semi-mature, which was an accepted part of landscape gardening. Loudon also explains why these trees may not have lasted long, 'some trees die when transplanted after they are eight to ten feet high, as the Pine and the Fir tribe'.[32] In fact it would not have mattered if the trees had not survived because within eight years the whole garden would be redesigned.

LEFT John van Nost, *The Hampton Court Moor*, a painted lead figure, kneeling and supporting a Portland stone salver with bronze sundial. The life-size figure, cast in 1701, cost £30. It was painted by Thomas Highmore and was originally sited in the Privy Garden at Hampton Court. By descent to George IV until c.1829. Reproduced by courtesy of Christie's.

ARCHITECTURAL FORMALITY
IN THE GARDEN

'There is an august simplicity that astonished me'.

— HORACE WALPOLE, 1785.[33]

IN 1795 HENRY Holland drew up proposals to extend the Marine Pavilion. Looking at the plan, it can be seen that Weltje's house was to be demolished and replaced by a circular formal garden. It filled the space exactly. The outline extended to what was the front building line of Weltje's house, facing Great East Street. Holland had included a similar design in his own London garden. It was an architectural response to garden making, and one that he repeated at other houses. Five years earlier, drawings had been made for Lord Spencer at Althorp House in Northamptonshire. In one of his proposals for altering the grounds around that house, Holland drew a circular formal garden. It was a flower garden with open trellis around the enclosure; the same device may have been planned at Brighton. At Althorp it was a kind of secret garden, separated from the wider landscape, but accessible from the house. It is easy to imagine the surprise and delight of entering this ordered, coloured and scented seclusion. Holland's father-in-law, Capability Brown, had disguised areas for flower gardens in his parks with dense planting, not trellis. They were hidden in separate enclosures so as not to confuse his grand, simple formula of uninterrupted landscape. It is amusing to think that flowers would have spoilt the view!

RIGHT Henry Holland, *Ground Floor Plan of the Marine Pavilion with Proposed Alterations*, 1795. The Royal Collection © 2003, Her Majesty Queen Elizabeth II.

BELOW Henry Holland, *Proposal for a Formal Garden at Althorp, Northamptonshire* (detail), 1790. © The British Library.

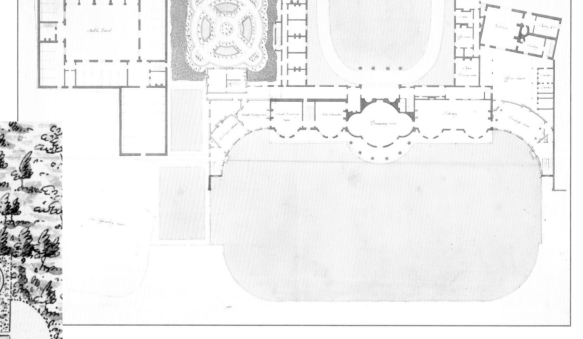

LEFT Detail from the margin of the drawing. The sophisticated design for the trellis and door into the enclosure show that Henry Holland's architectural style extended to garden structures. He had designed architectural trellis for the Prince of Wales at Carlton House.

It was a bold and sophisticated idea to include a formal garden at Brighton when the accepted fashion was for the exact opposite. It was typical of the Prince's indifference to current trends. The Prince would later give Repton specific instructions to disregard gardening fashions, 'I wish you to consider the subject well, and to give me your opinion unbiased by anything you may have heard to be mine, or by any prevailing taste or fashion, by which the World is apt to be led'.[34] When a formal garden was proposed at Brighton, other gardens were just catching up with the earlier trend for 'naturalistic' landscapes and formal gardens were being dug up. Horace Walpole had been shocked that an old formal garden was replaced at an Oxford college: 'I forgot to mention what taste has penetrated to Oxford. At St John's College they have demolished a comely old square garden of about an acre, and bestowed upon it 3 yds of serpentine shrubs, five loose trees that are hopping between four walls; and I suppose will have an irregular lake of a hogshead [a large cask] of water − when the brewing season is over!'[35] The garden had been replaced with an attempt at a miniature, landscaped park. Such was the influence of 'Capability' Brown.

A tapestry depicting a garden at Stoke Edith in Herefordshire (above) shows a simple 'comely old square garden' of the seventeenth-century type, which was doomed to be swept away by Brown.[36] It illustrates the way that grass and flower beds were treated. The precious plants are seen almost botanically. The tulips, for example, are spaced so that they could be appreciated individually. A refinement of this style can be seen in Holland's proposal.

It was no surprise that the Prince was in the vanguard of taste. He knew of the latest gardening trends and would have seen the appropriateness of a formal garden to his Pavilion with its limited site. He would also have enjoyed commissioning something different. A further reason to find an innovative solution may have been that his father, George III, continued to support Brown's old-fashioned landscape style. This was not suited to such a small site at Brighton. A more urban solution was required.

Significantly, Holland had visited Paris in 1785. The Marine Pavilion at Brighton had a French neo-classical look to it and was, after all, called a pavilion. The Prince was enthusiastic for all things French, from food to furniture. The French architect Neufforge had drawn similar geometric layouts for the gardens of his town houses[37] and Holland may have seen examples on his visit.

ABOVE Needlework tapestry from Stoke Edith in Herefordshire, early eighteenth century.
Reproduced by courtesy the Board of Trustees of the Victoria and Albert Museum. Used as part of the decoration to a bedroom, the tapestry was so large that a slim gib door (a disguised opening) was cut in the tapestry above the central gate. Orange trees in decorative vases had been brought out of the orangery. At Brighton orange trees were used to decorate the final Royal Pavilion. The way the plants are used, the layout, and the use of sculpture recalls the much grander formal garden at Hampton Court Palace.

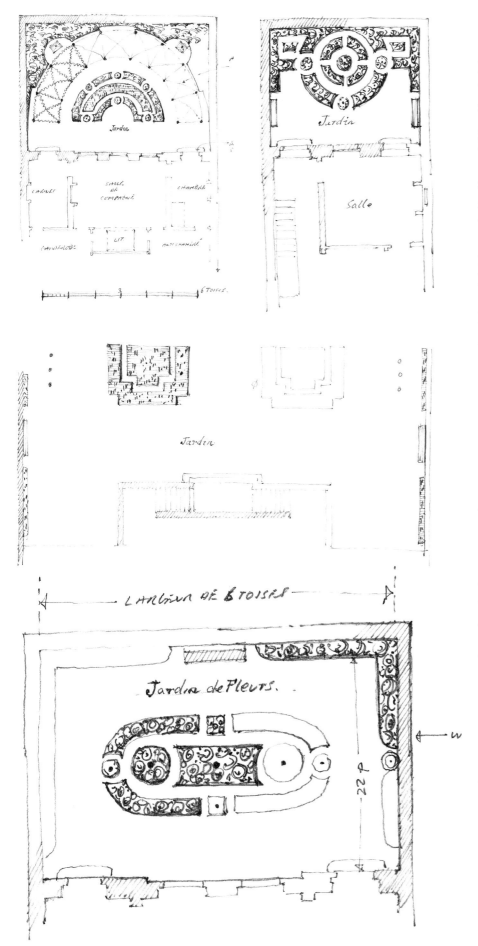

In some of the plates in Neufforge's volumes the gardens are reduced to simple rectangles of grass. In his Brighton proposal Holland had indicated simple rectangles of grass below the circular garden. The garden itself has similarities with Neufforge's designs and the geometric beds are surrounded by shrubbery as he had suggested.

This hard-edged simplification was completely new in England at this time. Repton also designed formal gardens as separate areas in parks but they were more romantic and lacked the austere French touch. Even so, they would be remarked upon by the knowing Prince. Repton and the Prince first met in Brighton after Holland had left. One of the reasons the Prince gave for calling him in was the confidence Repton had shown in going against the current fashions. Repton recalled the Prince saying, 'You dared to make a perfectly straight gravel walk. The moment I saw it, I was determined to see you before I proceeded further with this small plot … We then walked out and for nearly an hour he talked as if he had never thought on any other subject than gardens, Parks and Landscape.'[38] The daring of Repton's designs could be seen at Valleyfield (opposite), where the flower garden was centred on a long formal canal with straight walks either side. It had caused quite a stir in the gardening world.

Loudon was as surprised as the Prince by Repton's daring use of straight lines, but less appreciative, 'At Valleyfield, the barbarities committed upon a natural brook are almost incredible'.[39] At this time Loudon was still promoting natural planting, a style at complete variance with the formal garden proposed by Holland. In Holland's drawing for the alterations, there is no clear way into the garden's enclosure, suggesting that the design was forced into the space and had not been thought through. The planting of the geometric beds recalls the gardens in the Stoke Edith hanging. The plants were to be evenly spaced. This was so old-fashioned that it was new! However, the garden and the other alterations proposed at Brighton were not a success.

Weltje's house was not demolished and the plan was not realised. Perhaps one of the reasons was that Kempshot House, Hampshire, had been leased in 1788 for use as one of the Prince's hunting lodges, he had his own pack of stag hounds and would build kennels for them at Brighton.[40] Concurrent with the drawing for Brighton was Holland's proposals to extend Kempshot. There were similarities; the columns

REPTON AND INNOVATION

Flower garden, Valleyfield, Fife.
Illustration from Humphry Repton,
*Observations on the Theory and
Practice of Landscape Gardening*,
1803. In this view of Valleyfield the
daring of a Repton flower garden can
be clearly seen. It demonstrates the
astonishing speed with which garden
ideas were changing. It also shows
why Repton is considered to be the
starting point of present day
gardening. It demonstrates the idea of
compartmentalisation, the garden
planned as a series of contrasting
rooms or sensations with playful

architectural trellis to incorporate climbing plants. The straight walks are almost edged with herbaceous borders. At a quick
glance the garden could be a hundred years later. Repton in *Observations*, 1803, p.31, was concerned about the combination
of contrasting flowering plants that made up the borders, 'a long straight walk can have little variety: but the greatest source of
variety in a flower garden is derived from the selection and diversity of its shrubs and flowers'. The apparent tranquillity of the
scene was achieved by water passing underground with regulating sluices to maintain water height in the canal, as can be seen
in the foreground. In his words, outside the garden walls, was 'a river - rattling and foaming over rock' in the surrounding
landscape giving 'greater contrast with a smooth expanse of water in the flower garden'. As if to emphasise that the design of
small gardens required more skill than the design for the unlimited acres of his detractors, he declared that, 'I have occasionally
experienced more pleasure and more difficulties in a small flower garden, than amidst the wildest scenery of rocks and
mountains'. Repton was also quick to point out that Brown had never ventured out of England.

around the Saloon at the Marine Pavilion, becoming a central loggia at Kempshot. The viewing
balcony is almost identical and there is a shallow central bow. The Prince may have wanted something different, not more of the same at Brighton. Anyway, he could not proceed with either scheme
as he was hopelessly in debt. His marriage later that year would resolve the situation temporarily.
After a long period of reflection, Holland proposed an innovative new solution.

LEFT Henry Holland's proposal for the
enlargement of Kempshot House,
Hampshire, 1795.
The Royal Collection © 2003, Her
Majesty Queen Elizabeth II.

CHINESE DECORATIONS ARE EXTENDED INTO THE GARDEN

'The corridors … [are] ornamented in the peculiar style of the Chinese covered ways.'

– H. R. ATTREE, *Topography of Brighton*, 1809.

BELOW Henry Holland, *Plan of the Ground Floor of the Marine Pavilion with Alterations*, July 1801, watercolour and ink sketch. The Royal Collection © copyright 2003, Her Majesty Queen Elizabeth II.

SIX YEARS LATER, in 1801, Holland drew a new plan. Again it included a circular formal garden, but this time the plan is simpler, more confident and convincing. The gravel path around the shapes link the garden to the surrounding buildings, from the steps of Weltje's central garden door to the stables or the eastern lawn. The dotted line surrounding the circle may indicate a trellis as at Althorp. Weltje had died the year before and this allowed for a radical re-think of the area. Weltje's house was to be entirely remodelled and was to become part of the Marine Pavilion, Holland having valued and purchased the house on behalf of the Prince.[41]

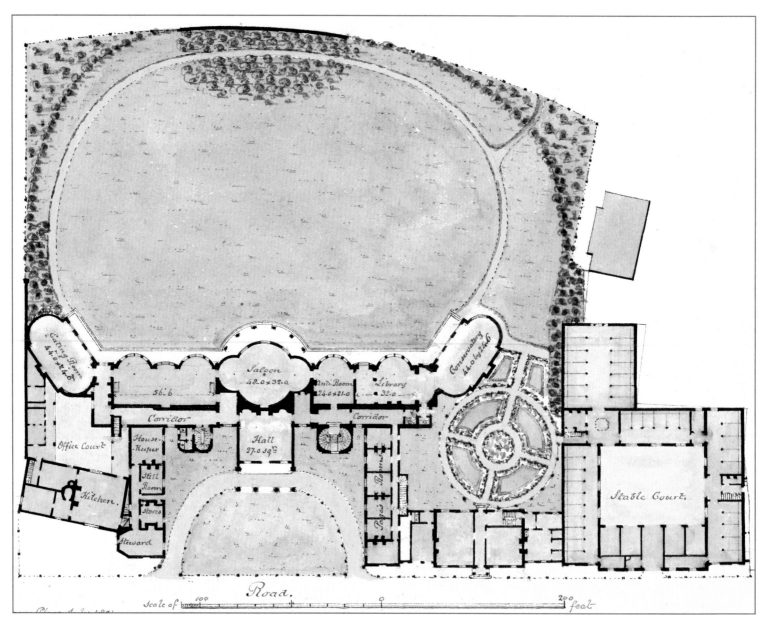

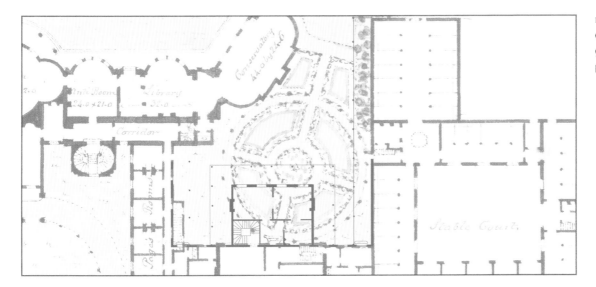

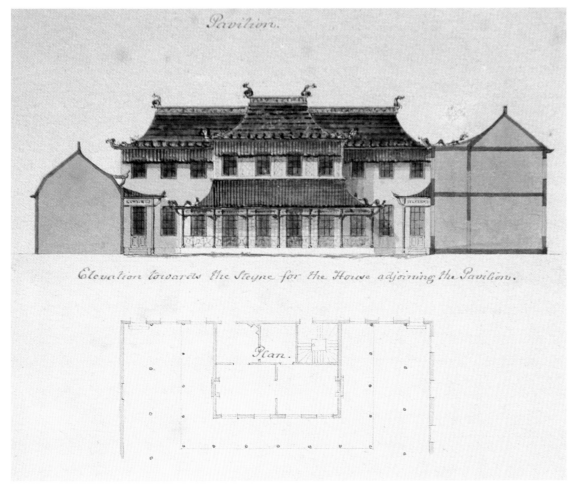

Pavilion.

Elevation towards the Steyne for the House adjoining the Pavilion.

Plan.

Holland was now able to propose a spectacular alternative to the formal garden; a Chinese covered way linking the house with the Marine Pavilion. This must have been a serious proposal because Holland drew accurate, measured elevations and plans for this Chinese courtyard garden. No such drawings survive for his extended Marine Pavilion. The Chinese courtyard garden faced the Steine. It would not have been visible from the Pavilion's entrance. On the entrance side Weltje's house had to conform to the Pavilion's simple classicism. A small part of the frontage of this building then facing the road still exists today, its handsome early cornice and squeezed-in windows, abutts the present Royal Pavilion. The shutter hooks are still there, as is a tiny part of the shallow break front.[42] The two single-storey side wings of Weltje's house, which had been used for his kitchen and carriage, were to be built full height.

This new idea would have linked and extended the new Chinese decorations that were being applied to the inside of the Marine Pavilion and which were to have such an influence on its future. Areas of the Marine Pavilion were being decorated as Chinese covered ways. The narrow internal corridors were ideal for this concept. Columns, separated by fretted balustrades supported boarded roofs and were open to the sky at the sides. It was a witty solution to the spaces, especially as it was mostly carried out in paint, using bold *trompe l'oeil* techniques to fool the eye. A later visitor described the overall effect, 'The Chinese scene is gay beyond description, and I am sure you would admire it, as well as the manner of living at the Pavilion, 'tho the extreme warmth of it might, perhaps, be too much for you'.[43]

RIGHT Drawing for the Marine Pavilion, c.1802. Reproduced by courtesy of the Cooper-Hewitt Museum, the Smithsonian Institution's National Museum of Design, New York. Entrance Hall with a Chinese Covered Way at first floor level.

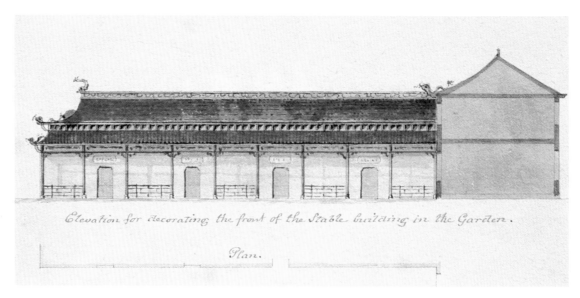

RIGHT Henry Holland, inscribed 'Elevation for decorating the front of the Stable building in the Garden', November 1802.

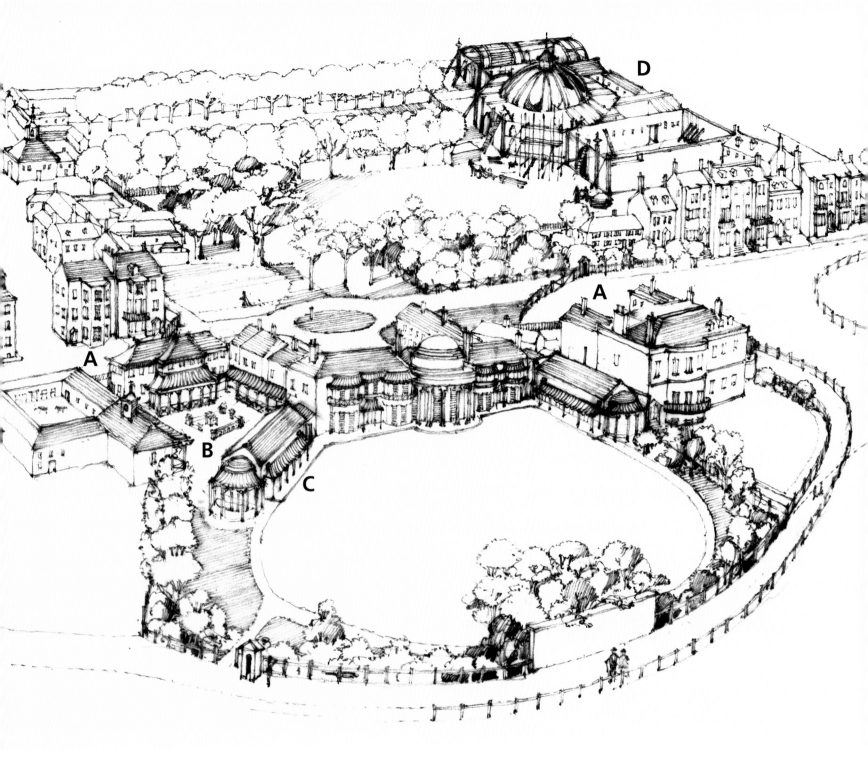

The accounts for Holland's 'Works at Brighton' include 'making Designs for Alterations and Additions to the Pavilion … making Designs for Chinese Decorations and directing the execution for Works and furniture'.[44] The alterations included the Entrance Hall, where 'a light gallery, with an awning crosses, beneath which are Mandarine [sic] figures, as large as life'.[45] The idea of a Chinese covered way as a gallery in the Entrance Hall occurs again with John Nash's alterations. This time it is given a delightful purpose; 'it will occasionally be used by His Royal Highness's band'.[46] The drawing for the stable wall (part of the covered way) is inscribed in Holland's own hand 'Elevations for decorating the front of the Stable building in the Garden'. The colours used in this exterior drawing correspond to the internal decorations. It would have been a logical and elegant progression to create a real Chinese covered way in the garden, though there is no conclusive evidence that this was built. Serious Chinese proposals were being considered for the whole exterior of the Marine Pavilion, some were to be submitted by rival architects. This area may have been seen as an early rehearsal. The Marine Pavilion was to remain, as extended by Holland, for fifteen years.

ABOVE Reconstruction of the site in about 1804. Great East Street (A) is now fenced off and the Entrance Front has a turning circle of grass. The Chinese Courtyard Garden (B) with its covered ways is behind the angled conservatory (C). The stables (D) and Riding House are awaiting completion. The two avenues of elms that formed Promenade Grove are still standing. The garden facing the Steine has been enlarged. The garden design connects the two new wings extending into the garden. The central section of the circular path is obscured by a group of trees and a length of wall.

THE BLUES AND BUFFS:
POLITICS COLOUR THE VIEW

'I am writing to you from our club at Brooke's'.

— GEORGE, PRINCE OF WALES, 1785.[47]

THE PRINCE OF WALES was a great friend of Charles Fox, the leader of the Whig Party and was so closely associated with their progressive ideas that he commissioned superb portrait busts of influential Party members to be displayed at Carlton House. It was understandable that the Prince would, until burdened with responsibilities, be attracted to the more adventurous 'movers and shakers'. Henry Holland was closely associated with the Whigs who were his major clients. He had designed their club, Brooke's, which the Prince frequented. Distinguished Whigs such as Lord

Spencer at Althorp, and the Duke of Bedford at Woburn Abbey, employed Holland to improve their estates in the most up to date fashion. The 5th Duke of Bedford was a young Whig of twenty-one when, impressed by Brooke's Club and Carlton House, yet to be completed, he first consulted Holland. The Prince's residence was to have a subtle influence on Holland's work at Woburn Abbey. The Whigs were as much a gardening club as a political party. Holland had taken an active part in founding the Architects' Club in 1791, whose members included James Wyatt, S. P. Cockerell, Robert Adam, John Soane and George Dance. He formed a partnership with his builder, Alexander Copland, to convert the former town house of the Duke of York, the Prince's brother, into what would become the first apartment block in Europe. By 1802 the former house had been remodelled inside and apartments or 'sets' were built over the garden. Albany, as it was called, would prove popular with gentlemen who did not want the expense of supporting their own establishments in town. Notable Whigs would become trustees. The long central passage between the blocks of chambers, built in the former Italian garden of York House became known as the Rope Walk and was a brilliant solution to linking the apartments. In Holland's scheme it became a remarkably early Chinese covered way, with upswept, boarded roof and supporting posts with a Chinese cut-out fret design (overleaf). It had echoes of his Chinese dairy at Woburn and the Chinese courtyard

BELOW *The Marine Pavilion, East Front*, c.1787, a watercolour from Henry Holland's office. The simple elegance of the building is enhanced by blue shutters and buff tiled walls. They also gave a sophisticated French elegance to the town, mostly built of brick and flint.

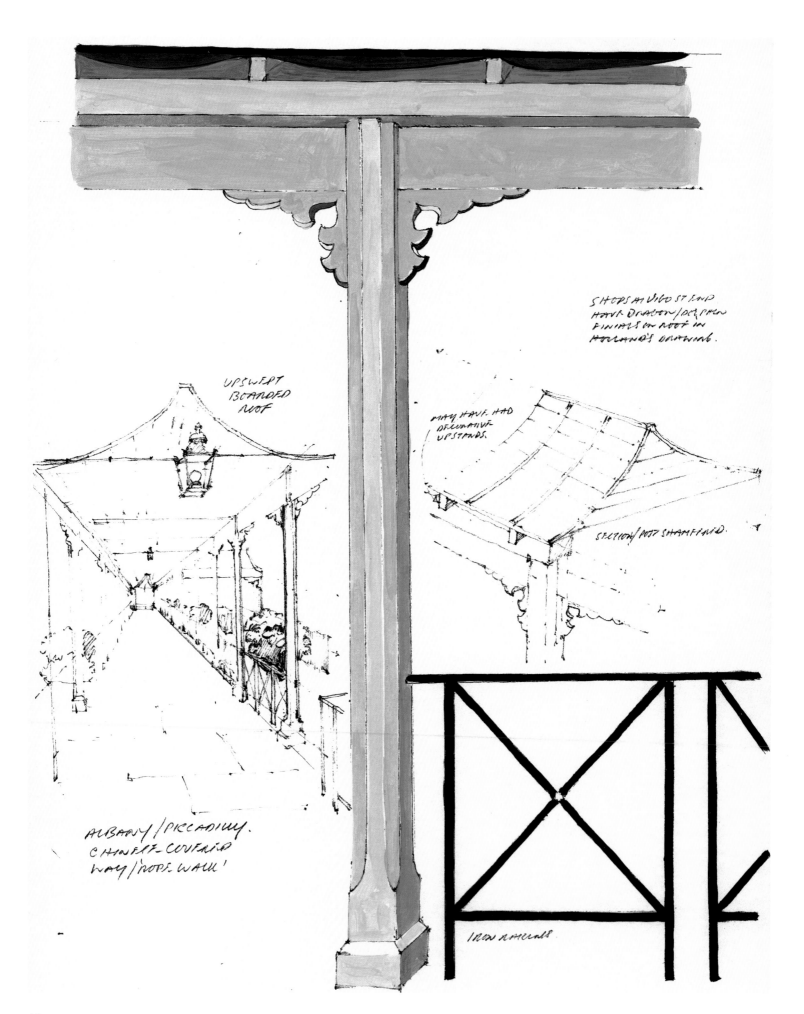

SHOPS AT VIGO ST END
HAVE DRAGON/DOLPHIN
FINIALS ON ROOF IN
HOLLAND'S DRAWING.

UPSWEPT
BOARDED
ROOF

MAY HAVE HAD
DECORATIVE
UPSTANDS.

SECTION/POST CHAMFERED.

ALBANY/PICCADILLY.
CHINESE-COVERED
WAY/'ROPE WALK'

IRON RAILINGS

garden at Brighton. His eventual solution to the east front at the Marine Pavilion also adapted these motifs. Repton later copied the idea for his proposed covered flower corridors, which extended the building into the garden on the west front. The Prince had a Chinese drawing room, designed by Holland, at Carlton House as early as 1790.

Although it was to be expected that the circle the Prince gathered round him at Brighton would generate radical ideas, it is surprising that they influenced the appearance of the town. The Whig colours were blue and buff and the Marine Pavilion had blue shutters and buff tiled walls. The Prince had nailed his colours to the Steine for all to see, confirming his membership of the club for the time being. The new row of houses opposite the Pavilion, with their blue walls and buff-coloured woodwork shown in Spornberg's watercolour, (below) were called the 'Blue and Buffs'. Later, as if to publicly distance himself from the Whigs, the new Marine Pavilion was to change colour on the outside and the garden became an enclosed space. The main concern during the next phase of the development of the garden would be the provision of more privacy.

LEFT Sketch of the existing 'Rope Walk', Albany, Piccadilly, c.1802. The drawing shows Henry Holland's Chinese supporting posts and the upswept roof of the covered way connecting the long ranges of apartments. The cream colour is modern.

ABOVE-RIGHT Humphry Repton, Woburn Abbey, Bedfordshire. Detail of the Chinese Garden prepared for the Red Book, 1804. By kind permission of His Grace the Duke of Bedford and the Trustees of the Bedford Estates. Detail of the posts from Henry Holland's Chinese Dairy, c.1794. The timber columns form a loggia in front of the dairy. A conforming covered way connected the dairy to two game larders.

ABOVE Humphry Repton, *Designs for the Pavillon* [sic] *at Brighton*, 1808. Detail of the covered way proposed for the garden opposite the new stables. In Summer the glazed windows, between the posts, were removed.

LEFT Jacob Spornberg, *View of the Pavilion and the Steine*, watercolour, 1796. The library on the right is now surrounded with new houses, compared to Donowell's earlier view. The 'Blues and Buffs' are the row of houses beyond the library. They project towards the Marine Pavilion and together contrast with all the nearby brick buildings.

7

THE TRIUMPH OF THE
GARDEN OVER THE HOUSE

'Only one step from the ground, so that you may
be instantly out of doors'.

– MRS LYBBE POWYS, *Diaries*, 1776.

BELOW Henry Holland, ink and watercolour, c.1801. The Royal Collection © 2003, Her Majesty Queen Elizabeth II. Top: inscribed: *'Elevation to the Steyne, as executing'*. Below: A design for the same elevation of the Marine Pavilion in chinoiserie style.

AT THE SAME time as Holland proposed the Chinese courtyard garden, he drew a sketch of the entire east front as a Chinese building. This would have completely disguised his earlier neo-classical Marine Pavilion. The dome of the central room, the Saloon, would be replaced by a pagoda. It was fanciful, yet stripped of its Chinese dress, the basic architectural elements were in place. Several other architects also submitted proposals to extend the building in the Chinese style. The architect William Porden, who was to design the stables, submitted elaborate finished designs. These would have turned the Marine Pavilion into a vast Chinese palace.[48] Repton was to suggest a more modest and practical idea, a large canopy as a Chinese addition to the Saloon. They were all trying to satisfy the Prince's enthusiasm, to relate the new Chinese interiors to a corresponding exterior. In the end the only Chinese motif used on the enlarged Marine Pavilion would be four simple frets, ending the sweep of the new side verandahs, as shown in the reconstructed drawing on page 44. They had appeared in the earlier Chinese drawing room at Carlton House as superb capitals to the ottoman, or sofa, area.[49]

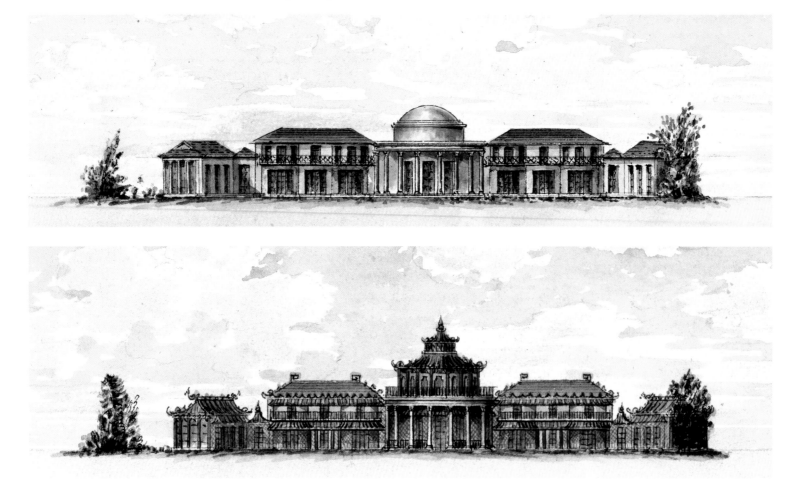

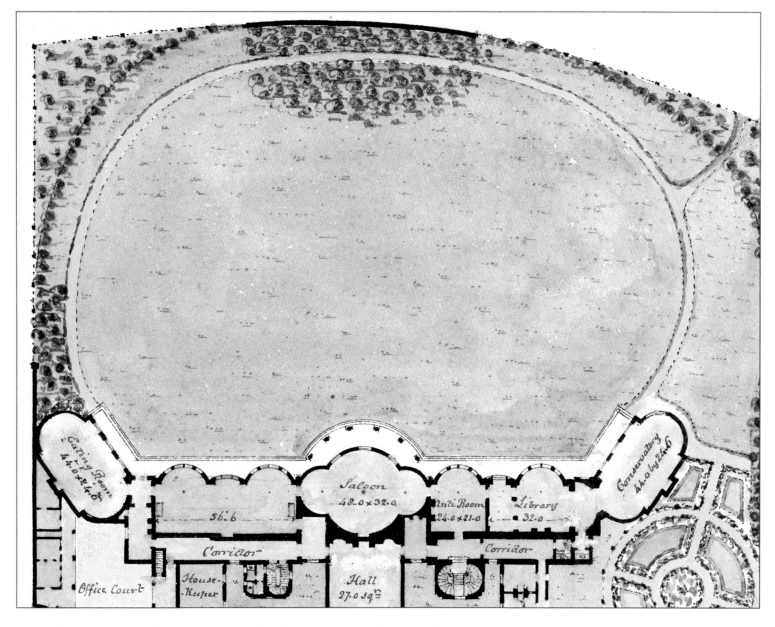

Within the plan, the following labels are visible:

Eating Room
40.0 x 16.6

Saloon
48.0 x 32.0

Anti Room
24.0 x 21.0

Library
32.0

Conservatory
44.0 by 24.6

56.6

Corridor

Corridor

Office Court

House-Keeper

Hall
27.0 sq

Holland's 1801 plan for extending his building shows two large, single-storey wings project–ing into the garden. For the first time the garden has become an important part of the composition. The angled extension at the north end abutted the wall of 'old' Grove House, now called Marlborough House, having been purchased by the Duke of Marlborough in 1790. On the plan above the thick black line on the extreme left indicates Marlborough House. The Duke and the Prince had adjoining gardens in London; Marlborough House and Carlton House both faced The Mall. Together the Prince and the Duke of Marlborough had paid to have the Steine drained in 1793. In return they were allowed to take in some of the valuable land to extend their gardens. The low-lying ground tended to flood in the winter and so establishing a garden here would be an ongoing problem. Their friendship and their adjoining properties would have a decisive effect on the development of the site, not just their adjoining gardens facing the Steine.

The new building at Brighton was in a state of flux as the Prince's changing ideas for the Pavilion were explored. The dimensions of the wings were enlarged as they were built.[50] The eventual solution used to extend the building exactly matched the latest ideas of how to plan and use houses. It was to be more informal and forward looking, taking elements associated with the garden and using them to transform and unite the composition. There was always access to the garden from the Marine Pavilion, but it would now become a crucial part of the composition. The ability to walk straight from a room into a garden was now developed.

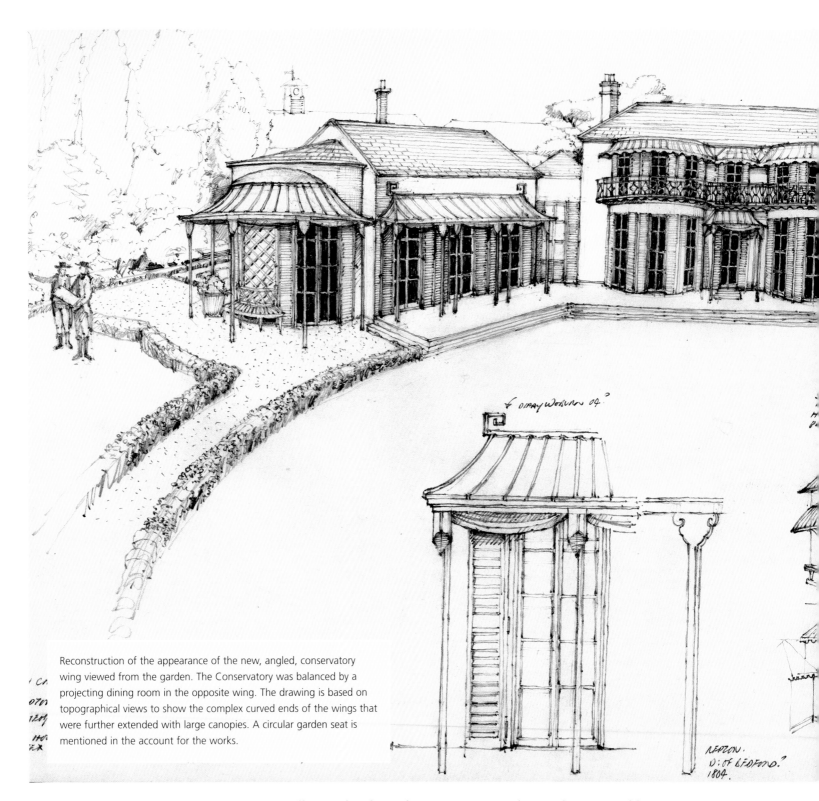

Reconstruction of the appearance of the new, angled, conservatory wing viewed from the garden. The Conservatory was balanced by a projecting dining room in the opposite wing. The drawing is based on topographical views to show the complex curved ends of the wings that were further extended with large canopies. A circular garden seat is mentioned in the account for the works.

In a typically grand eighteenth-century country house, the main public rooms were upstairs. However, Mrs Lybbe Powys, an avid country-house visitor, was delighted to find at Lord Radnor's seat, Longford Castle, that the rooms were 'only one step from the ground, so that you may instantly be out of doors'.[51]

At Brighton the new extensions, incorporating forty French windows from all the main rooms, brought the garden inside. The Saloon, the central circular room, lost its internal classical decoration from 1802 and had a stylised, imported 'paper' garden on the walls. The Chinese hand-painted paper depicted some of the new plants that were arriving in England. The wallpaper also featured fabulous birds. There was a pheasantry of exotic birds on the site as early as 1794 and the later garden accounts would include '2 birds for the lawns', presumably peacocks.[52] The wallpaper in the

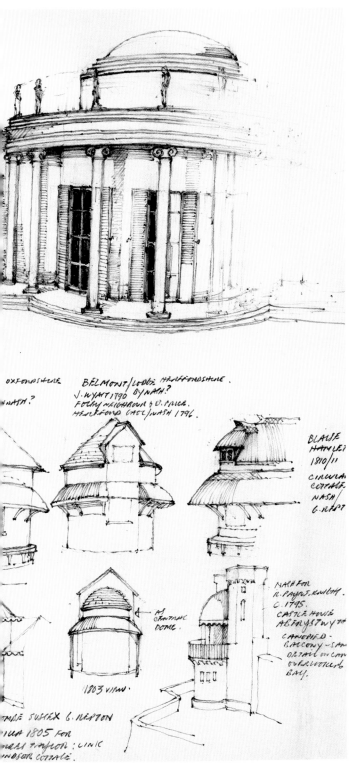

Saloon contributed to the transformation of the room into a luxurious garden arbour, open to the sky, which was painted on the ceiling. The real garden was 'only one step away'. It is no wonder that Repton would soon suggest a Chinese garden outside its windows.

The changes to the building provided a new link with the garden. The line between them became blurred with verandahs, curved canopies, trellis and a conservatory. The conservatory at Brighton would further blur the divide between outside and inside as the exterior and the interior were painted in exactly the same way. The Italian Louis Barzago, one of the artisans working for Henry Holland, painted the conservatory in fresco. Barzago had formerly been employed as a scene painter at the Drury Lane and Covent Garden Theatres, London, from 1794, his theatrical skills would be used to transform the Marine Pavilion. He modelled the interior and exterior surfaces of the conservatory with paint to simulate stone blocks, with all its variety of subtle colour, gradations and tonal imperfections, giving the flat surface the liveliness of real stone. Not only were the inside and outside walls given this effect, but the ceiling of the conservatory was also frescoed to match.[53] Nash later insisted on this treatment for the outside of his terraces at Regent's Park, where a similar finish was applied to the stucco.

The effect of the new conservatory at Brighton must have reinforced the idea that it was completely built of stone. The idea of using paint to create an alternative reality would become a major element in the decoration of the Pavilion. Later the Prince had floor cloths painted to resemble India matting and had brought the lawn inside at Carlton House with a cloth painted to look like grass! The tradition of painting an interior with stone blocking

LEFT External rendering on the Royal Pavilion painted in 1985 to resemble stone (left) by Gordon Grant, senior conservator at The Royal Pavilion, although now degraded it is still very convincing!

ABOVE Drawing for the Marine Pavilion, c.1802. Reproduced by courtesy of the Cooper-Hewitt Museum, the Smithsonian Institution's National Museum of Design, New York.
One of the few drawings with stone blocking and a stove that could relate to the conservatory.

is common in France. Holland may have seen this conceit on his visit in 1785. It would certainly have appealed to his austere, sophisticated taste. Among the many Chinese designs prepared for the Marine Pavilion at this time were a series of watercolours with *trompe l'oeil* masonry. They may refer to Barzargo's conservatory. The 'masonry' would also have provided a superb neutral background for exotic plants. In the accounts for the dispatch of plants from Kew at this time Brighton is mentioned. It is possible that the Royal Gardener had raised plants at Kew to contribute to the display in the conservatory at Brighton.

By applying these devices to the Marine Pavilion it looked like a completely different building. The eighteenth-century building now became a long, low villa, anticipating what has come to be known as the Regency style. The addition of the new curved structures projecting into the garden also gave an opportunity to link the building to the garden with colour. The buff tiles were rendered over and painted as stonework. The former blue shutters and all the decorative additions were painted green. The 'Blues and Buffs', the overtly Whig houses opposite, were losing their appeal for the Prince as his enthusiasm for the Whigs was declining.

The new garden was now a more irregular shape. The careful, hard geometry of the earlier lawn would change and with it the need for the Ha-Ha! to define and protect the garden. The open views over the Downs and the Steine crowded with visitors, were to be replaced with planting

BELOW G. T. Cracklow (figures by W. M. Craig), *View of the Pavilion and Steyne at Brighton with the Promenade*, 1806. The dome of the new stables can be seen behind the Marine Pavilion with its 1801 additions. The Prince of Wales, on the black horse, has joined the promenade. As with all topographical views, too much emphasis on the planting or its density would have detracted from the architectural composition and obscured the Pavilion.

and fencing as for the first time it became an enclosed space. The forty-year-old Prince now required more privacy in his garden. Repton, on his first visit in 1805, described the Pavilion as 'perverted, surrounded by houses on every side; and what was only a small fishing town is now become equal to some cities in extent and population'.[54]

The accounts include 'The Fences & West Fronts, a large Drain carried across the Lawn towards the Steine and Garden Seat at Circular end of Conservatory – £392. 11s. 7d.'[55] Holland's simple, yet brilliantly effective, garden design introduced a linear ring of planting within the irregular plot. This loop of dense planting connected the garden to the building making the most of the space, yet helping to disguise the wall next to Marlborough House, the stables and the Assembly Rooms on the opposite side. The inset gravel walk follows the same outline and responds to the curved ends of the new wings and the bow of the Saloon. From the new dining room in one of the angled wings, it was possible by stepping through large French windows to take a short tour round the grounds. The walk was designed as a circuit to admire the enclosure and planting on the way out and, as the path turned, the view of the building on the way back to the conservatory at the opposite end of the other angled wing (p.43). The corners of the grounds were given a more open planting. In topographical views the path to the Steine is shown to end in a sentry box positioned along the new fencing. In the centre of the circuit the clustered planting becomes most dense so

that someone strolling in the garden would be hidden from view. The visitor would be shaded walking through the trees. The thick black line on Holland's plan behind this cluster must represent a wall for extra privacy.

The large drain running diagonally across the lawn to the Steine, referred to in the accounts, would have connected to the drainage system put in earlier. This related to the problems of the flat, low-lying ground and another attempt at establishing trees in this area by the provision of additional measures to try to drain the ground. A description of this garden is given in a guidebook to the town, which describes the difficulties of establishing a garden on this site, 'Two wings were lately added to the fabric, which complete its proportions, and increase its accommodations … while the accompaniments of gravel-walks, grass-plats, and an *attempt* at plantation, towards the Steyne, (for trees can scarcely be *forced* to grow here), give a finished appearance to the whole … towards the street, the front forms a square … looking over a green, formerly the road'.[56]

In 1784, Holland was 'Making a small alteration in the Groundwork and planting'[57] for the Prince of Wales at Carlton House, to link his new stables to the 'Pallace' [sic]. This was the kind of work that he would have employed Samuel Lapidge to carry out. Lapidge had been 'Capability' Brown's surveyor and continued to work from Brown's business premises at Hampton Court after his death.[58] Lapidge's experience of surveying and laying out grounds with such a famous and influential figure enabled him to continue after Brown's death. [59] Among his many commissions was a surprising request to 'naturalise' the celebrated formal gardens at Chiswick House. Lapidge and Holland worked together at Althorp, Holland on the house and Lapidge on the garden. The work on the house was suspended when Holland was summoned to Brighton by the Prince of Wales. On Holland's return he would also take over the garden design from Lapidge, the formal garden already referred to was one of his proposals for the grounds[60].

Eleven years later Holland employed Lapidge to make the garden alterations at Brighton. Holland's letter of 1803 shows that the work of extending the Marine Pavilion was chaotic. He encloses an abstract of 'such bills as I have, and are likely to come to my hands … for the amount *above* the abstract … I have no bills or any guide, but an estimate of the sum … Mr Lapidge has a just charge … I have his bill. He is not employ'd now, Mr Eaton succeeds him'.[61] Holland's abstract simply stated, 'For the Ground Work and planting by Sam. Lapidge - £384. 3s. 2d.'.[62]

Repton had also employed Lapidge. After Brown's death there was a gap waiting to be filled and Repton was as keen as others to become his successor. In his third gardening publication, after what he thought was a successful visit to Brighton, he took a swipe at the competition. This may have been aimed at Lapidge; Repton needed to gain the upper hand and dismiss any rivals; 'Mr Brown after his death was immediately succeeded by a numerous herd of his foremen and working gardeners, who from having executed his designs became *consulted*, as well as *employed*, in the works which he had entrusted them to superintend. Among these, one person had deservedly acquired great credit … by the execution of gravel walks, the planting of shrubberies, and details belonging to the pleasure grounds … he fancied he might *improve* by *enlarging* his plans. This introduced all that bad taste, attributed to his great master Brown. Hence came the mistaken notion, that greatness of dimensions would produce greatness of character.'[63]

The contradictory Repton who disliked the garden would also have disapproved of the new building. He wrote in 1806 '[Fashion] should be guided by common sense or we may perpetuate absurdities. The rage for destroying old English buildings; and for introducing the Architecture of a hot country, ill adapted to a cold one'. Such absurdities included porticos and 'the Indian *verandah* as a shelter from the cold east wind of this climate'.[64] Of course, by this time the east front

BELOW G. Wise, Engraving c.1810. The extensions and canopied Marine Pavilion now resembles a fashionable 'Regency' villa.

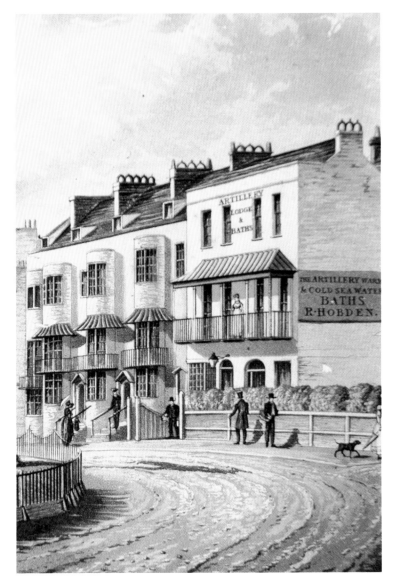

at Brighton was covered in verandahs. Repton was about to reveal his designs for enlarging Holland's building. The result would have been an entire building ill adapted to a cold climate with a garden adapted from sunnier climes to match!

The canopies and verandahs were later to appear in most seaside towns. It was architecture on holiday. They gave shade and a liveliness to buildings, many of which had incorporated the bow window for panoramic views. Canopies and verandahs were to be painted in stripes to simulate colourful awnings. A French visitor to Brighton was delighted by them. He would not have seen the Marine Pavilion, as by then it had been transformed into the building we know today. He was commenting on the influence of these ideas:

'But that which I like above all is the "veranda", a sort of iron trellis work in various designs which projects from each floor like a balcony and is surmounted by a zinc "tent", striped in different colours. Over most of them rambler-roses or other climbing plants are trained, seeming to transport the onlooker to some tropic clime and giving ... an indolent gaiety of the Indies. Everything about these dwellings seem designed for people who will go on enjoying them ... yet, in fact, their occupants are the merest birds-of-passage'.[65]

The Marine Pavilion transformed with Holland's verandahs and canopies would remain in place for fifteen years. The next priority was securing the surrounding land and building the new stables. It was the start of the final grand plan. The stables would necessitate a new Pavilion with a new accompanying garden. William Porden was on site a year after Holland's final account was submitted.

ABOVE-LEFT *The Battery, Brighton,* now King's Road. Aquatint after a sketch by Edward Fox, 1825. The influence of the Marine Pavilion on the town of Brighton. Canopies, shutters and verandahs became synonymous with 'architecture on holiday'.

ABOVE-RIGHT Photograph 2005, terraced houses in Brighton, c.1850, still transporting the onlooker to the 'indolent gaiety of the Indies'. The agave, a fashionable Regency plant, has modern associations with warmer climes as tequila is distilled from the blue succulent.

8

PRECIOUS CARGOES TO AND FROM CHINA

'Packed ... by Mr Kerr, Botanist at Canton'.

– LORD STEWARD'S ACCOUNT BOOK FOR KEW, 1811.

BELOW The peony has a long history of cultivation in Europe since the thirteenth century. The peonies from the Pavilion's garden are illustrated below. The Tree Peony *P. suffruticosa*, a precious new plant was depicted on imported hand-painted Chinese wallpaper.

IN 1804 HOLLAND'S account was settled and the Marine Pavilion's first Chinese decorations were in place. At the same time exotic new plants were arriving from China. These would add significantly to the range of plant material available to gardeners and quickly became available through the expanding nursery trade. It is not difficult to imagine the delight of first seeing a completely new plant, such as the Peony. Rarities that were once known only to a select few are now taken for granted and available in the local garden centre and it is difficult to imagine the ingenuity and care required to transport them to these shores. Seeds and plants were collected from all over the world and China was one of the new destinations for plant hunters. William Townsend

Paeonia lactiflora

Paeonia officinalis
'Rubra Plena'

Paeonia peregrina

Paeonia suffruticosa

Aiton, the Royal Gardener at Kew, was responsible for negotiating and looking after the new introductions that were sent to him for propagating at Kew. By 1813 he listed 120 species that were recent introductions from China to Kew. The quest for new plants was a hazardous and highly competitive business, as collectors and nurseries were anxious to be the first to offer new varieties. Enormous trouble and expense was required to locate new plants and to secure their safe passage to this country.

The problems of transporting plants and ensuring their survival on the long sea voyage, which might last six months, prompted experiments, which resulted in the invention of a special travelling case in 1829. It was designed by Nathaniel Ward, a doctor, botanist and inventor. The cases protected plants from extremes of temperature and salt spray. These were based on a simple idea that water vapour could condense on the glass of the sealed box and water the soil in a continuous cycle. It was like a portable miniature greenhouse with carrying handles. A modern version which works on the same principle is the large sealed glass plant bottle. At this time Aiton's itemised bills record 'fitting up a Greenhouse on Board the Ship *Hope* lying off Gravesend, bound for China, with a collection of Plants For His Majesty's Garden at Canton – 2 men, 12 days with expenses £11. 6s. 2d.'.[66] The ship was to take fifty-two assorted fruit trees, twelve vines in pots, six roses of sorts, mustard and cress, herbs, eighteen fruit bushes and 'potatoes and bag' all valued at £9. 17s. 6d.[67] This cargo, which included bed linen, a hammock and even a washbasin, was to be sent to William Kerr at Canton. They all must have appeared very exotic to the Chinese.

Kerria japonica, named after William Kerr.

ABOVE Ward's travelling case. The 'miniature greenhouse' protected plants from salt spray, and could be easily moved and lashed to the deck of a ship to prevent storm damage or movement. Fiji was the last recipient of a delivery of plants by Wardian Case from Kew in 1962.

RIGHT Chinese hand-painted wallpapers were imported by the East India Company in sets of up to forty lengths or drops. The tree and flowers designs were hung to form a continuous mural round a room. Pattern gaps or joins were disguised with cut-out birds or butterflies. The papers depicted exotic plants, many unfamiliar to Europeans. The paper in the Saloon, (photograph below) c.1790 has stylised flowering plants that could later be seen in the garden.

A. The Autumn-flowering chrysanthemums reached England from China in 1795.

B. The first tree peony *Paeonia suffruticosa* was sent to Sir Joseph Banks at Kew by Alexander Duncan, a surgeon with the East India Company, in 1787. It flowered six years later, five more arrived the next year to be distributed between Banks and the King. The first Chinese magnolia *M.denudata* appeared in 1780, again introduced by Banks. The well known *Magnolia grandiflora* had arrived from South Carolina in 1734.

C. *Camellia japonica* was given its Latinised name in 1753. It had arrived in England in 1739, treated as a greenhouse subject. *Camellia sinensis*, the tea plant, arrived from China in 1768. Tea had become a fashionable drink and the Wardian case was later used to transport ten of thousands of plants from China to start the tea trade in India. By 1816 John Reeves, a tea inspector for the East India Company in China, had potted up one hundred plants including camellias and one variety *C. Welbankiana* was named after the ship's captain Welbank. The ship docked with ninety plants still alive. The cargo included the Chinese *Wisteria sinensis* which flowered in 1818.

D. *Physalis alkekengi*, the Chinese Lantern was known in England since the sixteenth century. It grew wild from Europe to Asia and Japan.The green bud on the right represents a poppy. Opium is derived from the *Papaver somniferum* and the Oriental poppy, *P. bracteatum* arrived in 1817

E. The first living Hydrangea was brought from China to Banks at Kew in 1789. The American *H. arborescens* had arrived in 1736.

F. The hanging basket includes the exotic *Zea mays* (maize). It was an important cereal crop in tropical and temperate regions. It had been grown in England since the sixteenth century.

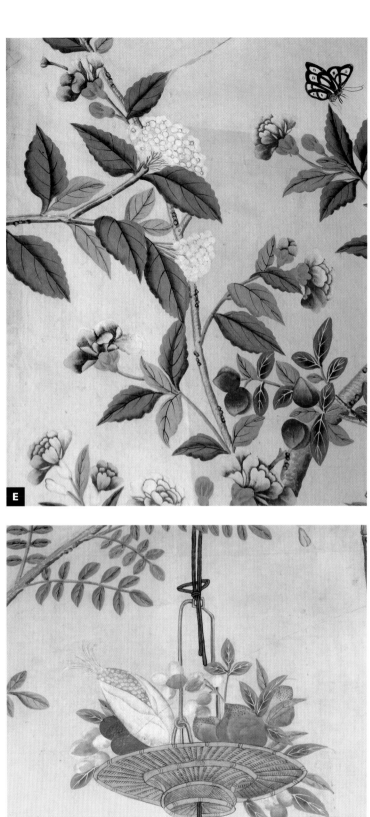

ABOVE *Lilium lancifolium* (Tiger Lily). To correspond to the Brighton garden accounts forty-eight bulbs have now been planted in the restored garden.

BELOW Page from the Lord Steward's accounts recording the dispatch of plants, 1802.
© The National archives, Kew.

In 1803 Kerr, a gardener who had been trained at Kew, was sent to China by Sir Joseph Banks. Banks was a wealthy patron, plant collector and advisor to Kew. He and Aiton arranged for Kerr to collect and send back Chinese plants for Kew. He remained there for eight years on a salary of £100 sponsored by Banks. Aiton's accounts show that there was a huge influx of plant material arriving at Britain at this time. 'Cargoes of living plants have been received from the Governor of New South Wales: and His Majesty's collectors, Mr Mason in Upper Canada, and Mr Kerr at Canton, have added their proportions yearly … Sir Joseph Banks has procured loads of seeds and plants from all Parts of the World at his own expense … upwards of 4,000 papers of seeds and roots have been received from different Correspondents since the year 1802, many of which have vegetated … it has been found necessary to increase the labour of the garden … the workmen's wages have remained at nine shillings a week'.[68] A special cargo arrived three years later, a Chinese gardener! The bills include 'weekly disbursements for keeping Au-Hey, the Chinese gardener – £16.17s. 0.3/4d. for the Christmas Quarter'.[69] In April the following year, 'The necessaries provided for the Chinese Gardener included 'Taking him down to the ship'.[70] Au-Hey was given an engraved silver watch by Aiton as a leaving present, which was itemised at £5. 10s. 0d. The list continues to record the arrival of plants, some from the Cape of Good Hope. In 1811 a Mr Bennet was paid ten guineas for looking after a garden cabin at sea with Chinese plants for Kew. These had been 'packed under Bennet's care by Mr Kerr, Botanist at Canton'.[71] Unfortunately the plants arriving are not listed or named. From this exciting period the Pavilion garden has *Kerria japonica*, named after Kerr. He also sent the Tiger Lily (*Lilium lancifolium*), that Aiton subsequently propagated and by 1812 had distributed over 10,000 bulbs.[72] Ironically, the Chinese grew them for their edible bulbs. Other new Chinese introductions to this country included the Peony, the Chrysanthemum and the Hydrangea. Plants in the garden would now relate to those painted on the Chinese wallpapers inside the Marine Pavilion.

The interest generated by the arrival of new plants resulted in what is now the Royal Horticultural Society, being established in 1804; Banks and Aiton were among the founding members. Such was the craze for plants that the Empress Josephine continued with her English Garden while England and France were at war! Many of her plant orders were despatched from James Lee and Lewis Kennedy's 'Vineyard' Nursery in Hammersmith. Kennedy was issued with a special passport enabling him to bring plants to her house, Malmaison. The Admiralty was warned about intercepting these delicate cargoes. By 1803 £2,600 had been spent on plants from the London nursery. It is highly likely that these consignments were a major contribution to the fame of Malmaison's collection of roses. Lee and Kennedy also supplied Aiton at Kew with fifteen named varieties of rose.

With Aiton's accounts at Kew are details of making packing cases and the kind of journeys that he made to collect precious plant cargoes from the docks. Travelling to Rochester by coach – boat to Sheerness – sculler from the boat to the ship, waiting for the captain, boat to Chatham Custom House, dinners, bed and breakfasts, helpers to unload and the return journey. This, itemised under 'attending upon a cargo of plants from Malta', took seven days and cost £14. 8s .6d.[73] Malta was captured from the French by Nelson in 1799 and its botanic garden was used by Sir

From 10th Oct. 1802 to 6th Jan. 1803.
Christmas Quarter 1802.

1802			
	Mrs Layton's Carriage Bill Contd.	6	12
Nov 26	Basket of Plants from Mincing Lane		2
	Porterage		1
Nov 16	2 Bags of Seeds from the Borough		1
23	Box of Seeds from the Glasgow waggon		1
27	Basket of Plants from Halfmoon St.		2
Dec 4	Box of Seeds from Moorfields		
	Box of Seeds from the Brighton Coach		
	2 large Baskets of Plants from Queenhithe		
13	Box of Seeds from Moorfields		5
18	2 Bundles of Trees from Putney		1
20	2 Baskets of Plants to the Brighton Waggon for H. R. H. the Prince of Wales		5
	Porterage and Booking		2
	Bundle of Trees from Putney		2
22	Bundle of Trees to the Brighton Waggon for H. R. H. the Prince of Wales		2
	Porterage and Booking		1
	Bundle of Trees to Charing Cross for H. R. H. the Duke of Kent		2
	Porterage		1
28	Parcel of Plants from Mr Gillespy		1
	Receipted and Signed		8
	James Layton		

Joseph Banks to supply new plants for Kew. Kew supplied other Royal gardens with plants. In the constant arrival or dispatch of plants Brighton is mentioned for the first time. The plants sent must relate to the garden being planted by Lapidge. 'Christmas Quarter 1802, 2 baskets of Plants to the Brighton wagon for HRH the Prince of Wales, with porterage and booking - £2. 0s. 6d'. Two days later on 22 December 'A Bundle of Trees to the Brighton waggon – 3 shillings'.[74] Unfortunately the varieties are not named. To have been sent from Kew they must have been special. These costs were for taking the plants from Kew to a wagon office in London for onward dispatch to Brighton. The George Inn at Borough in Southwark, was a popular coaching inn with its large forecourt and overlooking balconies. It was a good connecting point for wagons, which also took luggage. Coaches took visitors to Brighton from this inn. It still exists today.

Holland had built a Chinese Dairy at Woburn Abbey for the Duke of Bedford. With the arrival of Chinese plants it was now possible to create a more authentic Chinese setting for the dairy. (below) The garden was planted by Repton with plants which had only just arrived in this country. He wrote that 'The Chinese buildings were proposed to be decorated by an assemblage of Chinese Plants, such as the Acuba, Cameilla [sic] Japonica and Hydrangea'.[75] Sir Joseph Banks had brought back one of the first hydrangeas from China and the variety named after him has now been planted in the Pavilion gardens. It was from Woburn that Repton was summoned to Brighton by the Prince in November 1805. Repton could now respond to the Chinese decorations that were in place at the Marine Pavilion with a Chinese garden for the East Front using authentic plants. The Prince would have known of the innovations that Repton and Holland had made at Woburn. The Chinese garden indicated on the plan for improvements at Brighton was in fact a carefully considered arrangement of circular beds filled with changeable plants throughout the seasons. The beds were designed to look like large baskets by surrounding the edges with an interlaced decorative upstand. This reinforced their ordered appearance and enabled them to be scattered over the lawn as a witty conceit within the landscaped grounds.

BELOW Humphry Repton, *Woburn Abbey, Bedfordshire. The Lake, Dairy and Chinese Garden* prepared for the Red Book, watercolour, 1804. By kind permission of His Grace the Duke of Bedford and the Trustees of the Bedford Estates.
The Chinese canopy on the right-hand side relates to the new verandahs on the extensions at Brighton, it would also echo in Repton's Chinese garden proposals for the Marine Pavilion. The plants in the foreground include the hydrangea.

9

THE GROUNDS IN 1805

'It is better to trust in the Lord than to put any confidence in Princes ...'

– HUMPHRY REPTON, *Memoir.*

ABOVE Humphry Repton *Designs for the Pavillon* (sic) *at Brighton* 1808. (detail) see p.67. Circular flower beds, edged as baskets provide a foreground to a proposed sea view.

HOLLAND'S FINAL ACCOUNT reveals that he had valued and purchased land and nearby property to enlarge the grounds. He had negotiated for Weltje's house, the site of the Chinese court-yard extension already referred to. The same account indicates that he had inherited Weltje's role as go-between after Weltje's death. By using Holland to make enquiries the Prince hoped to continue to keep his identity secret and prices lower. The first important test of Holland's negotiating skills concerned the land opposite the Marine Pavilion on the other side of Great East Street. Up to this point the road had formed a natural barrier to the Prince's grounds preventing expansion. The Prince would never have been able to increase the size of his estate without crossing the main road and all future developments depended on it.

As early as 1801 Holland was 'valuing the Grove Estate and agreeing to purchase the same ... £25.10. 0'.[76] A guide book discloses that this land was owned by the Duke of Marlborough - 'in 1801 the Prince made a purchase of the Grove Elm gardens, the shrubberies and pleasure-ground of the Duke of Marlborough, which the London Road intersected'.[77] The Duke would have known of the Prince's future intentions for the whole site, including his house. The Prince had tried unsuccessfully to acquire the Grove Estate through Weltje three months before it was leased by the Duke.[78] It is clear that the Prince had wanted this piece of land and was prepared to wait until funds were available. Although the house itself and its garden were not finally purchased until 1812 it is significant that it was included in the instructions to Repton as early as 1805.

Holland also valued 'Mr Kemp's estate, the Dairy House and treating for the same - £5.5.0'.[79] This accounted for the two pieces of land immediately opposite the Marine Pavilion. Negotiations now began with the Town Commissioners to enable the Prince to divert Great East Street and hence to combine the parcels of land on either side. This was agreed in 1803 on condition that the Prince provided an alternative route. The Holland estimate for 'Fences E[n] & W[n] £323'[80] must relate to the new combined grounds.[81] The closure of the road and the fencing of the enlarged estate marked the end of Holland's involvement with the Marine Pavilion and its gardens. From now on the only architect on site was William Porden who was building the stables. He took over from Holland and completed the complex negotiations to purchase the land and property required for the new and increasingly elaborate plans for the house, stables and adjoining gardens.

It is extraordinary that by 1801 a plan was in place that would take some twenty years to re-alise. Porden arranged to buy and demolish two entire rows of buildings to construct his stables. One of the crucial pieces of land required to enable the plan to proceed was the market garden belonging to the Furner family. With this purchase Porden had now acquired the land that would mark the edge of the Pavilion's estate. Two documents in the Royal Archives illustrate the complexity of this process. Porden's letters describe in detail the sums required for these plots of land. They included the houses on Church Street. One owner would only sell on condition that a new house was built nearby.[82] The cost of building New Road was partly met by selling off the ground that was not required. The whole of the Furners' property, including the house, was purchased for £4,000 but, cleverly, the parts that were not required were sold straight away for £3,000.[83] The 'Dairy House, Cow House and fencing the field' would require another £5,000, this negotiation had already been initiated by Holland. Porden's estimate also included the Quakers Ground, at a

ABOVE Repton's method of presenting his designs with 'before' and 'after' views shows the existing view from the Marine Pavilion with the flap lifted to glimpse his seductive alterations.

cost of £850. The final estimate was for 'sundry Expences [sic] in levelling, planting and Compleating [sic] the Pleasure Ground, supposed £500'. The nearly completed stables and road were priced at £25,750.0s.2d. The estimated cost of 'the Coach Horse Stables, Coach Houses and Grooms Apartments, the Riding House' was another £11,900. For all this wheeling and dealing Porden put in an estimate 'to the architects Commission, the Clerk of the Works, Travelling Expences and Contingencies, supposed to be about 10 per cent - £4,533.16s.0d.'[84] We have no clear idea of what this pleasure ground looked like until Repton arrived in 1805.

Repton's proposals for the grounds were presented to the Prince in his typical seductive way. A portfolio of watercolours with 'before' and 'after' views, were mounted so that comparisons between the existing garden and his proposals could be easily made, by lifting or sliding a flap, and were accompanied by descriptive, reasoned text that supported his designs. The 'before' views are always drawn to appear as if they would benefit from his suggestions made in the 'after' view. It showed instant garden 'makeovers' that could be seen and enjoyed at a glance without waiting for years to see it happen. They were a large part of Repton's success as clients could enjoy their own 'Red Book' (as they were called as most were bound in red covers) even if the commission went no further. Loudon later criticised Repton over the way he presented his proposals, 'Mr Repton has a considerable share of what may be called tinsel ability in his art … the sameness and tameness of manner which must certainly … prevail in his red-books'. He goes on to give six reasons why, in his opinion, the before and after slides could deceive. He knew they were Repton's calling card and had helped to make him famous. The most obvious flaw was that, 'The upper slip would never please so much as the one under it, because the line which marks the boundary of the slip disturbs the harmony of the one composition'. Loudon thought they should be separate landscapes and his final opinion was that 'The whole is evidently a mere piece of QUACKERY'.[85]

Repton realised that the garden at Brighton presented a wonderful opportunity to show off his design talent. He proposed a completely inward-looking garden, a garden as a 'Work of Art' not 'Nature', the exact opposite of the kind of gardens that had been appreciated by Mrs Lybbe Powys. It exactly suited the mood of the time, as gardens were becoming smaller and related to his proposals for an enlarged Pavilion. He was asked to include his suggestions for a new house as well as the garden, as the Prince now required a more complex and innovative solution to extend the building and balance it with the new stables. It was a masterstroke to combine the style of his proposed new building with the new stables, linking them with a garden that exactly complemented both.

Before he was summoned to Brighton Repton was assisting the architect Samuel Pepys Cockerell at Sezincote in Gloucestershire. Cockerell's brother had just returned from India a rich man and wanted a house in an Indian-style. The house, the first domestic Indian-style building in

England, was to take as its design source the drawings of Indian buildings by Thomas and William Daniell. Their influential *Oriental Scenery* was published from 1795-1808.[86] The drawings had opened up a new vocabulary for architectural innovation. Repton advised on which details from the drawings would combine well for the exterior and made suggestions for the grounds. There were three kinds of garden at Sezincote, the entrance front faced rolling English countryside in the Landscape tradition. The formal garden was centred on a stone basin that has similarities with the base of the aviary in Repton's proposal for Brighton (p.63). The most dramatic garden, called The Thornery, could be glimpsed from the carriage drive over an Indian bridge. The banks were planted to imitate the kind of vegetation seen in the Daniells' drawings and included an Indian shrine that would appear again at Brighton drawn by Repton. The combination of the Daniells' drawings and the architectural talent of William Porden were to provide spectacular innovations at Brighton. Repton knew that India was the latest source of architectural variety that had already

This outline shews the heights of the Trees as they appeared in Winter, forming three distinct distances
it also shews the relative height of a Man with a Rod of Ten feet long at different stations
This Building was totally hid by the Trees near the Pavillon some of which have been removed
The farther Avenue remaining
The first Avenue cut down
A great number of Young Trees stood here, some of which are removed to the same distance on the other side, to hide the Town as there represented

ABOVE Humphry Repton, the view from the Marine Pavilion, 1808. All the land immediately opposite the entrance was purchased through Holland and Porden. In this view the enclosed fenced land included from the foreground Dairy Field, Grove Elm Gardens, the Quakers' Ground, and a portion of the market gardens belonging to the Furner family. It illustrates the complexity of securing a large garden in a booming town.

been used for the new Stables at Brighton and he was keen to win the approval of the Prince. As if to reinforce this he wrote 'we are on the eve of some great future change … in consequence of our having lately become acquainted with Scenery and Buildings in the interior provinces of India … such beautiful forms as have never before been adopted in Europe … when a partiality for such forms is patronised and supported by the highest rank … it becomes the duty of the professor to raise the importance by increasing the variety of his "art"'.[87]

Repton's illustrated 'before' views are the only known record of the grounds at this time. Looking at his proposals in the Pavilion's 'Red Book', the Western Lawn is viewed from the new turning circle, after the road was closed. In his accompanying text he noted that works had already begun, 'on my arrival … there was to have been a Coach Road, to enter by a pair of lodges, and to proceed to the House through a serpentine line of approach.'[88] In Repton's thinking, the idea of making a curved carriage drive through a small plot of land was old fashioned. He saw it as part of the mistaken idea of trying to make that garden look like a miniature landscaped park. He wanted his garden to be seen as a completely artificial setting, which linked to the new style of the stables and could be used as an outdoor room. He even drew the attention of visitors to the garden by providing an orchestra stand in the centre of his design. The Prince had his own band of musicians and his idea was to welcome guests in a way that reinforced their arrival to an enclosed exotic setting.

In this 'before' view (above) the men by the wheelbarrows on the left are ready to cart away the earth to shape the ground. It was a clever move to include them, as if with one nod from the Prince, they could begin. Repton would publish his method of shaping ground explaining 'that it may be raised and sunk according to the stakes by which the ground is divided into squares. This was done under my direction at the gardens of the Pavilion at Brighton; and the whole surface altered accordingly'.[89] He had demonstrated his method to the Prince on his first visit (see illustration opposite).

Repton's notes on the flap of this view explain that the stables were 'totally hidden by a great number of trees'. As a temporary solution to the problems of the site the new building had been screened so that it would not detract from the long, low Marine Pavilion and could not be seen

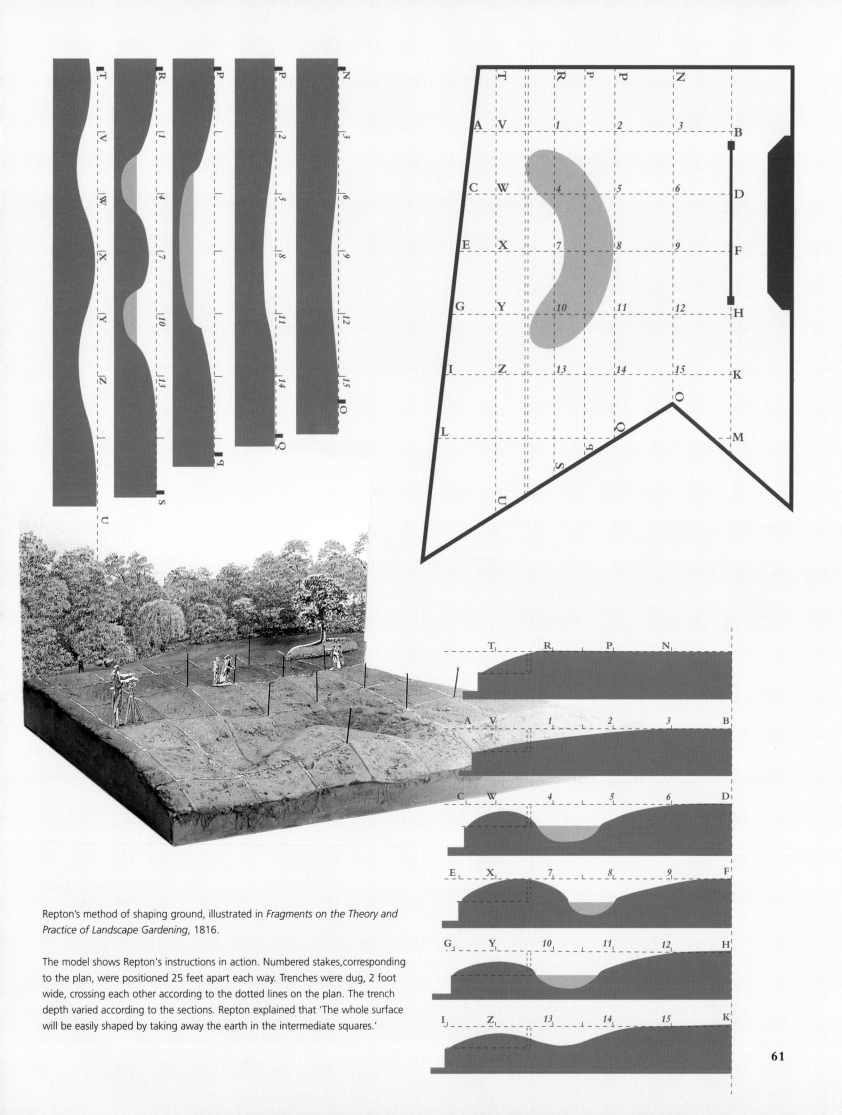

Repton's method of shaping ground, illustrated in *Fragments on the Theory and Practice of Landscape Gardening*, 1816.

The model shows Repton's instructions in action. Numbered stakes, corresponding to the plan, were positioned 25 feet apart each way. Trenches were dug, 2 foot wide, crossing each other according to the dotted lines on the plan. The trench depth varied according to the sections. Repton explained that 'The whole surface will be easily shaped by taking away the earth in the intermediate squares.'

61

from it. Repton suggests that the trees should be moved to hide the town shown on the left. The men are holding ten-foot high rods at different positions to give scale. By this measure the trees were then already over twenty feet high. Repton had delayed his visit so that the trees would be bare and he could see the extent of the grounds through them. Not answering the Prince's summons immediately was a serious mistake, as works were already under way. He tried to salvage his position with a cleverly worded letter, explaining that 'The Duke of Bedford told me the Prince wishes my opinion for the operations of the next year, and did not command my immediate attendance ... therefore I deferred seeing the spot, till all the leaves being off the trees, I might not form an erroneous opinion of what they now concealed. The high honor of being in any degree useful to his Royal Highness, was so flattering that I have lately been turning my attention to representations of Indian Scenery, and hoped to have produced some effects particularly connected with that style in the Gardens at Brighton'.[90]

The excuse and the bait worked. After thirteen days he received a reply. This time Repton turned his 'horse's head round and set off immediately to answer this letter in person'. The first meeting went well and Repton reassured the Prince that five acres were more than enough to make the gardens 'perfect of the kind'. After a subsequent visit his completed Red Book was well received at Carlton House, 'Mr Repton I consider the whole of this book as <u>perfect</u> – <u>I will have every part of it carried into immediate execution</u>'. Repton later waited for instructions to proceed with his final grand plans at the entrance to the Marine Pavilion, from where he had drawn the view of the existing grounds. He described the scene, 'I attended at the Pavillon [sic], and saw 20 others also waiting an audience – among whom was the Architect who built his Stables, he was in the open air and sitting down on the grass, and I was told it was the best way to catch the Prince's attention: but I preferred waiting under cover not being used to this sort of attendance. After nearly three hours (during which time the travelling carriages had been waiting at the door). The Prince entered, my working plans in his hand, he opened them, and pointed to three or four <u>little</u> alterations ... and explained them as if he had been – like myself – thinking of nothing else. Then he said he should expect to see the Cellars, and all the foundations finished by the time he return'd, and urged me to lose no time ... and with his Suite he hurried away'.[91] So did the entire project, although he was not to know this. Most of the trees in Repton's 'before' view would be moved later. Only the ancient elms and the furthest avenue would remain

Surprisingly moving large trees was not considered a major problem, as Sir Henry Steuart had demonstrated at his own estate. He had planted seven hundred trees, 'the largest not exceeding thirty foot ... the whole appeared like a spot at least forty years planted ... by the power of the Transplanting Machine ... *with no loss of health or vigour in the Trees*.[92] As an example of the low cost he estimated an eighteen-foot high tree at 6s. 6d. and a twenty-five foot one at 12s. 6d.[93] He cre-

BELOW Henry Steuart's machine in action. Plate from *The Planter's Guide*, 1828. © The British Library.

BELOW-RIGHT Plate from *The Planter's Guide*, 1828. © The British Library. Steuart's transplanting machine had 'wooded' the park at Allanton House between 1816 and 1821.

ated a wood around his lodge within a month and the cost was £20. 9s. 0d. It included a single horse with the driver to draw the machine and eight workmen for twenty-six days![94] He thought that if 'the sum had been double or even treble, it could not be regarded as a very exorbitant purchase!' Similar machines had been used by landscape gardeners and had enabled trees to be transported horizontally. The roots were cut around, three foot out from the tree and the machine brought up on its wheels to the trunk. The upright pole was lashed to it and forcibly drawn down by the workforce.

Repton's 'after' view of the same ground from the same viewpoint shows his proposals for its transformation. The stables are now completely revealed and the ground has been shaped. The levelling referred to in Porden's account has now become varied by moving earth from the centre of the grounds to form gentle banks and a square pool. The transformation also shows his debt to Sezincote and T & W Daniell, *Oriental Scenery*. (p.63) The aviary on the left is a witty adaptation of a Hindu temple from one of Daniell's illustrations. The kiosk at the end of the covered way is taken from the same source. It was adapted and simplified at Sezincote for the temple of Surya, a Hindu deity, set by a pool. Repton's version at Brighton is a direct copy. The lantern tower in the

RIGHT Humphry Repton, *Designs for the Pavillon* [sic] *at Brighton*, 1808. 'After' view of the Western Lawn, from the stables. On the steps of the square pool the musicians have been replaced by gardeners collecting water. A laburnum tree is given prominence in the planting. Repton's notes state that 'a pool is absolutely necessary in this place, because no Indian building is ever seen without'.

RIGHT Humphry Repton, *Designs for the Pavillon* [sic] *at Brighton*, 1808. 'After' view looking towards his proposed Pavilion.

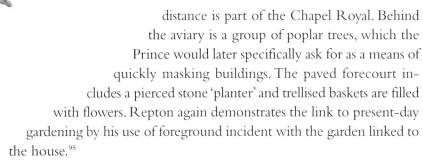

distance is part of the Chapel Royal. Behind the aviary is a group of poplar trees, which the Prince would later specifically ask for as a means of quickly masking buildings. The paved forecourt includes a pierced stone 'planter' and trellised baskets are filled with flowers. Repton again demonstrates the link to present-day gardening by his use of foreground incident with the garden linked to the house.[95]

From this view it is clear that an element of formality had returned to garden design, which would gain momentum, proving adaptable to smaller gardens. The artificial layout suited the new interest in horticulture and the extended range of plants that became available. Formal gardens were the perfect way to display new plants. Repton's garden, had it been realised, would have been a highly original example of an almost Moghal garden, unique in England. The square-shaped pool may have been included to please the Prince, who had applauded Repton's use of straight lines. The view also shows the way that Repton had tried to increase the interest within a small space, providing areas that enabled different plants to be grown or displayed. The paved entrance was used for display rather like a modern patio. The glazed corridors meant that the garden could not only be used all year round, but also provided areas to display tender plants. Eventually no fashionable house would be without a conservatory.

Looking from the stables towards the Pavilion in the same proposal (opposite), Repton's spectacular transformation can be seen. His oriental palace is revealed. It looks like a backdrop for the popular Regency toy theatres. It fails to convince unlike Nash's later simpler more solid building, which was based on the same sources. Porden's stables are decorated with plants, even the drainpipe has been utilised. The flower corridors, especially those on the far left, look remarkably similar to Holland's design for Albany in Piccadilly. They also relate to Holland's East front at Brighton and the covered walk next to the Chinese dairy at Woburn Abbey. The gardener in the foreground is planting up a container with seasonal plants. This idea was not new. In 1800 John Trusler published advice on the design and laying out of pleasure grounds for gentlemen suggesting, 'in flower gardens, by having a succession of various flowers in pots, they might be buried in the ground, and as they fell away in bloom, might be removed and others brought to supply their place … a constant succession and the flowers never seen but in the height of their beauty'.[96] He also advised that festoons of honeysuckles could be trained between the trees, led along a wire fixed between them. Repton used a similar device in the foreground tree.

LEFT *Laburnum anagyroides* (Golden Rain Tree) from woodland and mountain areas of south-east Europe and western Asia grown in England since c.1560 for their profuse, pendent, pea-like flowers. In early Summer the bright yellow dangling racemes give the tree its common name. Repton suggested 'this shower of yellow' in his proposal for the pool side at Brighton. In the restored Regency garden the Laburnum was planted, as suggested by period designers in groups to maximise their effect.

On the other side of the Marine Pavilion facing the Steine, Repton's 'before' view of the East Front shows a deliberately played-down scene. As always, it had to look completely unworthy and the planting inadequate to make his point. The subtle Holland plan and Lapidge's planting is reduced to a path right up to the perimeter bed. The border comprises low flowering shrubs in regular clumps. There are few trees. The surrounding red brick buildings and the Venetian window of the Castle Tavern ballroom are given prominence. To Repton they were both eyesores to be hidden from sight. He called them *scarlet sins* against good taste. 'New red houses, with all the fanciful apertures of Venetian … windows, which disgust the traveller, who looks in vain for the picturesque shapes … of former times'.[97] The grounds are cleverly depicted as if they had no privacy from the visitors and windows on the Steine or the overlooking Castle Tavern.

It was at the Castle Tavern, in Repton's lodging rooms, that the Prince first saw his designs for the garden. The Prince spent an hour looking at them and was so excited by the ideas that he arranged for them to be shown to Mrs Fitzherbert at her new house on the Steine, next to the Castle Tavern. Repton described the fateful meeting, 'Here – half reclining on a Sofa – surrounded by cushions and footstools – was the favourite friend, and (Wife as she thought herself) of the future King of England! Her person was large, and loaded with lace, and drapery'. She did not respond with the same enthusiasm to the drawings 'and as to the maps, they were totally incomprehensible to eyes which shone to be admired, rather to admire anything. There is no accounting for the species of charm by which the most opposite Natures are brought to coalliance! … All the remark she made on the subject so interesting to him was – "and pray what is all this to cost?"[98]

Repton's 'after' proposal for the East Front from the same viewpoint is hardly recognisable as the same place. The columns of the Saloon have become supports for climbing plants. The classical dress has been changed to a simplified Chinese canopy. It is similar to that facing Holland's Chinese dairy at Woburn, for which Repton had just designed the garden. The Castle Tavern, what

can be seen of it, has now been rendered a stone colour. All the 'scarlet sins' and the Venetian window have been obscured with huge trees. Repton had experience of tree-moving early in his career at Blandsbury. He had created an instant garden for his seventy year old client Lady Salisbury 'By employing a number of labourers to plant a great many trees … of the largest size that it was possible to move … to the great delight of the Venerable Owner, who lived nearly twenty years to enjoy it'.[99]

At Brighton there were to be two rows of trees with a raised terrace between them to hide the Steine. He had shown his concern about this ambitious tree planting in a letter to Lord Sheffield at nearby Sheffield Park, 'I have completed my plans for the Gardens of the Pavilion so much to the satisfaction of the Prince, that I am only anxious how to do them justice in the execution'. Repton asks Lord Sheffield for a quantity of sharpened birch trees, without roots, to act as 'wet nurses' for the proposed new plantings at Brighton, as the Prince was anxious about their exposure to wind from the sea.[100] In his proposal the gap in the planting gave a sea view and reduced the amount of the grounds that could be overlooked. The houses in the centre distance have conveniently disappeared. The angled conservatory of the Marine Pavilion has also vanished. To complete the artifice the lawn is scattered with circular beds of flowers edged as baskets. These plants were intended to be replaced each season as were the plants in his flower corridors on the western lawns.

Repton would use the idea of shaped beds edged as baskets in many of his designs. His Marine Pavilion proposed the most spectacular use of them. Such flower beds were formed as a low mound of earth highest at the centre, 'the first year they were planted with annuals, herbaceous plants, roses, shrubs, and geraniums in pots. The following autumn the main beds were to be planted with a hedge of dwarf roses, "with or without basket work". and filled with low flowers and roses'.[101]

TOP Humphry Repton, *Designs for the Pavillon* [sic] *at Brighton*, 1808. 'Before' view of the existing approach to the Pavilion.

ABOVE Humphry Repton, *Designs for the Pavillon* [sic] *at Brighton*, 1808. The same viewpoint of the approach with the flaps removed to show his 'after' view.

Repton's 'before' view of the northern approach to the Pavilion at this time shows the enormous bulk of Marlborough House, dominating the Marine Pavilion. Repton had been told to include it in his plans for a new house and gardens even though the Prince did not purchase it until 1812. The eventual purchase and landscaping of it was described in 1818: 'The Prince Regent purchased … a piece of land to the North of Marlborough House … and enclosed it with a flint wall, ornamented with a low palisading … planted with shrubs and laid out in grass plats, walks and so on, which add considerably to the rural beauties of the enclosures.'[102]

Marlborough Row, seen on the right, had also been included in Repton's instructions. The row of eight houses and a smithy were demolished sequentially, 1-4 in 1820, and a year later numbers 5-7. In his 'after' view the whole row has been removed revealing the stables behind a flint wall. Number eight is still standing today and is known as Northgate House.[103] The Prince Regent had to use these houses as accommodation until the Royal Pavilion was finished. The projecting wing on the left of Repton's proposal was to be the Prince's private apartments. From the viewing platform on the roof, the sea and the Chinese garden on the east front could be enjoyed. Loudon later commented on this proposal, 'the private apartments were never built and the consequence is, that the sea is not seen at all from any part of the Pavilion; a circumstance which renders it altogether ridiculous as a marine palace'.[104]

Repton's innovative designs for the Marine Pavilion were to come to nothing. Mrs Fitzherbert's cautious and sensible response to his drawings were based on fact. She knew there was no money to finance this palatial scheme as the Prince was hopelessly in debt. In the letter informing Repton of the situation was an apology for wasting his time. 'So ended my Royal hopes!' The formal moghul garden overlooked by perpetual flowering covered walks were only realised on paper. His Oriental palace would not be built, yet in it were elements that would be used in a simpler, more confident and unifying design. That design would be made by his one-time friend, business partner and eventual rival, John Nash. Looking back on the events of his life, the result of the Brighton commission was seen as a devastating but temporary defeat, "The two cleverest men in England" – The one was a fool and the other? – ah well! *He* has indeed "carried all the *World before him*" but he has left me behind for the present'.[105]

Part of Repton's manuscript autobiography was, ironically, discovered in Brighton in a 'job lot' bought by a local bookseller in 1976 and subsequently sold at Christie's five years later. The manuscript includes a long, detailed account of the sequence of events at Brighton. It is heartbreaking, yet gives a vivid picture of the time. The Brighton proposals would never be mentioned again. The following year, 1807, the Prince of Wales was in

Romford reviewing troops. Repton lived nearby and in the breakfast tent afterwards he was seated at the same table as the Prince. It must have been a difficult moment. '"Ah! Mr Repton I am glad to see you, how are your engagements for next week?"'. Repton was now asked to advise on the gardens at Carlton House. Again, his proposals came to nothing and he was later even refused admittance to Carlton House. 'I was superseded without the least ceremony or consideration. Again all my hopes from Royal favor faded away'. As if to pile on the agony he added, 'I heard no more of Brighton for 10 years – but being there one day … I called at the Pavillon [*sic*], and was refused admittance!'[106] His concluding comment was 'that it is better to trust in the Lord than to put any confidence in man. It is better to trust in the Lord than to put any confidence in Princes'.

In spite of Repton's disappointment over losing the Pavilion commission he published the Red Book. He was further disappointed that the Prince had never asked for the original back from the publishers. The Pavilion Red Book was included in Loudon's later reprint of Repton's works where many people saw it.

After the Repton interlude, beginning in 1805, no changes were made to the grounds for eight years. The site remained as Holland and Porden had left it. The Prince was, however, still searching for a way to extend the Marine Pavilion and harmonise it with the stables. It was still a disjointed range of buildings that included Marlborough House. It was not until 1813 that changes were planned and Nash completely transformed and unified the building and the garden.

Meanwhile the existing gardens had to be looked after and the first bill for their maintenance appears at this time. Two important names who would be involved in the future transformation of the garden are first mentioned, William Townsend Aiton, the Royal Gardener at Kew, and John Furner, the Brighton gardener. Furner, his father William and his brother Thomas, had lived in a house next to their large market garden. Their whole property had been bought by Porden and New Road, as it is still called today, was built over part of their land, which enabled the Prince's plans for the Marine Pavilion to proceed. These negotiations resulted in new opportunities for the gardening family. They moved to two houses nearby and were employed by the Royal Household as gardeners. From now on the garden at Brighton was included in the itemised quarterly expenditure for all the Royal Gardens, 'Mr Furner has a salary of £146 per annum or £36.10s. payable quarterly'.[107] Furner's first bill was for 'extra labour at the Royal Gardens at Brighton'. The first itemised bill covers the period from October 1812 to January 1813 and lists the extra labour of two men, with 'cash paid for new flower pots, scythes, brooms and annual flower seeds - 9s.4d'. The maintenance of the lawns was a high priority as most of the following year the costs relate to them, labour, grass baskets (to collect the scythed grass) and 128 bushels of soot as a top dressing for the grass.

BELOW Humphry Repton's proposal for the garden at Carlton House, watercolour, 1807.
The Royal Collection © 2003 Her Majesty Queen Elizabeth II. The former dense boundary of trees has been thinned out to provide variety of outline and to give a glimpse of Westminster Abbey. The ground is shaped and irregular shrubberies give interest to the lawn.

In November Aiton records 'Mr John Furners account, expenses to London visiting Mr Aiton and Mr Nash, respecting the new work – £3.17s.5d'.[108] This was to signal the transformation of the grounds and the meeting was to brief Furner on the grand scheme ahead. By this time the Prince had become Regent and Nash was responsible for all his personal residences. He would design the gardens for all four of them, and they would be planted by Aiton. There were some very grand schemes ahead. The Regency period in gardening was about to take off with a concurrent series of private and spectacular public projects that would give the Prince Regent and the new era a focus and a setting. All of them would influence the layout and the planting of the garden at Brighton.

VIEW FROM THE PRINCIPAL FLOOR OF CARLETON-HOUSE

the foreground supposed a balcony in the style of the House whether GOTHIC or GRECIAN

A New Park and Three New Gardens for the Prince Regent

*The presence of his majesty here [Brighton] …
acts as a powerful drawback to the pleasures of the
metropolis'.*

– *The Brighton Magazine*, FEBRUARY 1822.

BELOW George Stanley Repton, *Cronkhill, Shropshire*, watercolour, c.1802. Reproduced by courtesy of the Trustees of Sir John Soane's Museum. Repton, son of Humphry Repton, was draughtsman in Nash's office from 1801-1817. Cronkhill was one of the earliest Italinate villas. The 'Tuscan' projecting eaves would be used at Park Village East and West, Regent's Park, on land Nash leased in 1823. The beautifully composed ornamental shrubbery in the watercolour has similarities to Brighton and would require serious future maintenance.

THE PRINCE OF WALES became Regent in 1811 and was King in all but name. For John Nash this period was the busiest and most creative of his life; he was by then almost sixty. Four new projects were initiated that ran concurrently. They all involved him in the design of outdoor spaces. They ranged from a new landscaped park and the garden of the Prince Regent's London house, to a Royal Cottage at Windsor and the garden at Brighton. They were to be followed by the garden at Buckingham Palace.

Nash, unlike Repton, was not concerned with creating elaborate artificial effects near the house or of providing separate areas in a garden designated for the display of particular plants. As an architect, his idea of a garden as a setting for his buildings derived from his friendship and working relationship with Richard Payne Knight and Sir Uvedale Price, the two main exponents of a more exciting, emotional response to landscape. These two Herefordshire squires used wild, un-

kempt and dramatic natural scenery as inspiration for gardens. They thought that this would 'naturalise' or anchor a building to its surroundings.[109] Nash assimilated their ideas and use the effects found in natural scenery to provide a setting that exactly complemented his new buildings. The landscape setting of his houses would contribute to the immediate feeling and sensation of the building. A generalised 'broad brush' approach was required, rather than a detailed intricate garden design, which would have diluted the overall impression and competed with the architecture. Nash popularised the irregular 'castle' style, which had been used earlier by Payne Knight for his own house, Downton Castle in Herefordshire. It was one of the first deliberately planned asymmetrical buildings in England to which Nash may have also contributed. Knight had a comprehensive collection of Claude drawings that Nash would have seen.[110] He had designed Cronkhill, which looks like a Claude drawing of an Italian vernacular building in rural Shropshire. By 1811 he had reinterpreted the English vernacular style, most inventively at Blaise Hamlet, outside Bristol, with a cluster of irregular thatched cottages that were a precursor to Royal Lodge. In comparison Holland's symmetrical designs at Brighton must have seemed very old fashioned and dull.

ABOVE Engravings from drawings by Thomas Shepherd, from J. Elmes, *Metropolitan Improvements*, 1827. © The British Library. Top: Albany Villa, Regent's Park, designed by Samuel Pepys Cockerell. Below: The Holme, Regent's Park, designed by Decimus Burton.

The creation of Regent's Park was one of the first London projects that Nash undertook. It celebrated and subsequently defined the Regency era. From its inception it was composed as a landscape picture on a grand scale, with the sweep of the scenic terraces and separate villas set in and around extensive vistas of trees. It was submitted and approved in 1811. It would replace Marylebone Park, which had reverted to the Crown that year. The plan was revised many times, yet retained the strong parkland setting. The park would be the first open space within a city to be designed as a landscaped housing development. So important was the planting element that it was established first. Over 14,000 trees were planted as a setting for the future buildings. The setting was seen as part of the attractions of living there, making designed open green space part of town planning for the first time and so raising revenue for the Crown. The idea was that the trees could be cut as timber and sold when the plots were cleared for building. The gardens of the villas, completed from 1817, would relate to the gardens at Brighton. The illustrations show shrubs and trees composed in the same way, with mixed planting forming irregular shrubberies. The villas and their gardens sum up the ideal of the Regency house. James Elmes, who wrote about improvements in the Metropolis in the 1820s, explained the idea behind the project, 'John Nash … embraced all those beauties of landscape gardening which his friend, the late Humphry Repton, so successfully introduced … they began by planting the whole demise … it has therefore had the advantage of so many years growth while the buildings are in progress. There is another advantage in this process, much in favour of the divine art of landscape gardening, which is, that from the moment of finishing either, buildings or planting, the former begins to decay, and the latter to flourish'. He described two of the new villas, 'The Holme', designed by Decimus Burton, was 'the work of a young architect

and is creditable to his rising abilities'. It was praised for its 'charming plantations and lovely ever-greens'. Burton also designed grand architectural schemes for Brighton. Albany Villa was designed by Samuel Pepys Cockerell. Elmes thought that the villas were 'garnished with horticultural decorations … looking with a pictorial eye, at their present capabilities and prospects of future growth, they are beautifully diversified, and give a characteristic back-ground and accompaniment to the principle feature – the house'.[111] This comment could equally have applied to the completed Pavilion at Brighton.

Regent's Park was cleverly laid out to maintain the impression of uninterrupted landscape. The separate villas, and their gardens were screened from each other by the surrounding trees that also concealed the houses from the wider park scenery. The plan was to connect the park to central London. A new thoroughfare, aptly named Regent Street, was driven through a hotch-potch of streets to terminate in front of the Prince Regent's own house. In a brilliant grand plan for London and the Prince Regent, Regent's Park was linked by Regent Street to the Prince Regent's London headquarters, Carlton House. The main axis of Nash's new street was even centred on the entrance colonnade of Carlton House.

At Carlton House itself Nash contributed a suite of rooms giving on to the garden. The garden was transformed into an enormous outdoor room. It would become an extension of the house, covered with temporary buildings and up to twenty tents, which would be used for a series of events or fêtes. They demonstrated the Prince Regent's showmanship, theatrical flare and his ability to lead and represent the country in hosting and celebrating national events. At last he was in his element. The events planned for 1813 were to celebrate Wellington's victories over the French. In the accounts were itemised 'Carver and gilders work, fitting up the Pagoda and Chinese Pavillion [*sic*] in the gardens at Carlton House'.[112] The events culminated in 1814 with a grand fête to

celebrate peace. For this Nash constructed a rotunda 120 feet in diameter. The distinctive upswept tent roof would have obvious repercussions at Brighton and may have been in his mind at the time, as a possible solution for extending the Royal Pavilion. The illustration, (above) shows that a similar tented roof was to form part of the distinctive silhouette of the final Pavilion, which was begun the following year.

The rotunda would remain in the garden of Carlton House for five years. It was then presented to The Royal Regiment of Artillery as a museum at Woolwich. Nash reconstructed the twenty-four-sided perimeter wall in brick and covered the oiled-cloth roof with lead, as can be seen today. The irony is that all that is left of Carlton House is a temporary structure used for parties in the garden. It was also an early indication of the eventual solution to the Royal Pavilion.

William Townsend Aiton's bills for work on the garden at Carlton House appear in 1812. There were many references to the making and remaking of the lawn.[113] The reason was given in Aiton's account on 7 September 1813, 'The extra expences [sic] incurred in the gardens at Carlton House preparatory to the Grand Fetes of HRH the Prince Regent'.[114] In June of that year the garden bills reflected the preparation required. The bill for up to forty-nine men on site for nine days from 28 June came to £60. 3s. 3d. The extra cost of four and a half gallons of beer, 161 pounds of cheese and seventy loaves totalled £28. 8s. 8d.[115] Yew boughs and two wagon loads of orange trees were brought from Kensington Gardens. Flowers were delivered, decorators' work was itemised along with the arrival of trees, columns, ivy, laurel and Norfolk Island pines. Garden seats and chairs were hired. The delivery of bog earth and plants, noted as an extraneous bill, no doubt referred to a special display of American plants such as the spectacular rhododendrons. Shrubs from America, which grew in bog earth (acid loam) were highly fashionable. The rhododendron would later be introduced to the Pavilion's gardens.

The Carlton House display must have been superb. The activities, including the carpentry work, make it sound like an early Chelsea Flower Show. The decoration of Nash's rotunda included painting the inside of the upswept roof to imitate white muslin with gilt cords as ribs. 1,448 yards of artificial flowers were supplied along with mirrors, muslin drapery and twelve glass chandeliers of twenty-four lights each. It must have been some party! The necessity of using the garden for such festivities was one of the reasons the Prince Regent would move to what became Buckingham Palace since Carlton House lacked space. In a desperate move, he even considered taking possession of Marlborough House, which adjoined his garden on The Mall.

As a complete contrast to this public party atmosphere, Aiton and Nash were at the same time planning a completely private domain for the Prince Regent. The account for 'Labour and bills for executing the Works of the New Garden at the Cottage of HRH The Prince Regent in Windsor Great Park' was submitted in October 1815'.[116] The itemised lists include the carting of turf, gravel, plants and ice for filling the ice house. The plants and shrubs, from six suppliers, were costed at £108. 7s. 6d. The whole bill came to £633. 3s. 5d. Nash and Aiton were to surround the cottage with plantations to disguise its vast size. It was renamed Royal Lodge. It would become one of the grandest cottages ever built, with forests of chimney stacks. To add the final rustic touch it would be thatched with bonneted windows, a verandah and a huge conservatory. The slender cast iron structure, with Nash's signature roof trusses, were to pioneer the use of this material at Brighton. Cast iron made possible the construction of the domes, minarets and staircases. At Windsor the supports were covered with climbing plants and exotics could be viewed from the stone walkways between avenues of luxurious trees, treated as standards.

The kind of plants that are listed as being sent to the Windsor cottage in May 1816[117] would make another appearance at Brighton, in similar quantities. It is a long list: 175 laurels, 80 laurustinus (much used at Brighton), 130 tree box, 31 *arbor vitaes*, 148 hollies, another 300 laurels, 100 Portugal laurels, 18 almond trees, 100 large tree box, 125 large rhododendrons, 4 aristolochias (this did not appear at Brighton and is a woody, twining climber with heart-shaped leaves and curious syphon-like, yellow-green and brown-mouthed flowers, resembling a Dutchman's pipe'), two *buddlia blobosa*' (an amusing misspelling of *Buddleia globosa*), four Irish ivies (this would be *Hibernica*, which is very vigorous with large leaves) and ten parcels of hardy annuals. The illustrations of the cottage show it beautifully furnished with plants. The bulk of the above order was to conceal it completely

BELOW Top: *Entrance (north) front of His Majesty's Cottage, Windsor Great Park*. Below: His Majesty's Cottage, as seen from the lawn (south) from *Ackermann's Repository*, 1823. The Royal Collection © 2003 Her Majesty Queen Elizabeth II. The gabled roofs of the Cottage and its verandah are thatched. The conservatory is on the left.

from the outside world. Perhaps the aristolochias were intended to climb the rustic verandah posts.[118] Being mostly frost tender they probably added another exotic touch to the enormous cast iron conservatory, where birds flew around. Peacocks are depicted on the lawn. It must have been a magical place, tucked away in a glade, approached through densely planted woodland. Nash's inventiveness and versatility as an architect were demonstrated in the diverse projects that were taking place concurrently. As well as Windsor Cottage, Regent's Park was still continuing and so were the fêtes at Carlton House.

Aiton, like Nash, adapted to new responsibilities, far removed from his original contract of 1796. At that time he was 'cropping with oats and barley' the twenty-six acres in front of the pagoda at Kew, 'to moving His Majesty's Sheep, four times a year' so that the lawns could be fed, 'to keeping the waters in Kew Gardens clean and free from weeds … and to take care of the fish'[119] and the kangaroos from Botany Bay. Now he was also organising and planting the new gardens for the Prince Regent, as well as running Kew with its influx of new plants from around the world. The pace of work continued unabated for both Aiton and Nash with the transformation of the Marine Pavilion and its Regency garden.

RIGHT *Buddleia globosa* 'Chilian Orange Ball Tree'. This was planted at the Windsor cottage and at Brighton.

REGENCY GARDENS

'Looking at the finest passages of forest scenery ...
what beauties would be added to the park by imitating
such scenery'.

— J. C. LOUDON, *Treatise on Forming, Improving, and Managing Country Estates,* 1806.

BELOW *Aster amellus* (Violet Queen).

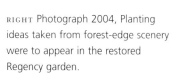

THE REGENCY GARDEN style can be summarised as a group of trees, shrubs, herbaceous plants, bulbs and annuals mixed together in a relaxed composition. It was a contrived version of forest edge scenery where Nature would be assisted with the introduction of 'accent' plants within the basic, contrasting arrangement of 'greens'. The irregularly shaped shrubberies were packed with plants, which would be of interest throughout the year. The idea of a succession of flowering plants and shrubs was new at the time though it is now taken for granted in garden design. The idea was to recreate in the garden the subtle, accidental effects seen in the countryside. Shrubs and trees were looked at more closely; leaf shapes, texture, seedpods, colour and seasonal changes were celebrated and combined.

Regency architects planned houses to have a more irregular appearance to reflect a more informal, relaxed lifestyle. The same principles were applied to gardens. In 1803 Repton made an important comment on irregularity and its advantages for architects and gardeners, 'Symmetry ... assists the eye in viewing and comprehending the whole object at once, but irregularity retards the progress of vision; and from the difficulty of comprehending the whole, its magnitude increases on the imagination'.[120] The completed Pavilion and its garden, where the mature planting partly obscures the building in deliberately framed views as it is approached, would bear this out and added to the mystery and magical first impressions for the visitor.

Guests at the Pavilion could be surrounded by planting in one area and have open views across the lawns in others. The Regency colour palette was not subdued or tonal, the colour combinations seen in the garden reflected those inside the Pavilion. Lilac and yellow were seen as harmonious and with an Autumn flowering plant such as *Aster amellus* 'Violet Queen', they were combined in the same flower with its lilac petals and yellow centres. The colours of flowers, used

RIGHT Photograph 2004, Planting ideas taken from forest-edge scenery were to appear in the restored Regency garden.

as jewel-like accents, were offset by the surrounding greenery and foliage, unlike later blazing minia-ture bedding, where flowers were used as Berlin wool-work tufts without greenery or the careful toning herbaceous clumps of the Edwardians. The Regency colour scheme is fashionable again as designers and gardeners have moved on from the predominately pastel 'heritage' gardening era of the 1980s.

A conservatory extended the Regency house into the garden giving greater scope for archi-tectural irregularity and new possibilities for horticultural display. It also brought the garden into the house. The popularity of linking the garden to the house with a conservatory was commented on in the letters of the writer and playwright, Maria Edgeworth, 'Small conservatories added to drawing-room and library make them both cheerful. How this luxury of conservatories added to rooms and opening into them has become general'.[121] The completed Pavilion can be seen as an enormous garden building. The main rooms all opened into the garden through French windows.

The completed Pavilion included over sixty French windows, opening on to the lawns or balconies, with views over the gardens. Repton had realised that the position of the glazing bars was crucial to ensure an uninterrupted view of the garden, 'There is no subject connected with landscape gardening of more importance, or less attended to than the Window through which the landscape is seen … which has never before been mentioned in books on Architecture, viz. the situation of the bar, which is too apt to cross the eye and injure the view'.[122] He recommended that the bar should not be more than 4 feet 9 inches, nor less than 4 feet 6 inches from the floor, then sitting or standing it would not obstruct the view. Jane Austen used the idea of the fashion-able cut-down windows to form an enticing image, 'A young woman, pretty, lively, with a harp as elegant as herself; and both placed near a window cut down to the ground, and opening on a little lawn, surrounded by shrubs in the rich foliage of summer, was enough to catch any man's heart'.[123]

ABOVE The Regency garden adapted planting ideas taken from the accidental effects seen in the countyside. Native plants are 'assisted' with garden hybrids. *Robinia hispida* 'Rose Acacia' can be seen above the peony in the restored garden.

Digitalis purpurea

RIGHT The planting is used to frame
and compose the building. The
Chrysanthemum maxima was
introduced in 1816.

BELOW The foxglove and forget-me-
not, (drawn on the right), appear in
the restored garden as if naturalised
under trees.

The desire to incorporate the outside world led to a new appreciation of Nature and the lessons that could be learnt by gardeners in studying the natural accidental plant combinations found in the countryside. Several rival garden writers were advocating a return to Nature as a new direction for gardeners.

As early as 1796 the landscape gardener and surveyor, William Marshall, was promoting a more natural look for gardens and suggested that inspiration could be taken from how plants are found growing together in the wild, 'how often do we see in natural scenery, the holly and the foxglove flourishing at the foot of an oak and the primrose and campion adding to the hawthorn, scattered over the pastured lawns … single trees footed with evergreens and native flowers and tufts, as well as borders of shrubs are admirable in *ornamental*, as well as *natural* scenery'.[124]

The Pavilion garden incorporated some native roses listed by Marshall. 'The *Rosa Canina*: the dog rose, common in our hedges. The *Rosa Pimpernellifolia*: the Burnet Rose, natural to England. *Rosa Centifolia*, the hundred leaved rose, Rosa Gallica, grown naturally in Europe. The evergreen or musk rose *Sempervivens*, and *Rosa Alba*'.[125] These were all to contribute to the natural, native, relaxed look. They have an elegant natural habit with small-leaved foliage. The flowers have a simplicity that melds into informal planting, unlike their highly-bred garden cousins. Marshall makes a special case for the laurustinus, 'It is one of the great ornaments of our gardens in the winter months … a fine evergreen … it will either be in full blow [flower], or … exhibit its flowers and buds in large bunches ready to burst open … at a time when other flowers and trees shrink under oppressive cold, is a matter of wonder and pleasure'.[126] Over 240 laurustinus were ordered for Brighton, ensuring the garden looked splendid for the winter visits of the court.

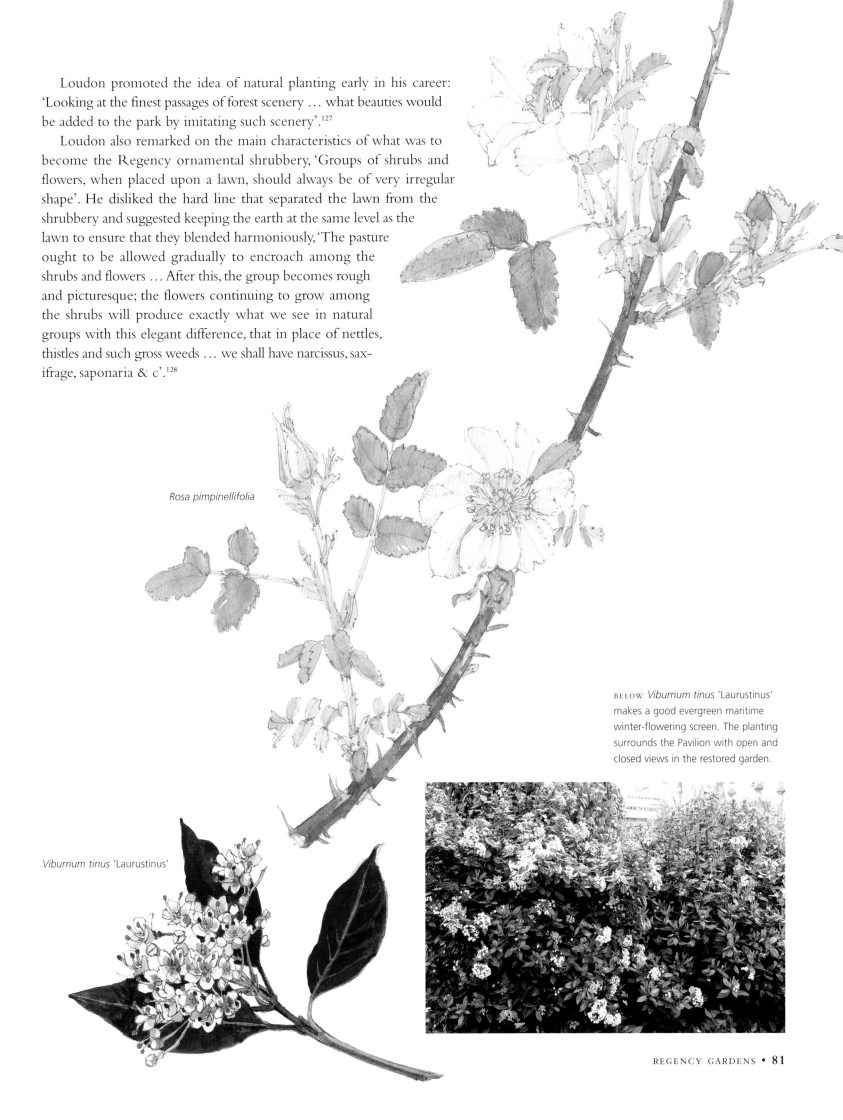

Loudon promoted the idea of natural planting early in his career: 'Looking at the finest passages of forest scenery … what beauties would be added to the park by imitating such scenery'.[127]

Loudon also remarked on the main characteristics of what was to become the Regency ornamental shrubbery, 'Groups of shrubs and flowers, when placed upon a lawn, should always be of very irregular shape'. He disliked the hard line that separated the lawn from the shrubbery and suggested keeping the earth at the same level as the lawn to ensure that they blended harmoniously, 'The pasture ought to be allowed gradually to encroach among the shrubs and flowers … After this, the group becomes rough and picturesque; the flowers continuing to grow among the shrubs will produce exactly what we see in natural groups with this elegant difference, that in place of nettles, thistles and such gross weeds … we shall have narcissus, saxifrage, saponaria & c'.[128]

Rosa pimpinellifolia

BELOW *Viburnum tinus* 'Laurustinus' makes a good evergreen maritime winter-flowering screen. The planting surrounds the Pavilion with open and closed views in the restored garden.

Viburnum tinus 'Laurustinus'

RIGHT Plants arranged in a haphazard way to look as natural as possible.

BELOW The planting under the white lilac (below) includes the *Rosa chinensis* 'Mutabilis'.

BELOW-RIGHT In the restored garden the shrubberies, of irregular outline, meander and project into the lawns. The railings are a modern addition.

As well as the irregular-shaped beds, the plants within them should be arranged as though in a haphazard way, 'In planting the shrubs in these groups, the great art is to put them in irregularly … as if no outline or form of group existed. This, however, is never done … the shrubs are regularly distributed over every part of it … an appearance as different from the irregular group thickets of nature'.[129]

Primula vulgaris
(primrose)

One of the disadvantages of this style was identified by Loudon: 'According to Repton and all the followers of the picturesque school, trees, shrubs, and flowers were indiscriminately mixed, and crowded together, in shrubberies … and they were generally left to grow up and destroy one another'.[130] Loudon realised that the ornamental shrubberies required constant maintenance or the planting would eventually degenerate into what became the gloomy Victorian shrubbery. For this reason the style was short lived. It will constitute a major challenge in the restored garden at Brighton as the shrubberies will need to be coppiced. Established trees within the beds need to be replaced with younger, smaller examples, otherwise the trees, if left to mature, will grow to shade out all the other plants and their eventual height will turn the grounds into a dense forest!

The lawn became a crucial link between the house and the garden and its use, maintenance and appearance was a major concern. If the house had direct access to the lawn, the gardens could be used as outside rooms. The architect and designer, John Buonarotti Papworth, refers to the use of lawns as a 'green carpet', which could be used as an extension to the ground floor rooms of a house. 'By the lawn is meant that portion of grass-plat … which is constantly kept mown, forming a verdant carpet on which the building stands, and amongst the improvements that have resulted from the modern practice of gardening it merits particular notice … in fact, the lawn has become a favourite auxiliary to every apartment on the ground floor'.[131] Loudon suggested that the lawn should be left as a natural meadow, which would also save on the cost of mowing. Instead of 'mere grasses; which re-

Viola odorata
(violet)

quire continual mowing and present one dull, vapid, surface of uniform green. They should be composed of primroses, violets, common and garden daisy, camomile (and three kinds of grasses), the whole of them judiciously mixed, would form a variegated carpet of gay flowers from April to December, the effect … compared to a mown lawn, would be as gaiety to gloom, or insipidity to expression – All the expense of mowing would be avoided … with such a variety of roughness as would give the whole a natural appearance'.[132] This kind of meadow lawn sounds very modern. Loudon did not advocate such views for long. It was a logical, if extreme, reaction to the unnatural look of perfect short grass, but it did not catch on at the time. An immaculate shaved lawn is still an obsession with some gardeners. Loudon would have been disappointed by the appearance of the Brighton lawns as recurring entries in the accounts record 'Cash paid for weeding turf'.[133]

Bellis perennis
(common daisy)

Lawns needed constant maintenance. The introduction of grass-cutting machinery revolutionised the task. It signalled the arrival of the lawn as an essential element in the gardens of new suburban detached houses. Lawns had been the preserve of the rich who could afford the upkeep with scything, rolling and sweeping. The lawn mower also improved the recreational grounds for cricket, tennis, bowling and croquet.

The first mechanical lawn mower was invented by Edwin Budding, a freelance engineer. The idea of cutting grass with a rotary (cylindrical) cutter came to him after seeing rotary cutters designed to trim the nap off wool cloth at a Gloucestershire mill. With his business partner, John Ferrabee, a mill owner, the new machine was marketed after the agreement between them was signed on 18 May 1830, 'Whereas the said Budding hath invented and applied a new combination of machinery for the purpose of cropping and shearing the vegetable surface of Lawns, Grassplots and Pleasure Grounds, consisting of a machine which may be used with advantage instead of a sithe [sic] for that purpose'.[134] In the specification accompanying the patent (October 1830) Budding advised that 'Country gentlemen may find that using my machine themselves an amusing, useful and healthy exercise'.[135] It revolutionised the task, as it enabled gardeners to maintain their own lawns.[136] Even one hundred years later the *Gardener's Assistant* could report that 'Since the invention of the lawn-mower, lawns are kept in better condition and at much less cost than when the scythe alone was used'.[137] In the Regency garden, as earlier, lawns were hand scythed. An American visitor to Regency England, Louis Simond, was impressed by the lawns he had seen, 'I have been induced by the beauty of English lawns … The rolling is principally done in the spring when the surface is sufficiently firm not to poach [to be cut up by horses' hooves]. The mowing, or rather the shaving of this smooth surface, is done once a week … once a month does in dry weather.

ABOVE The first lawn mower, produced by Ferrabee of Stroud to Budding's patent in 1830. The gentleman using the new machine was illustrated in Loudon's *Encyclopaedia of Gardening* (reprint 1835). The grass box is the flat tray (d), the small roller to regulate height (b) is directly behind the cylinder (c).

The grass must be wet with dew or rain, and the scythe very sharp; the blade is wide, and set so obliquely on the handle, as to lye very flat on the sod'.[138]

Scything required a very keen blade to cut the grass quickly. The noise of keeping the scythe sharp was commented upon: 'the silly habit that the mower has of indicating his industry, by the frequent use of the grit-stone in sharpening his scythe; and generally at the time of the morning when such noises are most tormenting'.[139]

Unlike mowing with a machine, which should be done when the grass is dry, scything was done when the grass was wet. It was a skilled, but laborious job and depended on the swinging rhythm of the scythe. The cut had to be made cleanly, in one go, or the grass would just bend. The invention of the lawn mower gave gardeners more civilised hours and nearby residents more sleep.

As soon as turf was laid at Brighton in 1814 there follow bills for eight scythes, four dozen garden brooms, batts and rubbers for sharpening the scythes, two grass rakes and new grass baskets.[140]

Sylva Florifera, by Henry Phillips, a Brighton botanist and garden designer, was a useful and popular manual published in 1823, which provided an understandable, practical textbook for gardeners. His book brought the grand theories of the naturalistic style to a wider audience. It was to be invaluable during the restoration of the Pavilion's Regency garden, which began in 1982.

In his introduction, Phillips claims that 'The shrubbery originated in England and is as peculiar to the British nation as landscape planting, (unlike the other arts) this has indisputably sprung from the genius of our soil'.

Phillips's book was subtitled *Observations on the Forming of Ornamental Plantations and Picturesque Scenery*. It describes over fifty trees and shrubs suitable for creating shrubberies. He would have seen the garden being planted at the Pavilion. By 1823 Furner and Aiton had spent ten years shaping and planting the Pavilion's garden, parts of which would, by this stage, be maturing. Phillips followed Nash in suggesting that lawns should have an undulating surface and 'It should appear in different places to retire into the plantation, so as to give an idea of greater extent, especially when viewed from the windows of the villa. Where the coach road is carried through the lawn, it should be occasionally obscured by irregular clumps of shrubs'.[141] The restored shrubberies at Brighton would relate to Phillips's list of trees and shrubs and have been planted according to his suggestions.

LEFT Nash's *Views*, 1826, West Front, detail showing a scythe being sharpened on the turning circle in front of the Royal pavilion. Scything was best done very early in the morning, although the noise could become a nuisance.

The grouping of the 'shades of green' (the basic, permanent framework of trees and shrubs) as he called them, are an important element in the composition of the beds. 'Flowers continue but for a short period, in comparison to the duration of foliage; therefore the picture should be formed by judiciously contrasting the greens'.[142] Phillips also suggests using plants in a painterly way to help perspective. A foreground of bright or yellow greens with cooler tints behind gave an impression of distance. The 'shades of green' included the evergreens, variegated leaves and the consideration of the many berried shrubs and trees as part of the overall composition. It would also ensure interest throughout the year. 'A well planned shrubbery depends not so much for its beauty on the expense or rarity of the plants it contains, as on the selection of trees and shrubs which succeed each other in blossoming throughout the year'.[143] 'Four or six lilacs should be grouped in one place and as many laburnums in another'.[144] In the accounts for the Pavilion's garden, among the enormous quantity of plants listed, are over thirty-six syringas, two dozen purple lilacs, a dozen each of Siberian and white lilac, and eighteen dwarf syringas. There were also two dozen laburnums ordered.[145] They have been used in groups in the restored garden to form slabs of colour, rather than dotted throughout the garden.

ABOVE A foreground of yellow green with comfrey, *Symphytum caucasicus*, helps perspective.

RIGHT A selection of trees and plants that rely on composition rather than rarity.

Comfrey. *Symphytum caucasicus*.

*Philadelphus
coronarius* 'Aureus'
(opposite)

LEFT & BELOW The shrubberies near
the Pavilion are planted with more
variety than those at a distance. The
flowers are seen against surrounding
greenery Trees footed with flowering
plants as advised by Regency garden
designers

Crataegus oxycantha
'Coccinea Plena'. Hawthorn (above)

The general bold effect of the combination of plant material was to vary as the shrubberies receded away from the house. The more cultivated and 'showy' plants would be used in the beds near the house with more native varieties used further away. 'In proportion as the shrubbery or plantation recedes from the dwelling, it should become more rural in its character'.[146] This has been followed at Brighton for the restored garden. The main concentration of varied planting is around the carriage drive to the Pavilion's entrance. The distant walks assume a more natural character as at the edge of a forest, with less colour and incident.

In 1824 Henry Phillips published *Flora Historica, Observations on a Regular Succession of Flowers from Spring to Autumn.* This was a companion to *Sylva Florifera* and concentrated on flowers. Phillips advised that 'The bolder flowers should be half obscured by shrubs, for by being partially seen their effect is materially heightened'. Flowers should be used in the foreground 'in such situations they seem to have planted themselves as if for the sake of shelter whilst the boldness of the trees and shrubs add much to the delicacy of their blossoming'.[147]

The boldness of the grouping of trees and shrubs with flowering seasonal plants in the foreground was illustrated later with a rare published planting plan for an ornamental shrubbery. Prince Pückler-Muskau, who had toured England, Ireland and France between 1826-1829 had watched and admired the planting of Nash's shrubberies in St James's Park, after the Pavilion had been completed. He copied the ideas for his own elaborate park at Muskau in Germany. The plan was published in his book on the landscaped park at Muskau. He became a celebrated landscape gardener and was welcomed to many European courts. He stayed at Windsor in 1847 after he sold Muskau.

ABOVE A plan of a Nash-type ornamental shubbery from Prince Pückler-Muskau's *Hints on Landscape Gardening*, 1834. The unshaded areas on the plan indicate spring. The irregular-shaped shubbery, intepreted by the drawing shows how the plan might look if realised. It has similarities with photographs of planting in the Victorian grounds at Brighton p.117.

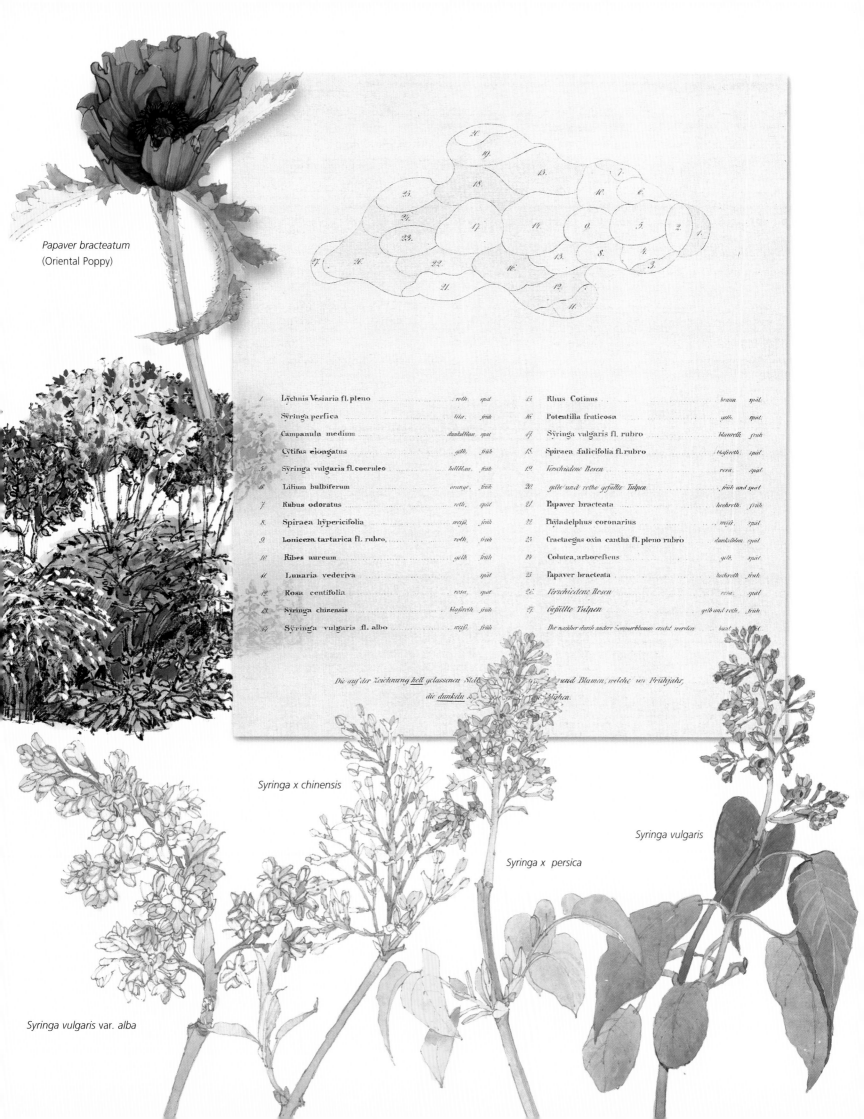

Papaver bracteatum
(Oriental Poppy)

1	Lychnis Vesiaria fl. pleno	roth	spät	15	Rhus Cotinus	braun	spät
2	Syringa persica	lila	früh	16	Potentilla fruticosa	gelb	spät
3	Campanula medium	dunkelblau	spät	17	Syringa vulgaris fl. rubro	blauroth	früh
4	Cytifus elongatus	gelb	früh	18	Spiraea falicifolia fl. rubro	blaßroth	spät
5	Syringa vulgaris fl. coeruleo	hellblau	früh	19	Verschiedene Rosen	rosa	spät
6	Lilium bulbiferum	orange	früh	20	gelbe und rothe gefüllte Tulpen		früh und spät
7	Rubus odoratus	roth	spät	21	Papaver bracteata	hochroth	früh
8	Spiraea hypericifolia	weiß	früh	22	Phyladelphus coronarius	weiß	spät
9	Lonicera tartarica fl. rubro	roth	früh	23	Craetaegus oxin cantha fl. pleno rubro	dunkelblau	spät
10	Ribes aureum	gelb	früh	24	Colutea arborefcens	gelb	spät
11	Lunaria vederiva		spät	25	Papaver bracteata	hochroth	früh
12	Rosa centifolia	rosa	spät	26	Verschiedene Rosen	rosa	spät
13	Syringa chinensis	blaßroth	früh	27	Gefüllte Tulpen	gelb und roth	früh
14	Syringa vulgaris fl. albo	weiß	früh		Die nachher durch andere Sommerblumen ersetzt werden	bunt	spät

Die auf der Zeichnung hell gelassenen Stelle .... und Blumen, welche im Frühjahr,
die dunkeln .... blühen.

Syringa x chinensis

Syringa x persica

Syringa vulgaris

Syringa vulgaris var. alba

RIGHT *Narcissus pseudonarcissus*, the wild daffodil, is now under threat from more robust modern cultivars.

Narcissus poeticus var. recurvus
(Pheasant's eye)

In Spring, Phillips suggested 'narcissus, snowdrops, crocus and primroses should be planted in considerable quantities, scattered as it were from Nature's hand'.[148] In the Pavilion gardens the wild daffodil (*narcissus pseudonarcissus*) and the crocus would be strewn over the lawn. Tulips would be grouped, as recommended, six to eighteen in one spot. Violets and periwinkles are used in the shrubberies that are more distant and with ivies they help conceal the hoop-top railings, which, of course, would not originally have edged the paths.

The Summer flowering plants included the Rosebay willow herb, which Phillips says was native in Sussex woods. He recommended it should have its roots confined in pots to control its spread.

Narcissus pseudonarcissus

Crocus vernus

Epilobium angustifolium (Rosebay willow herb)

RIGHT Rosebay willow herb and Meadow cranesbill, (*Geranium pratense*), part of the composition of the restored shubberies.

Vinca major (Periwinkle)

Rosa 'Petite Lisette'

Rosa x centifolia 'Muscosa'

Pittosporum tobira

Roses were essential and the Brighton garden accounts have them arriving fifty at a time, although only the moss, briar and China rose are specifically named. Phillips used mostly well-known flowers, lavatera, foxgloves, poppies, astrantia, day lilies and the Marvel of Peru. He explains that the Marvel of Peru or *Mirabilis jalapa* is suitable for public gardens frequented in the evening as the flowers open late in the day, from four o'clock in the afternoon, hence the popular name 'Four o'clock flower'. There were annuals, such as love-in-the-mist, nasturtiums and snap dragons. Scented plants are positioned near the path edges: santolina, artemisia, broom (*Spartium junceum*), Marvel of Peru, jasmine (*Jasminium humile* 'Revolutum'), philadelphus, bergamot (*Monarda didyma*) and roses.

These well-known varieties were combined with more recent introductions that would have surprised and delighted Regency visitors. These included *Hydrangea* 'Joseph Banks' (this has now been planted at Brighton), *Kerria japonica* and *Pittosporum tobira*, both 1804, the snowberry, *Symphoricarpos laevigatus* and *Rosa* 'Petite Lisette', both 1817, *Fuchsia magellanica*, 1823 and *Paeonia lactiflora*, from 1784. Flowers, such as the peony, painted on the earlier Chinese wallpapers in the Pavilion, could now be seen in the garden. Phillips lists *P. officinalis* and *P. albiflora*, as well as the tree peony, which he says have frequently been brought from China, in a growing state since 1794[149] and is easier to grow and hardier than might be expected. One exciting new flower was the Tiger Lily (*Lilium lancifolium*), whose markings are spotted like a big cat, and was introduced from China in 1804. The Brighton garden accounts for December 1820 lists forty-eight of them, which would have provided a surprisingly exotic foreground, in complete contrast to the more familiar and native plants.

ABOVE John Tenniel's illustration from Louis Carroll's *Through the Looking-Glass* (first published in 1871). Alice was surprised that the tiger lily could talk: 'We can talk', said the Tiger-Lily: 'When there's anybody worth talking to'. The drawing is based on an observed plant, within a 'Regency' edged bed, recalling Repton's ideas for Brighton.

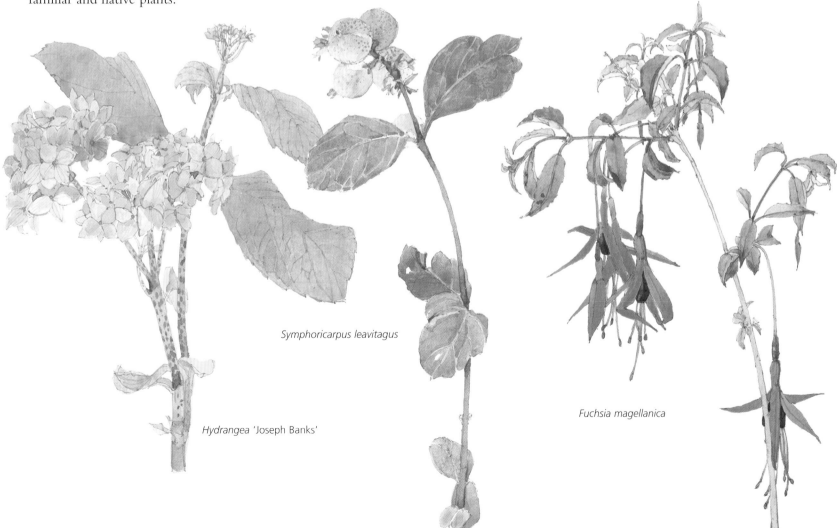

Symphoricarpus leavitagus

Hydrangea 'Joseph Banks'

Fuchsia magellanica

According to Phillips late Summer and Autumn flowers 'Are generally of larger size and richer colour, consequently they are more showy as many of them such as the hollyhock, sunflower and dahlia grow to considerable height, their proper place is among shrubs'.[150] The hollyhock, first brought to this country in the thirteenth century, was used as an important Regency spire plant. Phillips thought they were 'Appropriate for the decoration of the most princely grounds in clumps of 5 to 10 and added variety to the shrubbery late in the year'.[151] In the restored Brighton garden they make a bold and popular appearance, perfectly complementing the Pavilion's unique silhouette by echoing in the shrubbery the minarets and finials on the roof. It was as if Phillips had these 'princely grounds' in mind as he was writing.

The Regency garden style has become fashionable in the twenty-first century. Plants are now grouped together to avoid a 'bitty' result. There is a move towards a more relaxed, natural look for gardens. Naturalistic planting gave the impression that Nature had the upper hand again and represents a quintessential Englishness, as had the landscaped parks of the eighteenth century. Nowadays an award-winning garden at the Chelsea Flower Show is as likely to display naturalistic planting with native plants as it is to showcase the more elaborately staged traditional, 'artificial' gardening styles with new exotic plants. Such native plants as the Rosebay willow herb, considered a weed, are now coveted. Henry Phillips, who popularised the use of native plants in gardens, would have been delighted.

RIGHT *Alcea rosea* (hollyhock) Introduced from Spain in 1255 by Eleanor of Castile, the wife of Edward I. Tall spire plants draw the eye upwards and give variety and contrast in the restored shuberries.

BELOW Hollyhocks, *Alcea rosea*, compliment the Pavilion's silhouette.

12

THE REGENCY GARDEN
TAKES SHAPE

'A very agreeable plantation, occupying more than 7 acres'.

– C. WRIGHT, *The Brighton Ambulator*, 1818.

BELOW Ground plan of the Royal Pavilion, c.1821, from Nash's *Views*, published in 1826.

JOHN FURNER WAS now to plant the garden. He would have concentrated on the necessary preparatory work to realise Nash's plan and its desired effect. Nash had established the overview of the shapes of the beds, the carriage drives, paths and general massing and outlines to be achieved with the plants. Not surprisingly, no planting plans have come to light, as they do not usually

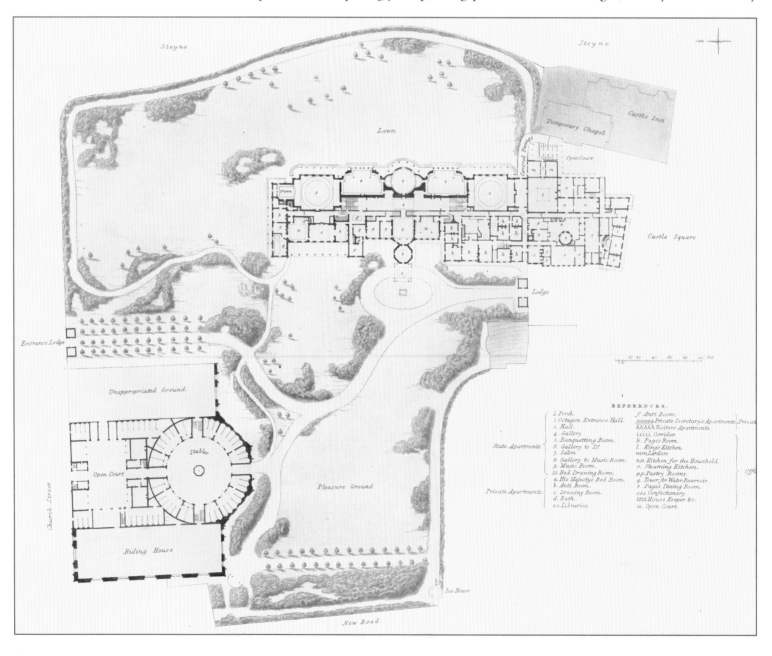

BELOW Ground plan of the Royal Pavilion, c.1821, from Nash's *Views*, published in 1826.

survive; they are by nature large working drawings and are liable to be drawn over, rained on and changed as the practical planting gets underway. A garden is a living, changing composition and the plan of the beds may have been sketched only with words at the first meeting between Nash, Aiton and Furner. A ground plan was published by Nash in 1826.[152] The plan illustrates Nash's proposals for the site, parts of which were not implemented. The lodges were not built and Northgate House (once part of Marlborough Row) was not demolished. From the initial meeting, Aiton would fill in the details and organise the content of the planting. He would contact the nurseries, choose the plants and arrange their collection or dispatch. Furner, who did the planting, would have known when the plants were required on site.

Work started a week after that first meeting in London on 20 November 1813 and with five hired gardeners, was to continue up to Christmas Eve.[153] In the following two years, the pattern of hired labour continued, using a maximum of fifteen men, two boys and two horses. The accounts for these years record the intense activity on the site and the preparation that was required to make this garden.

There were '987 loads of rubbish removed',[154] which would relate to the shaping, levelling and preparation of the ground and that was followed by its replacement with '1,105 loads of mould and marle', which was the imported new soil, mixed with the marle or general manure to improve the soil and form a good basis for the lawns and new beds. The large amount is accounted for by the fact that the perimeter beds were banked up with earth to provide privacy.

The drives and paths were then constructed using '69 loads for roads' (carriage drives) with '40 of small gravel'[155] for the surface of the paths, in the restored garden the drives and walks used a modern equivalent.

After the beds and paths were established there must have been great satisfaction on site to see the new turf arrive so that at last, after the initial hard preparatory work, the site would suddenly turn green with the first delivery of '73 waggon loads of turf … Mr Scrace's 1 1/2 acres of turf @ £25 an acre'.[156] As soon as the turf was laid its maintenance was accounted for. It was scythed, swept and the grass collected in baskets. '144 bushels of soot for the lawns'[157] was a top dressing, which was also used to compost grass and to deter slugs.

ABOVE *A view of the garden at Carlton House* etched by William Woollett, 1760 (detail). The garden was laid out by William Kent in the new informal style for Frederick, Prince of Wales. Grass maintenance remained a labour-intensive task until the invention of the lawnmower. Here the gardeners are brushing up lawn cuttings and sieving them into a basket after scything. Brushing was also used to raise the grass before scything. Rollers were used to maintain a smooth surface and to flatten worm casts before scything.

The accounts list '16 cart loads of dung', many more were to follow.[158] The nearby stables would have been a bonus for the gardens at Brighton. Repton thought that stables on an estate should be sited as near as possible to the garden so that the grounds were not cut up by the waggons bringing dung from a distance. In the eighteenth century the stables had been situated away from the main house. The quality of the animal may have been significant, as the accounts for Kew Garden separately itemise 'His Majesty's phaeton horses – 4 wks dung at £1. 2s. 0d.'[159] Dung had been categorised according to its various merits, with advice on its procurement and use, with stable dung considered the best at ten shillings a load. It was estimated that if a horse was stabled and well littered with straw or fern it would produce twenty-eight loads a year, enough to manure a good three acres. The stables at Brighton were a fabulous resource, as they could house sixty-two horses.

Other dung options were not for the squeamish, 'Horse-Dung. When fresh for stiff clays; when rotten, for all sorts of land'. Cow dung was considered 'Rich and cooling; fit for dry sandy ground'. Hog was too strong of itself but good for the compost heap, as was pigeon. Chicken, goose and duck dung were good for top dressing along with that of sheep, rabbits, goats and deer. Human dung was too hot but lime would remove the smell and make it spread. Human urine and that of cattle or dogs were, if mixed with water, good top dressings as was blood from butchers, with the proviso that it should be carried from the premises mixed with earth, sand or sawdust. As with the present day blood, fish and bone mixture that is a gardening staple, the shavings of bones, hoofs, animal hair or feathers were, with ground oyster shells all recommended.[160] The expense of grinding shells and bones to dust in a mill was amply repaid by the increase in their fertilizing power. Loudon listed the benefits: 'Salts, principally phosphate of lime, carbonate of lime, phosphate of magnesia, fat, gelatine, and cartilage, the same nature as coagulated albumen'.[161]

The benefit of improving the soil was well known to the ancient Greeks and Romans, who surprisingly, used human night soil and olive oil, 'Human dung is so much commended by the Ancients … the Nicety of some people, has perhaps kept them from using this Manure in their gardens in *England* … believing it will give an offensive relish to their Fruits and Salads'.[162] As if to reassure gardeners that human dung was quite safe, it was compared to any natural substance of the body, 'the Blood, the saliva, the urine, the sweat, and the milk, all separated from one another, only by passing through Strainers of different kinds … in a word dung let it be whatsoever, only contributes to promote the Growth and Luxuriance of a Plant, and cannot communicate its natural savour to any Part of a plant'.[163] Loudon again listed the beneficial qualities, 'night soil … is well known, as a very powerful manure … abounds in carbon hydrogen, azote [an old name for nitrogen], and oxygen … whatever state it is used, whether recent or fermented. It supplies abundance of food to plants … the Chinese … mix their night-soil with one third of its weight of fat marle, make it into cakes and dry it by exposure to the sun. Dessicated night-soil forms an article of commerce in France *(poudrette)*; in London it is mixed with quick lime and sold as cakes'.[164] Olive oil had been used by the Ancients to promote good cropping, mixed with urine. In Britain oil was replaced by fish. Loudon advised fish as a powerful manure, 'herrings and pilchards [oily fish] are used throughout the country with excellent effects. They are usually mixed with sand or soil, and sometimes seaweed, to prevent them from raising too luxuriant a crop'.[165] Americans in the 1780s had realised that fish was a good manure, 'inhabitants … have employed for the purpose of manure the white-fish; a species of herring remarkably fat and so full of bones, that it cannot conveniently be eaten. These fish … are caught in immense multitudes. No manure fertilizes ground in an equal degree'.[166]

LEFT William Heath, *Rusticating*, etching, 1824. George IV is shown gardening at his Cottage, Royal Lodge, with the Conyngham family. The King's shovel has a jewelled handle and a Royal Coat of Arms. Lady Conyngham is working the water pump. The conservatory can be seen in the background.

The grounds at Brighton were well manured, as the accounts indicate. There is no doubt that the experience of the Furner family, using resources from the stables, the sea and the Royal kitchens ensured that the site was properly prepared. At this stage with the beds ready, the planting could begin. 'Nursery man's account for trees and shrubs. £98. 14s .0d'.[167] The main supplier was John Willmott's nursery in Lewisham. Furner would make several trips to choose plants with Aiton and Furner would bring them back to Brighton. Loudon, in his *Encyclopaedia of Gardening* had listed eight pages of manures and Willmott's were cited as proof that fresh horse dung, rather than the more usual well rotted could also be used, 'recent dung is unquestionably to be preferred, and, in fact, is so by most market-gardeners; John Wilmot [sic], an extensive market-gardener … bears testimony to this fact. A given weight of recent stable dung he says, will not only go further … but will serve as a manuring for the succeeding crop'.[168]

The progress on site would have been checked by Nash on his first visit in January 1815. A friend of the Prince, the Earl of Chichester, from nearby Stanmer Park, would help with the new building and the garden. He supplied the fir poles to be used as scaffolding during the building and decoration of the Pavilion,[169] also stakes for the new trees, sticks to support the plants and hundreds of sacks of sawdust for the riding-house floor.

As soon as the trees and shrubs had been planted, they would require irrigation. As early as July 1814 a garden engine was delivered to Brighton by wagon from Chelsea in its own packing case, costing £14. 8s.[170] Watering engines were made to act on the principle of the force-pump and were still in use in the 1930s. *The Gardener's Assistant* of 1937 recommended Green's Garden Engine 'as one of the handiest of them all'.[171] The caricature of George gardening at his newly-planted Aiton/Nash cottage at Windsor shows a similar engine in use. In fact a two-wheel engine, costing nine guineas, was sent to the Windsor Garden in April 1817.[172]

Two years after Nash had arrived on site, the accounts make reference to a greenhouse. By 1817 the greenhouse is being repaired; the lights are re-puttied, so it had obviously leaked, requiring fifty-three squares to be replaced.[173] The only clue to the position of the greenhouse in the grounds is given in a local guidebook of that year, 'The spot of ground formerly known by the name of the Promenade-grove, is laid out in flower-gardens and a beautiful green-house; on the north side of which there is erected a truly magnificent range of buildings … these are the royal stables'.[174] In the same passage, the description of the grounds continues: 'Although the Downs are deprived of

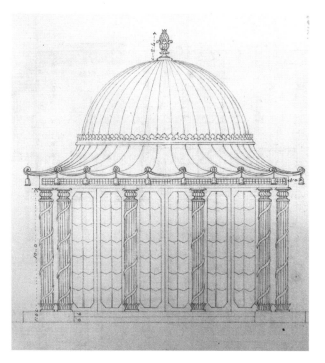

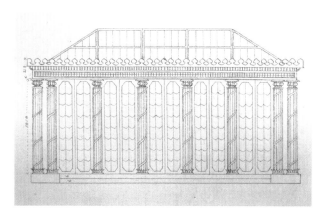

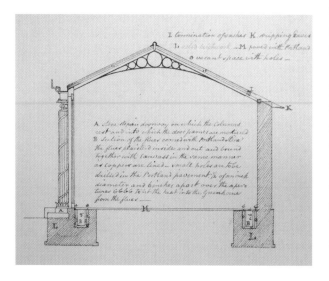

forest scenery, the Pavilion enclosures have numerous trees of large growth'. The gardens were 'a very agreeable plantation, occupying more than 7 acres, interspersed with gravel walks, grass plats etc. which gives a finished appearance to the whole'. We have no information as to the appearance of this 'beautiful green-house'. It does not appear on the Nash plan of the garden. The designs (left) would have complemented the site and look splendid set off by the remaining avenue of Promenade Grove as a backdrop.

A greenhouse would have given the grounds a more dressed 'Regency' look. From the accounts the frames would have been a lead colour and even the watering pots were painted green and white. There were flower stands, plant baskets and special flower pots '25 casts of new flower pots', perhaps they were modelled with the Prince Regent's emblem as later monarchs would mark their own flower pots. Tobacco is also listed, which was used to fumigate the greenhouse.[175] Controlling pests was dealt with by using a surprising range of products, some familiar to gardeners today, 'ingredients for destroying insects in the Royal Gardens, 5 lbs of tobacco, 2 lbs of soft soap [presumably for washing leaves to eradicate insects], 1 quart turpentine, 1 pint sweet oil and gunpowder. £2. 11s. 1d.[176]

The first named plants arrived in 1816. They were listed by their common names and there were to be an incredible quantity delivered to the Pavilion's garden over the next decade. The most frequently recurring names form a long list: privet, tamarisk, laurustinus, sumach, laburnum, viburnum, striped and green hollies, syringas, bupleurum fruticosa, acacia, cornus alba, moss, China and guelder roses, brooms, bay, Portugal laurels, groundsill trees and arbutus, as well as fifty globe artichoke plants and 400 purple and yellow crocus.[177] The plants all appear in the restored garden and form the basic elements of the shrubberies. Other plants listed in the accounts are less frequently mentioned and would have been used for ground cover, to climb bare trunks, as accents amongst the mixed foliage, or as foreground. Such varied plant material included 'dahlias, papion [sic] flowers, tiger lilies, ivies, mignonette, sweet peas, jasmines, clematis, periwinkle, rosemary, honeysuckles, myrtle, hypericum, lupins and tender annuals.'[178] The 'papion' flowers mentioned in the list must refer to the buddleia, the butterfly bush.

The garden was completed in stages, as the final rebuilding of the Pavilion progressed. The garden accounts reveal that at the same time as the first named plants arrived the activity on site included, 'To carriage of 8 loads of rubbish from the lawn in front of the new building and 2 young birds for the lawn', presumably peacocks. At this stage over £2,500 had been spent on the Brighton garden.[179] Great East Street, which had run in front of the old Pavilion, would have been used as access to and from the site. 'Making a new coach road in East Street' forms part of the garden accounts in 1819[180], which suggests that the building must have been sufficiently advanced to make a less direct link from the main carriage drive.

LEFT George Stanley Repton, two drawings for greenhouses, undated, from a sketchbook recording architectural designs while he was in Nash's employ. The columns are similar to those in the Entrance Hall of the Royal Pavilion. Both drawings show Nash's distinctive 'waved' glazing, the rectangular greenhouse his distinctive roof truss, as used at Royal Lodge.

FACING Two pages from The Lord Steward's accounts recording the creation of the garden. © The National Archives, Kew. The 1815 expenditure covers labour and grass maintenance. The most costly items in the first list of plants sent the following year are 'flower and other seeds' at £8.9 shillings, a dozen lilacs for example were itemised at just nine shillings.

Royal Gardens Brighton (215)

Brought forward ———————— £352 · 11 · —

For New { Carpenters' Bill — 8 · 17 · 5
Frames { Blacksmiths — 1 · 0 · 1½
{ Glaziers ———— 8 · 11 · 1½   18 " 8 " 8

4 New Scythes ——————————— 1 " 2 " —

1444 Bushels of Soot for the
Lawns, at 8 ——————— 4 · 16 · —

2 New Grass Baskets ———— — " 11 · —

5 New Spades ——————— — " 15 · —

New Flower Pots —————— 4 " 17 " 6

Syringes 4/6 —	—	12	6
1817 Package &c ————————	—	3	—
March 8 — Flower & other Seeds —————	— 8	9	—
12 Groundsell Trees 12/ — 12 Bladder Senna 12/	1	4	—
12 Scorpion Senna 9/ — 12 Red berried Evonymus 12/	1	1	—
6 White Evonymus 9/ — 12 Spanish Brooms 9/ —	—	18	—
12 Althaea frutex 12/ — 12 St Johns Wort 9/ —	1	1	—
6 Stone crop Trees 6/ — 18 Privets 9/ ————	—	15	—
12 Dutch Honeysuckles 9/ — 4 Passion flowers 8/ —	—	17	—
6 Venus Sumach 9/ — 12 Phillyreas 18/ ————	1	7	—
6 Cornus Alba 6/ — 12 Lilacs 9/ ————	—	15	—
6 Phillyreas of sorts 9/ — 18 Moss Roses 18/ ————	1	7	—
12 Persian Lilacs 9/ — 12 Tamarisk 9/ ————	—	18	—
12 Viburnums 9/ — 12 Laburnums 12/ ————	1	1	—
6 Cinquefoil Shrub 4/6 18 Syringes 13/6 ————	—	18	—
12 Laurustinus 18/ — 13 ——			

ABOVE Established elm trees, which were of a great age, seen in a detail from Repton's view of the Western Lawns, 1808. The trees may well be those still existing in this position, opposite the Pavilion's entrance.

BELOW North Front from Nash's *Views*, showing proposed planting.

The accounts show that over the entire period an extraordinary number of trees were planted, indicating the King's increasing need for privacy. The town was to be hidden by the use of trees. The quantity of trees listed in the accounts is astonishing: 125 Scotch firs, seventy-five chestnuts, 150 large laurels, eight limes, 200 scarlet firs, ninety-five elms and poplar trees. The poplar had appeared in Weltje's garden in the 1780s to disguise the nearby wall of the Castle Tavern. Repton had used poplars to screen the town behind his proposed aviary on the western lawn of the Pavilion. The poplar grows straight and close and quickly forms a good wind break. The Prince Regent had made enquiries as to the best trees for a quick effect. In one of her letters Maria Edgeworth recalls an incident involving poplar trees at Liverpool, where she had visited the Botanic Garden with its founder Mr Roscoe:'Mr Roscoe was to show His Royal Highness the Botanic garden. So he walked round it with him and as they went the Prince said, "Pray now Mr Roscoe what is the quickest growing tree you know?" Mr Roscoe mentioned a species of poplar. "I wish you would have the goodness to send me a few to hide a wall in a new building I am making at Brighton." Mr Roscoe sent ten pounds worth as a present. On meeting the Prince afterwards in London he was told that, "The trees are growing very well but there are not enough of them." Mr Roscoe sent ten pounds worth more.'[181] William Roscoe was a banker, botanist and Member of Parliament for Liverpool, who had started the botanic garden there in 1802. As well as trees from Liverpool and London, the Brighton bills show that some had been imported, 'Port of Shoreham, 22 May 1821, *The Printemps* – from Dieppe, customs, duties etc. on 3 cases of Trees and Plants for His Majesty … free'.[182] At the same time John Willmott's were sending '9 coboea [*sic*] scandens, a gloxinia superba [presumably for the greenhouse or conservatory], ice plants and 12 virginia creepers turned out of pots with 24 variegated ivies'.[183] Cobaea is a climb-

ing plant found in forests from Mexico to tropical South America. *Cobaea scandens* has large scented flowers shaped as a cathedral bell (its common name). The cream flowers age to purple. Loudon listed it as a greenhouse plant, 'known to grow a foot a day and must be kept within bounds'.[184] At a possible height of seventy feet, nine plants must have made a spectacular exotic show at Brighton.

By 1822 some of the established elm trees had been felled. The existing elm trees in the garden were of a great age, as can be seen in Repton's view of the western lawns. Some were in the wrong place for the intended new works and their roots were notorious for spreading. The garden accounts of 1819 record 'Labourers time employed in raising up & removing large Elm Trees in the Gardens on the West & North front of New building'.[185] The work took ten men nine days and must have involved the tree-moving machine. That same year works were directed to building the north front and the new apartments for the Prince Regent. The grounds to the north and the old coach road were to be dug up to allow for water pipes to be laid down East

ABOVE Mature planting in front of the former stables, 2005. The tree is *Koelreuteria paniculata* (Pride of India).

ABOVE View of the Stables from Nash's *Views*, possibly showing mature planting. The avenue on the left was retained from Promenade Grove. The planting on the right shows the accidental grouping of trees.

LEFT West Front from Nash's *Views*, immature shrubberies including perhaps the new Douglas Fir, providing an exciting foreground silhouette.

Street to the sea. This was an enormous disruption not only to the grounds of the Pavilion, but also to the town as East Street was one of its main thoroughfares. This disruption was caused by the Prince's desire to have his new bathroom supplied directly with sea water![186] The elm trees at the north end were removed 'To sink a subterraneous passage … across the lawn to the area in the north front'.[187] The underground passage would connect the Prince's new private apartments with the stables. The Prince would have direct access from his new rooms, which included his bedroom, to the stables without venturing outside.

There would be another fifty elm trees planted around the perimeter of the grounds. William Marshall advised that elms could be closely spaced 'So that a bird could not fly through between them … the elm will interweave with each other, in a manner we seldom see in any other species of tree'.[188] The tree and shrub planting continued after the Pavilion had been completed and Nash's *Views* were published. In Nash's published plan for the garden, John van Nost's sundial was to be placed in the centre of the turning circle outside the completed Pavilion. After the King's last visit to Brighton in 1827 it was presented to the Earl of Egmont at Cowdray Park. The views of the garden show areas that had reached maturity and others that look more recently planted. It was a work in progress. The final tree planting would concentrate on the perimeter to define, enclose and shelter the grounds. The garden accounts continue right up to 1830 the year of George IV's death. In addition to the elms the trees included catalpa, elders, poplars, twenty-five Scotch firs, fifty maritime pines and 100 evergreen oaks. Henry Steuart, who had advocated the instant effect of trees with his transplanting machine, would have applauded. He wrote in 1827 'His Majesty is the only prince in Europe, who, to a correct taste in the other Fine Arts, adds a perfect knowledge of one, that is truly indigenous and English … we may now hope to see a British monarch, in the vicinity of Windsor, GIVE IMMEDIATE EFFECT TO WOOD … and thus rival the great masters of design, in his Creations of Real Landscape'.[189]

In the garden accounts of 1824 two new names appear, John Williams is the new man on site and is described as the 'Foreman', whose work would be overseen by Richard Snart. Snart made many trips from London to Brighton over the next decade. He was the Royal Gardener at Buckingham (or the Queen's) House in St James's Park, which would shortly become Buckingham Palace.

BELOW *Le Pavillon*, 1825, lithograph, by the Thierry Brothers, after J. P. Smith. One of the few topographical views showing dense perimeter planting.

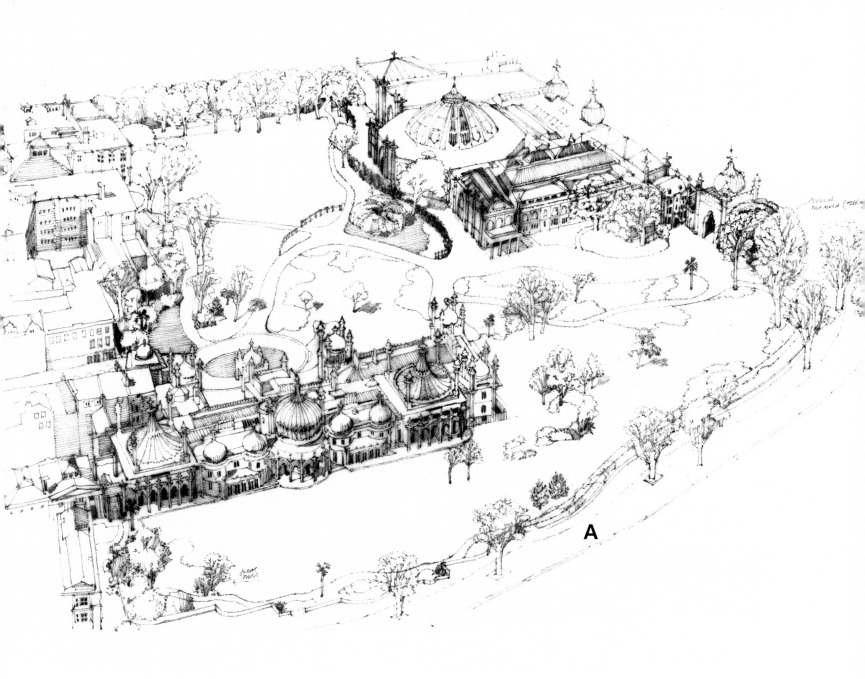

Snart's contract had been drawn up in 1803.[190] He was paid a comparable wage to Furner of £62. 4s. 0d. per quarter and had responsibility for grass keeping, the supply of a succession of flowers in the garden, the greenhouses, gravel walks and the workforce. A separate clause in his contract stipulated that no trees were to be cut down or lopped without licence from the Master of His Majesty's Household or a fine of £1,000 would be imposed; an early example of tree preservation orders. Among his jobs at Brighton, Snart was to complete the tree planting and travel by hired coach to Lewes to select yet more plants and shrubs. The shrubs included 100 each of privet, laurel and laurustinus and twenty-five rhododendrons.[191] The character of the garden was about to change.

William IV, on his first visit to the garden as the new King, had instructed Snart to make a new carriage road.[192] The garden accounts continue until 1831 and end with Snart's 'Travelling expenses, twice between Brighton and London on HM business relating to the Pavilion garden'.[193] Snart had, by this time, been a gardener to three monarchs. The new carriage drive and the planting marked the end of the Regency garden. The new drive ran once again straight to the front entrance of the Pavilion. The serpentine carriage approach through the shrubberies, with direct access from the palace to the lawns and the garden itself would have to wait 150 years to be reinstated.

ABOVE Drawing of the site as existing. Few changes were made to the extent of the grounds, which enabled the garden to be restored to its original layout. The most dramatic change was the perimeter boundary (A) taking ground from the garden to widen the road.

13

THE REGENCY GARDEN ADAPTS

ABOVE Photograph, 2005, of the remaining section of the flint wall and railings, which surrounded the Estate.

BELOW Photograph from the *Brighton Gazette*, 1964. The North Gate was considered so convincing that it represented the gates of Lahore for a B.B.C television series on the writer Rudyard Kipling.

'[The grounds] no longer, as formerly, prove an ornament to the town'.

– J. C. LOUDON, 'NOTES ON GARDENS AT BRIGHTON', 1842.

WHEN WILLIAM IV was Duke of Clarence he had his own apartment in the Pavilion and would have known the earlier garden. He was experienced in estate management since, when first married in 1818, he lived at Bushy House, where he was Ranger of the Park. It was reported (with some foreboding) that he was seen on the morning following his first visit to the Pavilion, as King, discussing changes to the grounds 'As early as nine o'clock … His Majesty was seen outside of the South Lodge, familiarly conversing with … Mr Nash, and sketching in the gravel, with the point of his walking-stick, the ground plan of some alteration which he intended making … Surely the new Monarch did not intend to emulate his predecessor in the way of "alterations" to the Pavilion!'[194]

William IV and Richard Snart, the gardener from Buckingham Palace, with John Williams as site foreman, simplified the layout of the garden. The plan they devised in 1830 was not altered in any fundamental way until the Pavilion was sold to the Town Commissioners in 1850. This twenty-year period saw the introduction of more evergreens, conifers, rhododendrons and laurels. They were used to make a dense barrier around the perimeter, adding to the banked shrubberies along the East Front. The high flint wall around the estate with the small run of railings on the top was retained, and a small section still exists. It had first been suggested by Repton in 1805 and appeared in his view of the North Front. There were sentry boxes positioned at strategic points along the walls and the new, well guarded, gatehouses incorporated sentry boxes in their design. William IV's contribution to the grounds was mostly architectural. He built two entrance lodges,

the South Gatehouse, with its extra staff accommodation and the North Gatehouse, which still exists. The provision of separate stables for the Queen's horses, a new requirement at Brighton, was met by building on the land that had been intended for George IV's indoor tennis court, behind the former Marlborough Row. The last house in the row, now called North Gate House, was retained and to conform to the rest of the estate, was orientalised at the same time. The additions to the grounds were ambitious and handsome. They unified and defined them in a sympathetic style.

The Pavilion is not an easy building to add to, without resorting to diluted pastiche, as later architects were to discover. When the south end was reconfigured after the town had bought the estate and the Indian Gateway we see today was erected, it was suggested that the original Pavilion's entrance portico should be removed. It was described as 'the pseudo Orientalism of Nash … false and even pretty. The real reveals the sham'. William IV's North Gate was considered a success as it was 'stately … copied from one at Delhi'.[195] The planting added to the architectural effect with a row of elm trees along the new straight drive. It was ironic that once again the estate was divided into two halves,

which George IV had waited years to unite. The Western Lawns, now one large expanse, were treated as a miniature landscape, broken up with three areas of ornamental shrubbery and existing trees. These islands of greenery were a precursor to the Victorian shrubbery, and later included the dotting of specimen trees on the lawns. The restoration of the Regency garden at Brighton had to take these existing, municipal specimen trees into account.

On his accession to the throne in 1830 William moved to Windsor Castle, where a new garden had recently been designed and planted by William Townsend Aiton in a revivalist, Italianate style. Central to the scheme were superb vases and statues that had been chosen and positioned by George IV. The garden, with its geometric beds and central fountain contained an impressive collection of garden statuary that had been acquired for other royal gardens by his predecessors, notably from the garden at Hampton Court, whence the 'Blackamoor' sundial had earlier been removed to Brighton. The formal style of garden at Windsor had not been seen since the baroque period. The planting was very different and new, a combination of azaleas, rhododendrons and kalmias with evergreen shrubs, lilacs and standard roses.

William IV's wife, Queen Adelaide, was a keen gardener. She grew 'florists' flowers' such as the tulip, auricula and carnation. A florist at this period was an amateur gardener who grew flowers that were cultivated to strictly laid down rules. Queen Adelaide had her own Flower Painter in Ordinary, the botanical artist Augusta Withers. The Queen sponsored the Metropolitan Society of Florists and Amateurs, founded in 1832, and provided a ten-guinea prize for the best tulips, with the winning flowers being presented to her. A new plant was the dahlia, which was consequently an expensive novelty. It was one of the later criticisms of the shows that they were only for the wealthy, who could afford to grow large numbers of exhibition flowers under glass. The new

ABOVE Reconstruction of the site c.1837. The garden is surrounded with dense planting and high walls. The North Gate (A) was then within the curtilage of the grounds, not on the pavement. The carriage drive ran straight to the South Gate (B), with Queen Adelaide's Stables at (C) The shrubberies (D) can be seen in a later photograph on p.117.

society rivalled the Horticultural Society of London, founded in 1804 by, among others, William Townsend Aiton, which became the Royal Horticultural Society. Flower societies were formed by small groups of enthusiasts who usually held shows in local inns, but this new society was on a much grander scale and was soon attracting large crowds. Royal patronage had increased its popularity to such an extent that when the show was held at the Surrey Zoological Society's gardens, 11,000 people attended. Queen Adelaide had a pelargonium and a carnation named after her.

The interest in the cultivation of flowers, botany and the role of women in gardens was expanded by Loudon's wife, Jane, after his early death in 1843. She published a series of books aimed primarily at women. They were handy manuals for planning and making a flower garden or for giving instructions to a jobbing gardener.

Flower shows became a popular competitive event where the blooms, grown to exacting display standards, were shown off by their proud owners who had nurtured them to an almost artificial perfection. Within thirty years gardening and the cultivation of show flowers had become such an accepted part of national life that the first Chelsea Flower Show was held by the Royal Horticultural Society in their Kensington grounds in 1862. At Brighton, flower shows became so popular that they were held three times a year in tents on the Pavilion lawns and in nearby buildings.

William IV reigned for only seven years. His admired North Gatehouse was elaborately decorated with greenery and flowers, including crowns made of dahlias, to welcome his successor, the young Queen Victoria on her first visit to Brighton in 1837.

By now the Pavilion grounds were completely concealed from public view. The dense planting around the perimeter shut out the town and destroyed any feeling of being by the seaside. Queen Victoria commented on the lack of sea views and the oppressive crowds. To the young Queen the Pavilion and its setting made no sense. She failed to see the point of it or its suitability as a holiday or future family home, although a delightful suite of rooms had been prepared for her visits, including a bedroom over the entrance facing the quiet garden, rather than the Steine. The room was papered with a hand-painted yellow-ground, Chinese wallpaper, covered with flowering plants and a foreground of fabulous birds.

The claustrophobic atmosphere of the Pavilion's setting was commented on by Queen Victoria's Maid of Honour, who wrote 'I have been walking in the Pavilion garden, which is odious; so low and damp, without a glimpse of the "deep and dark blue ocean"; one might as well pace round and round Berkeley Square. I suppose it *is* sea air, but so mixed with soot and smoke it loses half its value … the whole place was a strange specimen of royal eccentricity, and a most uncomfortable, dull residence'.[196]

Loudon thought the grounds 'so shut in by increasing the height of the wall, and boarding the inside of the iron railing, that they no longer, as formerly, prove an ornament to the town'.[197] His solution was to lower the wall and have open railings so that people could see in as there 'could be no annoyance

to a queen who is not averse to showing herself in public, even if she were walking within'. He even added that, if the town could afford it, all the houses around the Pavilion should be cleared away so that it could be surrounded with more lawns and trees. Yet more houses could be cleared 'so as to admit a view of the sea from the principal rooms'. The town would be compensated for this expense 'by inducing the Court to pay more frequent visits to Brighton'. One of the reasons the Queen made few visits was the lack of privacy and the crush of the crowds when she did venture out 'the crowd behaved worse than I have ever seen them do … we were mobbed by all the shopboys in the town, who ran and looked under my bonnet … We walked home as fast as we could'.[198]

In fact negotiations were already underway for the purchase of a private retreat on the Isle of Wight after rigorous enquiries were carried out to ensure that the proposed property had no footpaths or rights of way through the extensive grounds. Queen Victoria noted that 'The sea was so blue and calm that the Prince Consort said it was like Naples'.[199] The new house built on the site was designed by her husband, Prince Albert, to evoke Italy with its campaniles and loggias in the irregular Italianate style with fashionable formal terraces and garden facing the view over the Solent. Osborne House became a favourite seaside retreat with its own beach.

The use of vases, statuary and a central fountain recalled the garden at Windsor, although here they were part of a larger, more elaborately staged composition. The pergolas, flights of steps and balustraded walls were all perfect for the incorporation of the many, by now, mass-produced pieces of garden sculpture or vases that were available. Such was the popularity of the new revivalist formal styles of gardening that most of the garden ornaments were obtained from catalogues.

Coronilla emerus sketched in the Pavilion's restored garden.

BELOW Edward T. Fox, *Attree Villa, Queen's Park, Brighton*, 1835. Built by James Barry for Thomas Attree, Esq. The drawings show the Italianate building set on terraces where the main elements of the garden design was hard landscaping using fashionable ornaments, such as urns, statuary and balustrading.

THE ITALIANATE STYLE

The new Italianate fashions and the concentration on hard landscaping can be illustrated by a celebrated villa on the outskirts of Brighton. Attree Villa and its garden show the fashion for the Italianate style a decade before Osborne House. Loudon, on his visit to Brighton in 1842, was impressed with Barry's layout of Attree's garden on a steep terraced slope. The hard landscaping, constructions and ornamentation were the main design elements. 'The architectural garden, terrace walls … as a foreground to the park and the sea … flights of steps, beds edged with stone, and a handsome basin and fountain in the centre; some pedestals and vases, a handsome open temple or pavilion at one angle, and a massive stone seat at the other. The garden [on three levels] is bounded by a high retaining wall … terminated … by a rich parapet surmounted by vases'.[200] As Loudon said, they were all 'conspicuous ornaments to this villa'. Of Attree's planting the Coronilla emerus was singled out and his gardener was praised for always keeping a reserve of 'bushy wallflowers in pots ready to follow the summer bedding'. Beds were never left empty and Loudon listed other evergreen options to maintain interest in the beds through to May; 'pinks, sweetwilliams, saxifrages, creeping thyme, rue, sage, rosemary, perriwinkle, box and heaths'.[201] Loudon had proposed a good selection of different coloured greens and plant habits. Loudon referred to the conservatory, which linked to the drawing room, as a 'plant cabinet', no doubt filled with exotics. The striped awnings at the windows, a beguiling Italian touch, had similarities with the earlier canopies and verandahs. They also provided shade and relief to the flatness of façades. At Osborne House, a striped curved canopy above a viewing platform to the sea was to serve the same purpose.

The Victorian home required a density of objects and ornamentation that mass production satisfied. The same was true in gardens. A vast range of products from improved lawn mowers to ranges of seats or urns for flowers were produced. It was the beginning of a consumer market that would lead to the modern garden centre. Gardens, for now, were works of art again as Repton had championed at Brighton. He would have been horrified at the commercialism he had sensed with the coming of the Industrial Revolution as well as by the kind of gardens required by the newly rich.

The new style of garden had the significant advantage that it could be adapted or diluted to suit the aspirations of the new suburban gardener. The style became a craze. The gardening bible at the time was Loudon's *Encyclopaedia of Gardening*, published in 1822, and not surprisingly all the flower gardens in the book were geometric. The new formal style with its massed bedding would also appear later in the Brighton garden.

Meanwhile, since the estate at Osborne, purchased with private funds, was progressing without interference or the need for permits from the Treasury, the Royal Pavilion at Brighton was emptied with a view to demolition. The doors were locked and the keys sent to the Lord Chamberlain on 7 June 1848. The garden had also been emptied of plants, which had been sold at auction two months be-

fore. The sale was announced on bills pasted around the Stables where the event took place and listed the various lots, including tools. It also indicates that the garden already contained tender greenhouse plants that had been used as bedding.

The list itemised 'Geraniums, Cinerarias, Casserarias, Lobelias, Scarlet Verbenas, Petunias, Mimulus Andersonii and Mimulus Colei'. There were 156 lots of plants, most in bundles of a dozen. They included forty-eight 'choice fuchsias', with a further thirty-six treated as standards. There is also mention of Double Scarlet Ribes, Striped Tree Peony, Salvia Patens, Statice, Marvel of Peru and Striped Dahlia roots. There was a vast quantity of sized flower pots, 218 dozen in all and gardening equipment that ranged from an engine with syringe (for spraying), to a hand water barrow with iron wheels and the ice house tools. The long list of gardening tools indicates that the grounds were well maintained and the inclusion of edging and turfing irons with edging shears suggest that the lawns were immaculate. The list typifies the Victorian idea of the garden with its provision of colour and tender exotic blooms and gives an insight into the planting of the grounds during this period. (For a complete list of plants and garden equipment see p.113).

ABOVE Caleb Robert Stanley, watercolours painted as a record of the building for Queen Victoria, 1845. The Royal Collection © 2003, Her Majesty Queen Elizabeth II.
Top: *East Front*. Fashionable kidney-shaped flowerbeds cut into the lawn are planted with colourful annuals. The tented roofs were, at that time, painted stone-colour. Below: *West Front*. The foreground shows Weltje's house still intact with Holland's buff tiles. The grounds continued beyond the house to the main road. This land was sold off in plots when the Pavilion became the property of the town.

The sale marked the end of Royal gardening at Brighton and the beginning of a new era for the town. The proposed demolition of the Pavilion was met with a mixed response. Posters appeared both for and against. For those wishing to save the Pavilion emphasis was placed on the advantage of the grounds as a public open space: 'The Pavilion lawns would be an attraction to visitors on whom the Town entirely depends' and that it 'cannot otherwise have Public Gardens, Libraries, Museums … there being no locality for them'.[202]

There was the fear that if the demolition went ahead the ground 'will be covered with new shops and new tradesmen', it had also been rumoured that Mr Cubitt, the well-known developer and entrepreneur, who built Osborne, was interested in the site.

The eventual outcome, after over 27,000 people had inspected the empty rooms (such was the curiosity and interest shown) was that the whole estate, thought to be worth much more than the asking price of £50,000, was purchased by the town in June 1850. Within nine days the Pavilion gardens were opened to the public 'A new era seems to have burst upon us – a park in the centre of Brighton, with lofty trees, shady walks and a delightful lawn … for the grounds till now have been closed to the public, on Sunday, thousands of the residents visited the grounds'.[203]

ABOVE Engraving c. 1855. The grounds are now a public space in the town centre.

BELOW Edward Fox watercolour, 1850. The grounds are about to opened to the public. The shrubberies on the reconstructed site drawing on page 107 at (D) can be seen in the watercolour, viewed from the Dome.

CATALOGUE OF
GREEN-HOUSE PLANTS & GARDEN IMPLEMENTS,
REMOVED FROM THE PAVILION GARDEN,
TO BE SOLD BY AUCTION,

BY MR. PARSONS,

At the Stables of the Pavilion, in Church Street, Brighton, on Thursday,
April 13, 1848, at Twelve o' Clock punctually.

CONDITIONS OF SALE AS USUAL.

Beneath the Dome.

1—1 doz plants; viz. Verbenas, Petunias and Tilardas
2—Ditto
3—Ditto
4—Ditto
5—Ditto
6—Ditto
7—Ditto
8—Ditto
9—Ditto
10—Ditto
11—Ditto
12—16 ditto
13—14 ditto ; viz. Geraniums, Fuchsias, Cinerarias, Casserarias & Lobelias
14—Ditto
15—Ditto
16—Ditto
17—Ditto
18—Ditto
19—Ditto
20—Ditto
21—Ditto
22—Ditto
23—Ditto
24—25 struck plants of last year's Fuchsias
25—14 ditto, new Scarlet Verbena
26—14 plants; Geranium, Fuchsias, Cineráias, Casserarias and Lobelias
27—Ditto
28—Ditto
29—Ditto
30—Ditto
31—Ditto
32—Ditto
33—Ditto
34—Ditto
35—Ditto
36—Ditto
37—Ditto
38—12 plants of similar sorts to preceding 12 lots
39—Ditto
40—Ditto
41—Ditto
42—Ditto
43—Ditto
44—Ditto
45—Ditto
46—Ditto
47—Ditto
48—Ditto
49—Ditto
50—6 ditto, Geraniums, Mimulus Andersonii, Veronica
51—6 ditto
52—6 ditto ; Geraniums, Fuchsias, Casserarin, Mimulus Andersonii—6
53—3 Geraniums, 1 Fuchsia, 1 Casseraria, 1 Mimulus Andersonii,—6
54—3 Geraniums, 1 Fuchsia, 1 Veronica, 1 Mimulus Andersonii,—6
55—3 Geraniums, 1 Fuchsia, 1 Casseraria, 1 Mimulus Andersonii,—6
56—3 Geraniums, 1 Fuchsia, 1 Veronica, 1 Mimulus Andersonii,—6
57—3 Geraniums, 1 Fuchsia, 1 Casseraria, 1 Mimulus Colei,—6
58—4 Geraniums, 1 Casseraria, 1 Mimulus Andersonii,—6
59—5 Geraniums, 1 Mimulus Andersonii—6
60—4 Geraniums, 1 Teucrium Japonica, 1 Mimulus Colei,—6
61—14 plants; Geraniums, Salvias, Dianthus
62—Ditto
63—Ditto
64—Ditto
65—Ditto

66—Ditto
67—Ditto
68—Ditto
69—Ditto
70—Ditto
71—Ditto
72—Ditto
73—12 plants; Geraniums, Fuchsias, Lobelias, Cinerarias
74—Ditto
75—Ditto
76—Ditto
77—Ditto
78—Ditto
79—Ditto
80—Ditto
81—Ditto
82—Ditto
83—Ditto
84—Ditto
85—17 ditto, various
86—4 large Geraniums
87—Ditto
88—3 ditto, and Teucrium Japonica
89—4 large Geraniums
90—Ditto
91—Ditto
92—Ditto
93—Ditto
94—6 Fuchsias of sorts
95—16 plants ; Geraniums, Casserarias, and Cinerarias
96—Ditto
97—13 ditto
98—12 pots of struck Geraniums
99—Ditto
100—12 plants ; Verbenas, Petunias, and Tilardas
101—Ditto
102—Ditto
103—Ditto
104—Ditto
105—Ditto
106—Ditto
107—12 plants ; Geraniums, Fuchsias, Lobelias, Casserarias, Cinerarias
108—Ditto
109—Ditto
110—Ditto
111—Ditto
112—Ditto
113—Ditto
114—Ditto
115—Ditto
116—Ditto
117—Ditto
118—Ditto

Choice Fuchsias.

119—4 plants
120—Ditto
121—Ditto
122—Ditto
123—Ditto
124—Ditto
125—Ditto
126—Ditto
127—Ditto
128—Ditto
129—Ditto
130—Ditto
131—3 ditto, standards and half standards
132—Ditto
133—Ditto
134—Ditto
135—Ditto
136—Ditto
137—Ditto
138—Ditto
139—Ditto

140—Ditto
141—Ditto
142—Ditto

143—3 plants; Double Scarlet Ribes, Spiræa, Striped Tree Pæonia
144—2 ditto, Salvia Patens
145—14 plants ; Statice, Pseuda, Armeria, &c.
146—Quantity of Marvel of Peru roots
147—Ditto
148—Ditto Striped Dahlia roots
149—Ditto
150—33 doz. flower pots, 60's
151—25 doz. ditto
152—18 doz. ditto, 42's
153—Ditto
154—16 doz. ditto
155—16 doz. ditto
156—45 pots, 12's
157—47 ditto, 15's, and 3 large ditto

Stable Yard.

158—12 6ft 5-bar iron hurdles
160—Ditto
161—6 iron watering hoops
162—Wheel barrow
163—Ditto
164—Ditto
165—Hand water barrow with iron wheels
166—Ditto
167—28in iron roller
168—24in ditto
169—29in grindstone, and strong frame
170—Garden truck and bed
171—150 stakes
172—Ditto
173—Ditto
174—Ditto
175—6ft 3in garden seat
176—Ditto
177—2 large oval water tubs
178—7 leaf and packing baskets
179—6 ditto
180—5 ice beaters, 1 shovel, 1 rammer, 1 diamond, ice chopper
181—Shovel, 3 pairs shears, 3 saws, axe, auger, trowel, hammer, chisel and 2 nippers
182—Rammer, shovel, 5 ice beaters, 1 ditto chopper
183—2 daisy hooks, 2 road rakes, pruning shears and hoe
184—3 rakes, 3 dutch hoes, spade, turf beater and axe
185—3 dutch hoes, 3 rakes, 1 drag, spud, fork, edging shears, weeding fork, shovel and turf beater
186—12 brooms
187—3 rakes, 3 hoes, shovel, spud, pick-axe and fork
188—Trug basket, rammer, 3 mats and fall
189—3 rakes, 2 hoes, edging shears, edging iron, pickaxe, spud and spade
190—Hand garden engine and syringe
191—18 brooms
192—Cross cut saw, 2 pickaxes, crowbar and axe
193—4 iron shod wedges, grub axe and beetle
194—Turfing iron, 2 edging irons, beater, line reel and 10ft rod
195—2 scythes, 2 pouches and 2 rakes
196—3 watering pots, yoke and 3 sieves
197—4 watering pots and 3 sieves
198—Fumigating bellows and 2 watering pots

☞ **May be viewed the day preceding and morning of Sale, by Tickets only, to be had at Mr. Parsons's Offices, Marine Parade, Brighton.**
[*Sickelmore, Printer, High Street, Brighton.*]

LEFT Poster advertising the sale of plants from the Pavilion's garden, 1848.

14

FROM A PUBLIC PARK
TO A RESTORED GARDEN

'A lung to their magnificent town, they have that which no other town in the kingdom possesses – an extensive park of its own in its very centre'.

– *The Brighton Magazine*, JUNE 1850.

BELOW Photograph, c.1874, from The James Gray Collection of the Regency Society of Brighton and Hove. The Victorian shrubbery (left foreground) has yet to be cleared and replaced by the marble statue of Sir Cordy Burrows (see page 120).

AS SOON AS the Pavilion's garden became town property the emphasis shifted from a private garden to a public park. As a civic amenity it was subject to a wide variety of activities. These ranged from lawn tennis and the new game of croquet, to concerts, flower shows and temporary exhibitions. The grounds were often specially lit up at night with lanterns and oil lamps, including the addition of seventy glow worms on one July evening, which was 'thoroughly appreciated' for the many concerts.[204] The Floricultural Society was given permission to hang Chinese lanterns in the

RIGHT J. Paine & Sons' proposed illuminations of the East Front of the Royal Pavilion to celebrate Queen Victoria's Jubilee in 1897. Reproduced by courtesy of East Sussex Records Office. The tradition of illuminating the exterior of the building with coloured lights continued until the 1960s.

trees and burn coloured lights. Extreme caution was required in the flower tents as the use of portable oil lamps was forbidden. In 1884 electricity was extended to the grounds. When the Promenade Concerts were held on the Western Lawn a comparison was made to its former use 'nearly 100 years ago, when it was known as the "Promenade Grove" and was much patronised by George, Prince of Wales and the world of fashion at that period'.[205] The whole space was also lit up for Royal occasions, maintaining the tradition that was set with the Prince's first visit to the town. For Queen Victoria's Diamond Jubilee 30,000 coloured light bulbs were used as part of the illuminations. They 'wreathed ... every tree in the grounds; every flower bed twinkled with them'[206] and they transformed the Pavilion into 'an enchanted palace' by outlining the architectural detail. It must have looked magnificent, like a coloured Harrod's!

There were more outlandish proposals too, such as a suggestion to form a lake in the western lawn, using the water required to 'blow', or pump the bellows of the organ in the Dome[207] 'to form a small cascade when in use it would under any circumstances keep the lake always full'.[208] It was reasoned that this would cut down on mowing costs and produce revenue in the winter by charging sixpence to skate on the lake. Other amusing ideas, which were also declined, were the use of the grounds as a launch pad for balloon ascents and an offer from the Duke of Bedford of a peacock and two peahens as a suitable exotic decoration.

The horticultural aspects of the grounds were secondary, although within ten years of municipal ownership the planting was described by Philip Lockwood, the Borough Surveyor, as in a poor condition 'most of the Shrubberies and Flower borders in the Pavilion Grounds are getting into an exhausted condition: they require to be dug out and cleared away … new mould added and some new shrubs and plants supplied'.[209] This was agreed to and the Surveyor was later asked to design and cost a greenhouse for rearing plants, which was built on the north lawn, near the North Gatehouse in 1867. The state of the grounds were again on the agenda seven years later and this time the step was taken to appoint a head gardener, James Shrives, at a salary of £1.11.6. per week.[210] His new plan for the grounds was accepted within four months of his taking the job and concentrated on the Western Lawn.

With Shrives's new plan the latest fashions in popular gardening would be adapted to suit the site and take advantage of the open position. The existing planting, consisting of 'clumps', were removed as they were considered to be badly positioned under trees, obstructing the best views of the buildings.

The two photographs opposite predate Shrives's alterations to the grounds when the 'clumps', as he called them, were removed. The photographs are taken from the entrance to the Pavilion, looking towards the Dome. The garden retains the vestiges of the ornamental shrubbery that had survived from the time of William IV's more simplified layout. The straight carriage drive in the foreground had separated these lawns from the Pavilion. The shrubbery has amazing similarities to the kind of ornamental shrubberies that were designed by Nash for St James's Park after he had completed the Pavilion and were copied by Prince Pückler-Muskau. The shrubberies closely correspond to the photographs opposite (illustration p.88). The shrubbery is cut into the lawn in a flowing, irregular shape and filled with trees, shrubs and herbaceous plants. Since it is Spring, the foregrounds have clumps of flowering bulbs that again correspond with earlier planting recommendations, particularly by Henry Phillips. The young flower seller with the basket on his shoulders (opposite-below) has already made a few sales. To enhance the landscaped setting, the seats shown in the earlier photograph (opposite-top) were made from natural branches in a rustic gothic style. They had been used outside the spa in nearby Queen's Park. They were replaced by benches six feet in length, shown in the later photograph. In 1890 they were exchanged for seats measuring twelve feet in length that were costed at £24 for a dozen. The length of the grass and its natural-looking composition also conforms to earlier Regency ideas and would not be acceptable in an urban park today! The first 'patent mowing machine' was purchased for the grounds in 1863 for £10.10.0., so it would have been possible to have the grass immaculate.

With Shrives's new plan the garden became a showcase for tender bedding plants that filled colourful beds cut into the lawn. They took their outline from simple geometric motifs that broke up the space, ensuring that interest was concentrated in areas where it could be easily admired from the paths. The sunniest part was outside the Dome, on a gentle slope, and it was here that an extraordinary bed appeared that recalls Repton, and his simple geometric design for the rose garden at Ashridge.

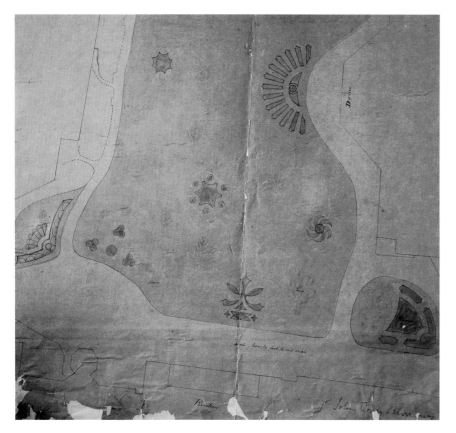

The plan also indicates the two important areas, detached from the lawn, that marked the entrances to the grounds. The bed opposite the Pavilion's entrance was given a narrow border that also picked up on Repton's idea of hooped basketwork, although it was interpreted with flat outline planting, as at Muskau.

At the north entrance was an island bed that Shrives suggested be divided up into four flower beds otherwise, due to its size, 'it would have to be planted chiefly with shrubs which would shut out the view of the Grass beyond whereas the beds which I propose making can all be planted with bedding plants and will give the entrance a bright appearance'.[211] The preference for low planting with bedding shows how far garden design had departed from Naturalism and the Regency idea of making open and closed views with ornamental shrubberies.

Shrives had three propagating houses built, each fifty-five feet long, on the outskirts of the town so that his plan could be realised. After his initial success he asked for an increase in salary the following year, with the explanation that '£1 per week in the country with a Gardener's usual allowance of house, coals and vegetables is far preferable to mine'.[212] His weekly wage was increased by eight shillings and sixpence to £2.

The bedding system was gardening as if 'painting by numbers', where an outline was made and filled in with plants. For the amateur gardener or suburban housewife the style became so popular that it was essential to know how to transfer a design to the ground. Jane Loudon advised that a similar technique to that of scaling up a design for embroidery be used. The design on paper was first squared up and the ground marked out as a grid with pegs and chalk-covered string then 'each string … is made to thrill by pulling it up about half-way between the pegs with a sudden jerk, and letting go again'. This transferred the chalk from the string to the ground, the result was a white squared ground so that the pattern could then be 'traced with a sharp-pointed stick, the proportion of each square being copied'. The advice to form circles was simple and effective 'a string the length of the diameter … with a piece of stick tied to each end, one stick … driven into the ground in the centre of the circle, and a line is traced with the stick at the extremity of the line, which is drawn out quite tight'.[213] It is amusing to imagine these newly confident garden designers 'thrilling' up and down the country.

Shrives's desire for a 'bright appearance' within these outlines was more than satisfied with the new range of plants available. 'Not a year passes', wrote Mrs Loudon in the 1860s, 'in which improvements on existing plants are not effected at home, and fresh introductions made from abroad'.[214] The colour palette that was available was not for the faint hearted and Mrs Loudon suggested that this should be exploited, 'The principal beauty … consists of the brilliancy of colours, masses of colour and the most striking contrast to each other'.[215] The glorious displays were achieved with 'yellow Calceolarias, scarlet Pelargoniums, white Petunias, scarlet and purple Verbenas, pegged down, blue Lobelias and pink Crucianella stylosa'.[216] In fact in an earlier book, addressed to a singular Lady her advice had produced a garden, 'now so brilliant … that you can scarcely gaze at it in the sunshine'.[217]

The degree of colour outside would be matched inside by the new aniline dyes that revolutionised the textile industry. A by-product resulting from the production of the magenta-based aniline dyes, was an arsenic compound, called 'London purple'. When mixed with water, it

was sprayed on to plants as an insecticide. It retained its colour when diluted so that it was easy to judge the quantities and an engine was invented to spray the solution by hand pump action. The sale of gardening equipment when the Pavilion was sold included 'an engine' which may have been an early insecticide dispenser. The introduction of chemicals led to concerns about the health of gardeners, wildlife and edible fruit that had been liberally sprayed with arsenic. The Victorian search for novelty and colour in gardens led to other, unforeseen consequences. Designers used the latest ideas for offsetting their patterns of planting with coloured coals, minerals, chalk or marble chippings. At Stoke Edith, in Herefordshire, to keep up with the latest fashions, a new formal garden design had been made using low clipped box plants to outline the pattern. The blue decorative dressing between the outlines contained lead, which killed all the plants! Gardening now reflected a dependence on the industrial age. New technology included improved glasshouse construction, using cast-iron curved bars and heating systems. Nurseries had acres under glass as the race was on to maximise production, just like a factory; 40,000 calla lilies and 30,000 fuchsias were produced in one season.[218]

The success of the bedding system depended on raising large quantities of annual tender plants to create the effects, and with the abolition of the tax on glass in 1845, this became popular. The greenhouse became an essential and prestigious area of the garden for growing new exotics, protecting them over winter, or producing large numbers of bedding plants that popularised the trend towards formality. It was the custom at Brighton, as elsewhere, of giving away the thousands of surplus plants at the end of the season reinforcing the link between the local community and its park. The quantity of plants required to 'put on a good show' was phenomenal. The number of bedding plants used could indicate wealth and status; 10,000 for a squire, 20,000 for a Baronet, 30,000 for an Earl, and 40,000 for a Duke. On the principle that 'if you've got it, flaunt it', a Rothschild could boast 41,000.[219]

At Brighton the displays could upstage those of a Duke as the Pavilion grounds used up to 60,287 plants, and would include the Echeveries (succulents)[220]. The continued success of the bedding style could be attributed to the guarantee of a long flowering period, from June to October, in contrast to the usual three weeks

The Pavilion Grounds

Gentlemen

With reference to these Grounds I beg say that I have carefully considered what is best to be done at the present time I have examin the Bedding Plants and find about Two thousa three hundred including those in the Greenhou to make a good show of these grounds it woula take seven times the number I would earnest recommend the purchasing a quantity of Plant at once that I may at the proper time propaga freely for next year

The existing beds & borders I find are very poor & recommend that they be thorough trenched manured, and fresh soil added

of herbaceous plants. It was given further impetus by the nursery trade who concentrated on supplying tender plants that gave little alternative. The style remained in fashion until the First World War and became synonymous with the sea-side, where it was part of the seasonal attraction of the resorts and a measure of civic pride. Brighton was well known for its bedding displays and hosted competitions between rival towns, right up to the 1980s. The *Sussex Daily News*, 11 April 1953, reported that 'Corporation flower-beds always have a spruce and military air about them; but most of us will not have them otherwise, for civic flowers are essentially public servants who owe a duty to popular taste'. The sea front displays formed an ordered, immaculate contrast to the skirmishes between the Mods and Rockers that were famously enacted in front of them.

The problem of anti-social behaviour and how to enforce byelaws in the Pavilion's grounds recur in the Pavilion Committee Minutes. They have a familiar ring to them and still apply today. From the earliest days there was pressure from the Head Gardener to appoint a caretaker 'to keep order' although a custodian was already making hourly patrols. From 1851 the list of rules to be observed included the prohibition of cycling, perambulators (banned until 1873), dogs without leads, smoking, carriages, begging, drinking, ragged attire, kites, balls, arrows, trundle hoops or games. The shrubberies, borders, flowers, and trees were not to be touched and there was a warning that any barriers or fences put up to protect areas were not to be crossed. The grounds were locked at 10.00pm. The fine was £5 for each infringement. The use of the grass had to be balanced with its maintenance as the lawns were in constant demand. They required frequent returfing and the areas set aside for events were often moved to allow grass to recover.

As well as bedding-out the fashion for incorporating new exotics or tropical plants was seen in the Pavilion grounds in 1878. The bed surrounding the new marble statue of Sir Cordy Burrows, an eminent benefactor and three times Mayor of the town, typified the latest ideas in plant associations. Plants now included the banana, canna lilies, abutilon and palms that gave height and added interest to the low bedding. They were particularly suitable for the sheltered area opposite the entrance. The sub-tropical displays must have surprised and delighted visitors as much as the 'new'

Regency plants had done in the Prince's time. They also brought a reminder of far-away countries and the extent of the British Empire. Queen Victoria was celebrated in many parks and at Brighton her statue still faces the Pavilion Gardens. These high maintenance, seasonal displays are still prepared in some parks today. St James's Park in London, which was re-landscaped by Nash after his designs for Brighton, had an area devoted to these tender 'fireworks', part of the foreground to a raised shrubbery. It was replaced in 2005 with a new planting in the original spirit of Nash and the immaculate edged lawns nearby were re-seeded with a mixture of grass and wild flowers. The exotic bed in the Pavilion grounds had been planted by Shrives, no doubt to demonstrate the benefits of his new greenhouses. He also purchased '60 American Arbor Vitae … at 1/6d each and potted for decorating the Pavilion Grounds'.[221] The form of this evergreen fir is not given, presumably *Thuya 'occidentalis'*, which makes a large, conical tree. They continued to be used as temporary decorations for the grounds until the 1980s (see p.128). Thirty-one Arbor Vitae had been used in Aiton's planting around Royal Lodge.

ABOVE Photograph from the Brighton Herald,1955. The entrance bed planted with palms and the same view (below) twenty years later.

The bedding style became very popular and was seen everywhere. It was natural that a reaction would set in and indeed a reaction, or revolution, was the response. Gardening had become a temporary display of massed low-growing flowers. What had happened to all the traditional plants that gardeners had known and used for centuries? The gardening prophet William Robinson created an influential garden at Gravetye Manor in Sussex, incorporating many different styles. He introduced the idea of the wild garden, growing native or hardy plants in a natural way. These were not stocked in nurs-eries in the 1870s as there was no demand. His idea of a wild garden corresponded with the rediscov-ery of Nature by members of the Arts and Crafts Movement and de-signers such as William Morris. Morris set up his own dye works at Merton Abbey in 1881 reviving old recipes in reaction to the artificial aniline prod-ucts. These dyes were used to print his famous designs, which were given names that recalled 'Olde England' and were a reaction to industrialisation; 'Borage', 'Bird and Anemone', 'Rose', and so on. Painters such as Millais had even incorporated 'weeds' in his fa-mous picture, *Ophelia*. The Purple Loosestrife, which appears in the re-stored Regency garden, is shown

Lythrum salicaria (Purple loosestrife).

growing on the banks along with other native favourites. The natural world was looked at with new interest as Henry Phillips had advocated when the Regency garden was first made.

This movement led to the kind of English gardening that has become world famous, notably, through Robinson and Gertrude Jekyll. Robinson knew Jekyll and had advised on her garden in Surrey. They both influenced informal planting in twentieth-century gardens. The way they used plants to give the impression of the garden merging slowly, imperceptibly, into woodland, with more native plants, had similarities with Regency principles. Changes were slow to gain widespread acceptance as the hardy herbaceous plants 'give an untidy appearance'.[222] The more 'tidy' bedding system was still popular in 1937 although 'more

WEST ELEVATION

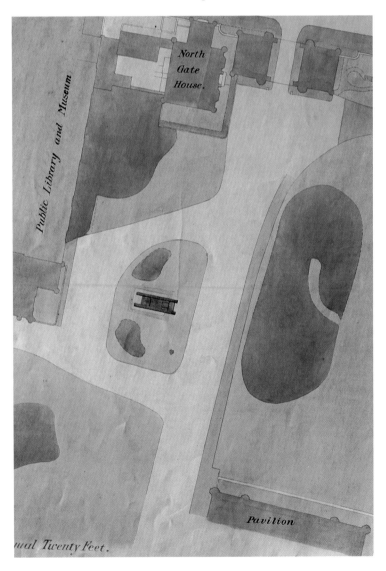

Public Library and Museum

North Gate House.

Pavilion

...ual Twenty Feet.

consideration is bestowed upon herbaceous borders than on the bedded out garden. This change of taste has so stimulated the cultivation of these plants'.[223] The grounds at Brighton had to wait over 100 years before its garden composition of natural looking beds and plants was reinstated.

Meanwhile they adapted to fashions in a very different way. The proposal for an enormous Winter Garden that would cover the whole of the North Lawns was given serious consideration in 1893. The Pavilion Committee's nervous reaction to it can be judged from the instructions to make a mock up of the building with posts, cords and a temporary wooden structure to approximate its impact. The same method had been suggested for unsure gardeners in the eighteenth century; battens to simulate a building or white sheets for a lake were advised as a try out. The Pavilion grounds survived intact, although within twenty years, they would be required for a more urgent use.

With the outbreak of the First World War the flower beds on the lawns were, in effect, replaced with iron beds for the wounded. The Pavilion itself, the Dome and the grounds were used as hospitals for Indian soldiers.[224] Fire precautions were provided by four firemen and a stationary engine in the grounds, although this did not prevent the 'destruction of a marquee in the centre of the Western Lawn by fire caused by patients smoking'.[225] The number of new patients were strictly limited by early 1920 and in May the Pavilion was emptied, disinfected and cleaned. The director was authorised to take the furniture out of store and open the grounds to the public after the workshops that were set up in them were removed. The Indian Memorial Gateway at the South Entrance to the grounds was presented to Brighton the following year by the people of India to commemorate the role of the town's Indian military hospitals in caring for the wounded. The strong design balanced that of the North Gate. The War Savings Association proposed that a military tank, be displayed near the North Gate. Fortunately an alternative site was suggested on the Steine.

The grounds were now looked at with a view to making improvements. Elaborate works were proposed outside the Dome, such as 'terraces, pergolas and temples … rock and water gardens', with plants labelled for educational purposes. It was thought that such schemes would 'absorb a large number of unemployed accounted for by those returning from military service'.[226] The Superintendent of Parks and Gardens, Captain B. H. MacLaren, devised a scheme to widen the road on the Steine by taking away some of the grounds, cutting them back to a straight line. The old, decayed elms, the railings and shrubberies were removed giving an open view into the grounds for the first time in 120 years. The local paper reported that MacLaren 'promised a charming scheme of flowers, rose covered pergolas, and other pretty devices to take the place of the railings and shrubs'.[227] The scheme was completed a year later for the Mayor's

garden party. It was described as a low concrete pierced 'oriental' wall, where 'fountains played in the new pools surrounded by scarlet geraniums and Ventia palms and semi-tropical plants'. There was a bandstand in the centre and a 'village' of tables and chairs under striped umbrellas and marquees'.[228]

The photographs show MacLaren's scheme being constructed. The large elm trees, now on the pavement, were inside the railings as part of the boundary of the original garden. The wall and railings shown in the photograph were an early attempt in 1900 to open up the view into the grounds. From 1879 the Pavilion

Committee wanted to lower the earlier high wall insisting that the 'character of the existing boulder [flint] wall will be preserved'. At the same time as these alterations were carried out, twelve large elm trees were removed, along with the dense border planting, 'so that the passing public … can obtain a better view of the Pavilion and Grounds'. The *Sussex Daily News*, 1 February 1922, reported that, 'New vistas have been opened up by the removal of the banking and railings all round … several old trees have been felled and the shrubs have been removed. The soil removed from the banking near the roadway is being taken to fill the hollow at the extreme southern corner of the lawn'. The original levels were designed for privacy so that the garden ground was sunk below the surrounding banked shrubbery, as had been suggested by Repton. The drop in levels and the path can be seen beyond the inner hurdle fence where the workmen's jackets are hanging. The view from the street also shows that the elms were planted on top of the banked up earth. Nash

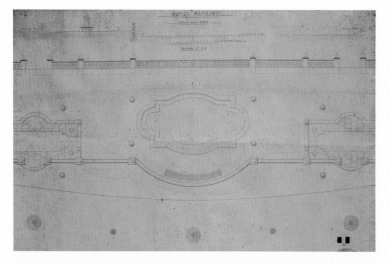

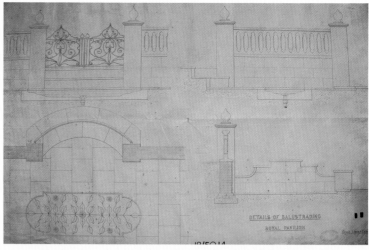

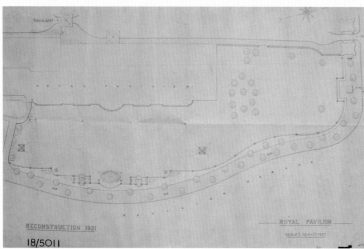

ABOVE Three drawings showing MacLaren's proposal for the East Front boundary.

BELOW Drawing showing how MacLaren's scheme took twenty feet away from the garden to widen the road and established the boundary as it appears today. The elm trees on the pavement were formerly in the garden.

ABOVE Postcard. The view predates the introduction of one-way traffic in 1926 and shows how cleverly the banked boundary levels were accommodated. The planting with palms and Agave (a succulent) give an exotic touch to the scene. The use of urns to contain accent points of colour and changing displays appear in the earliest photographs of the entrance front of the Pavilion from the 1870s. They gave the building a fashionable Victorian domesticity.

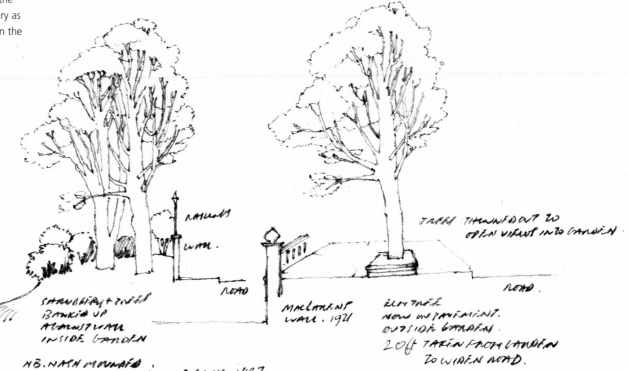

planted trees on artificial mounds at St James's Park. They gave variety and seclusion to the flat site. The wall and railings recorded in these photographs were about to be replaced with MacLaren's low pierced 'oriental wall', which still forms the boundary today.

In 1922 changes were also made to the Western Lawns. Twenty elm trees were removed opposite the Pavilion, six at a time, and new ones planted. This was done 'regretfully because they have an idea that Brighton is short of trees', it was reported in the *Sussex Daily News* 'poor old things (they had been planted by William IV) … are not trees at all: only deformities'.

The rejuvenation of the grounds at this time brought a radical proposal that had been famously suggested over 100 years before. That 'Indian buildings ought to have an Indian garden'. The present grounds were described to the Brighton and Hove Horticultural Society as 'too ordinary, too English'. Members were shown pictures of an alternative setting of formal lakes, edged with marble, fountains and tall cypresses 'to make the Pavilion grounds a place for the reading of Omar Khayyam and the Thousand and One Nights'. The speaker was thanked for 'showing what could be done in the restoration of old gardens and making them accord with the style and date of the buildings to which they are attached'. It was clear that the Parks and Garden Committee were not contemplating a 'restoration', as the proposal met with the same response as that given to Repton 'the trouble would be the money'.[229] The proposals would have seriously limited the use of the grounds, as by now there were open-air dances on the lawns, fêtes, markets (some selling plants) and staged pageants. Ironically, when the restoration of the Nash garden was first considered in the 1980s, there were some then who also would have preferred the Repton scheme. It too would not have adapted well to its use as a public space. Thankfully, it was agreed that Nash's scheme constituted the correct historic garden.

By 1925 the Annual Chrysanthemum Show at Brighton was considered second only to that held in the metropolis. The chrysanthemum was one of the plants collected by Robert Fortune on his last expedition to Japan in 1860. Fortune was the Curator of the Chelsea Physic Garden and was one of the first to use the Wardian Case to transport his many finds. The show become so popular that the Dome and Corn Exchange could not hold them all and the Museum was taken over as well. Chrysanthemums 'as big as an adult person's head' were displayed with carnations, violets, begonias and primulas. Trophies and medals were awarded with certificates for the best front and back gardens, hanging baskets and window boxes.

The success was such that annual Spring, Summer and Autumn shows were held. The *Sussex Daily News* (24 September 1927) reported on the 'triumphs' of Captain MacLaren who had worked through the night to prepare the autumn show, overseeing 'forty vanloads of palms, ferns and foliage plants. He had also planted the grounds with 'a riot of colour, never a finer show'. The

description of the beds gives an insight into inter-war municipal planting and showed what could be achieved in a garden in Autumn. Outside the Dome was a display of 'The Brighton Gem' (a dahlia), massed with asters that had replaced the summer planting of 'Paul Cramphal' geraniums and African marigolds. The detached bed by the North Entrance 'shows something out of the ordinary; red lilies share the centre of a circular bed with mammoth white asters, while mauve Victoria asters and lobelia provide the edging'. The adjacent square bed was filled with 'coleus, fine scarlet and white asters, edged with alyssum'. The bed opposite the Pavilion entrance displayed more 'asters in mauve, blues, reds, pinks and white, with red lilies and a background of eucalyptus and ornamental shrubs'. The final show bed on the East Front was the most popular 'mesembryanthemum, beetroot red, with blue ageratum, apricot and pale yellow antirrhinums'. There were many enquiries from people

wishing to know the varieties to 'secure these effects'.

Three months later there was a proposal to extend the Pavilion from the King's Apartments to the North Lawn. The 'Pavilionette', as it was called, met with such outrage that it was reported in the national press, from *The Times* to the *Daily Mail*. This additional 'first class banqueting accommodation' was abandoned as it was reasoned 'the Royal Pavilion needs isolation – it belongs to a world of its own'.[230] That world was soon to be dug up as the Second World War loomed.

The North Lawn was now turned into a specimen allotment to show planting for survival rather than for decoration. As a gesture of support the geranium beds outside Buckingham Palace were growing potatoes and the garden at Royal Lodge was ploughed for food production. Trenches were dug across the Western Lawn to link with the Dome for use in bomb attacks and a water tank holding 300,000 gallons was sunk into the ground, 'for fire fighting purposes' although there was a 'possibility of its conversion at a later date to an ornamental lake'.[231] The lighting in the grounds was concealed and as an extra blackout precaution the gilding on the minarets and roof of the Dome was 'obliterated'. It would never be put back. Demonstrations of animal husbandry were held. How to keep chickens, rabbits or pigs became a national concern, with advice on how to fatten them up or make a pigsty in your own back yard. Over 7,000 pig clubs were set-up across the country.

With the return of peace the ground was quickly reinstated 'to its pre-1939 condition', and it was decided that the simple treatment of 'natural undulations gives effect of breadth',[232] an opinion that was worthy of Repton and concurred with his theories on shaping ground. The new grounds were soon to be subject to yet more conflict and anxiety. There was concern in the press about the trees in the grounds, 'Trees have a life of 200 years. They should be at their best 120 years after starting. One would like to see

ABOVE Animal husbandry being demonstrated outside the King's Apartments during the Second World War. The basement of the Royal Pavilion was used as an air-raid shelter.

RIGHT An artist's impression of the proposal for a conference hall part of a £750,000 scheme to extend the Corn Exchange across the top of the Western Lawn. Illustrated in the *The Builder* magazine, 1955.

more trees planted now so that there are no gaps when the trees come down. It has been said that the elms in the Pavilion grounds will have to go for safety's sake and if the loss is to be made good, why not smaller and safer species such as cherry and laburnum?'[233]

There was an ambitious scheme (illustrated in *The Builder* magazine 25 March 1955) to build a two-story conference centre across the top of the western lawn that was reconsidered in 1959, by which time the threat to use the grounds as a car park was also quashed. In the early 1960s there were pleas in the local press 'to save our lawns'[234] as they had been used to demonstrate pre-fabricated buildings on dug foundations for a National Housing and Town Planning Conference. 'Desecration and Sabotage' were the headline descriptions; seventeen years after the war the grounds looked like a war zone again.[235] The space was valued as an open setting for the Pavilion, to attract visitors. Twenty palm trees costing a total of £200 were purchased. It was thought they would 'mingle with the weathered oaks and elms on the lawn' and give Brighton a new competitive edge: 'West Country resorts will be annoyed'.[236] The variety of palm (Trachycarpus Fortunii, or Chusan Palm) was first imported from China by Fortune in 1845. The palms for the Pavilion were brought from Guernsey so that 'they would match the Eastern minarets and being associated with warmer climes will be worth thousands of pounds in publicity'. At fourteen foot, fifty years old and weighing a ton they were ironically craned in place 'in cold drenching rain'.[237] The garden superintendent was quoted as saying 'I think they'll survive, but I'm keeping my fingers crossed'.[238] Six surviving palms are still in the grounds today. The restoration of the Regency garden took them into account as part of the history of the planting on the site. The cautious superintendent would have been surprised.

In effect, George IV's gardens had now become an urban park. Planting was reduced to the maintenance of a few shaped beds filled with seasonal colour. The bed near the North Entrance spelled out a welcome in bedding plants. Up until 1980 it was still being used to commemorate special events, such as The Queen's Silver Jubilee in 1977. The tradition continued MacLaren's 'riot of colour' that James Shrives had instigated 100 years before. The pressure to use the grounds as a place for cars, rather than people and plants, reflected more affluent, mobile times.

The 1980s saw the beginning of the 'heritage' era as the reappraisal and conservation of the past caught the public's imagination. Old houses, interiors, antiques and gardens were looked at with a new enthusiasm. It became a fashion that was boosted by many publications, ranging from scholarly research on aspects of the country house to 'how to do it' decorating books that fuelled a new interest in creating past styles. The conservation of houses and their contents was reflected outside with the interest in period gardens and plants, although the Garden History Society had been actively promoting conservation and research into gardens and landscape since it was founded in 1965. Historic buildings were at the forefront of the movement that led to campaigns for preservation and historical accuracy. At Brighton the full

structural restoration of the Royal Pavilion led to the authentic reinstatement of some of the original internal decorative schemes. Contemporary accounts, documentation and research were used to return the building to its original appearance as designed by John Nash.

At the same time the momentous decision was taken to restore the garden, presenting the whole building in an appropriate setting, as was originally intended.

ABOVE Photograph, 1970s, showing the garden in use as a car park.

LEFT The view from the top of the North Gate showing the grounds used as a thoroughfare with a blue Pavilion in 1975. The same view, 2005 showing the restored garden beds and paths in early spring. The building is reunited with its garden.

15

THE REGENCY GARDEN RESTORED

'It is most appropriate that the first major Regency garden restoration should be at Brighton, the focus of the Regency period'.

— MAVIS BATEY, *Regency Gardens*, 1995, P.71.

BELOW Preparations for the reinstatement of the garden plan while the building was undergoing restoration.

THROUGHOUT THE 1980s the Pavilion was covered in scaffolding wrapped in blue sheeting. When it was revealed, the fibreglass minarets, a 1960s attempt at restoration, had been removed and replaced with carved stone. The 'duck-egg' blue painted walls of the late 1950s were repainted to match the stone, as was the original intention. The light fibreglass minarets were used by an enterprising London gardener to embellish his roof-top garden. The Pavilion was finally taken seriously as an important historic building and, behind the scenes, documentation and research led to the reinstatement of the building to its original appearance. In the grounds a similar process was underway to realise the first major restoration of a Regency garden in England. Unlike the building, the Regency Garden was an uncharted area.

LEFT Photograph, Ianthe Ruthven, *The World of Interiors* magazine, 1985. A Chelsea roof garden with the light fibreglass minarets from the Pavilion used to transform the skyline.

As with any restoration project the results, to be successful, need to be as authentic as possible. Detailed research was required to make sense of the beds shown on Nash's plan, to establish the guiding principles that would be followed with the planting. Period garden reinstatements, such as The Privy Garden at Hampton Court, had the turf specially grown on Romney Marsh, using a grass mix typical of grazed heaths. The yews and hollies were propagated from surviving originals such was the determination to be historically accurate. At Brighton there were only a few surviving original trees, but no physical evidence of the original layout. Dutch Elm Disease and the hurricane storm of 1987, had taken its toll. (See photograph on p.132 from the 1970s showing the huge numbers.) Ironically the trees, planted in the late 19th and 20th centuries had grown out of scale with the Pavilion, creating areas of dense shade and poor soil. Their position in the garden would have made the present restoration impossible.

The Garden History Society, through Mavis Batey, was instrumental in bringing together, for the first time, the necessary research for an understanding of the complex theories behind the Regency garden, its evolution and creation. It also provided a useful practical guide for remaking the ornamental shrubberies. The organisations that promoted and funded the restoration project are credited in the acknowledgements.

ABOVE Aerial photograph, c.1970, the Pavilion Estate showing the density of elm trees.

BELOW Plan of the disposition of the restored beds translated to the site, based on Nash's design.

A list of suitable plants, known to have been available at the time, was drawn up and a planting plan devised. The shrubberies were designed by Virginia Hinze who with great enthusiasm and knowledge fulfilled her role as the twentieth-century Aiton.

For the first beds on the East Front, the plants listed by Aiton in the second edition of his father's *Hortus Kewensis*[239] were also used, along with contemporary nursery catalogues as a guide to the plants that were available at the time. It was a broad-brush approach that perfectly accorded with the watercolours prepared for Nash's *Views*.

Nash's plan for the garden, (see p.96) in the same publication, was a key document in the reinstatement of the Regency layout. Minor alterations allowed for twentieth-century operational requirements and the changes over time to the physical boundaries. The establishment of a new workable plan that could be linked, in phases, to the ongoing restoration of the building was crucial. In fact it has taken over two decades to complete the gardens.

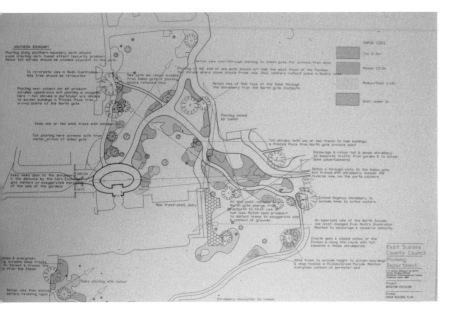

OPPOSITE Augustus C. Pugin, *The West Front*, watercolour, c.1822, preparatory watercolour for Nash's Views. The wide sweep of the foreground setting shows immature shrubbery.

OPPOSITE-BELOW Augustus C. Pugin, *The North Front*, c.1822, preparatory watercolour for Nash's Views. The loose rendering of the shrubbery shows the intended effect of the planting.

The completion of the garden had to wait until the building contractors had left and the scaffolding was struck, allowing the road in front of the Pavilion to be removed. It was the cause of much celebration in 1991 when the road, for the fourth time in the history of the grounds, was dug up. As in George IV's time the removal of the road allowed the unification of the building with its garden setting. The first paths and planting, linking the North Gate with the Pavilion were in place for the visit of The Prince of Wales in May 1995.

While the first experimental shrubberies were maturing and the rest of the grounds awaited transformation, research continued and an exciting and encouraging discovery was made. The complete record of the accounts relating to the Pavilion's garden were found amongst the many vellum-bound books that recorded the expenditure on all the Royal gardens at that time.[240] Meticulously written, detailed and dated they confirmed the garden's creation. They gave an insight to the initial ground preparation, plant lists, labour requirements, tools and, as usual, itemised 'beer for Mr Nash's men'.[241] The beer was certainly earned as the accounts revealed many pages of backbreaking work to change a building site and landscaped field into a garden that would be worthy of a newly-crowned King.

On site the restoration work proceeded with a new confidence and almost paralleled those accounts. The ground was prepared and the main carriage drive and turning circle, based exactly on Nash's plan, saw the grounds slowly resembling their former layout. The twentieth-century mechanical diggers and equipment took the place of Nash's men - only the beer was missing!

The upheaval on site recalled the days of the Nash building when local residents complained of the inconvenience, with letters to the Prince Regent asking for compensation of £100 per year

due to the work and noise: 'the repairs … at the Pavilion, for some years, have made bad, worse … millions of bricks have been heaped up in front of our windows - immense quantities of filth, mortar, timber and every noisome material … have been laid at our doors … we have received great injuries and our property much lessened in value'.[242] However, the disruption this time was planned around the needs of visitors and residents and the buildings remained open throughout the project.

ABOVE The Pavilion is once more united with its garden. The road is replaced with lawn and planting that frame and compose the buildings.

ABOVE Before and after views. The bed opposite the Museum entrance (top), the Western Lawn and the serpentine paths.

Tamarisk, a reliable shrub, is tolerant of coastal exposure and polution. It has feathery foliage and plumes of pink flowers from late summer.

The original plant lists confirmed those suggested by Phillips and, like his, were listed under their common names. The main supplier of the plants for the original garden was John Willmott of Lewisham. His nursery was one of the largest in southern England, with over 100 acres in 1822.[243] Later research revealed that plants had also been dispatched earlier from Kew, including seeds, and that additions were made from local nurseries in Lewes. What is clear is that the plants were chosen for their suitability for the seaside site, to be tolerant of wind and salt and reinforced the role of Aiton (and perhaps the King), who over a long period had experience of the site and its shortcomings. The density of the shrubberies and the perimeter beds packed with trees – the faster growing the better – also points to his impatience. The incredible quantities recall Aiton's earlier planting at the Royal Lodge, which ensured the King's privacy.

The new planting was completed to general acclaim, although the length of the grass was the cause of many complaints. Unfortunately this was before the shrubberies had grown and its appropriateness to the natural effect could be judged, and accepted. For a while it seemed that Shrives and MacLaren could be back and making 'tidy' suggestions again. The last perimeter areas next to the Dome were planted, after its refurbishment, in 2003. As a final acknowledgment of the years of hard work, patience and vision the garden has been added to the English Heritage Register of Parks and Gardens. The Royal Pavilion gardens are registered as Grade 2.

Two beds in the restored garden typify the ideas behind the planting. The emphasis of the shrubberies changed depending on their position within the garden. They conformed to Phillips's advice that, as they receded from a building, they should look more like natural scenery. The first bed (opposite) could be compared to the edge of a wood or at first glance it may seem that nature had been left alone, which was, of course, the intention. Although there are contrasting evergreens, there is additional seasonal interest throughout the year as is indicated by the accompanying sketches. This was the kind of shrubbery that would have pleased Nash. His shrubberies in St James's Park were devoid of showy flowers. This would probably have mystified the gardener Furner. The early enthusiasms of Loudon would have wished for a wilder lawn and as for Price and Knight the whole scheme would have been far too tame. They would have supported the proposal of a lake fed from the Dome but as a torrent rather than a gentle cascade. The sunken path, not on the Nash plan, at the side of this bed was put in during the restoration to allow people a crossing point that remained unseen from the Pavilion. It was exactly the kind of conceit that Phillips had recommended to obscure private walks in his *Sylva Florifera* of 1823.

RIGHT The strawberry tree, *Arbutus unedo*, forms part of a natural-looking landscaped shrubbery.

Arbutus unedo 'Rubra'
(strawberry tree)

Ruscus aculeatus
(butcher's broom)

Ulex europaeus (gorse)

Lavatera olbia (mallow)

Hydrangea arborescens

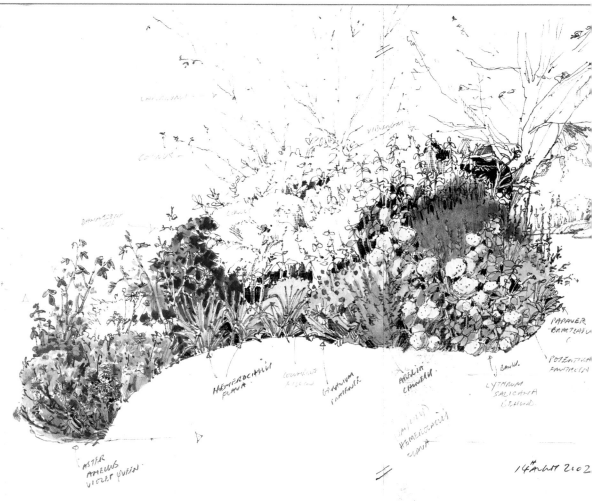

The second illustration (above) shows the plants grouped together near the Pavilion Entrance. This shrubbery is at its floriferous height in August and is deliberately planted with exciting colour accents throughout the year. It is part of the central group of irregular beds that form the main link to the Pavilion and can be seen from it. It is also part of the main carriage drive where the shrubberies are most visible to visitors and the more showy introductions are 'mixed and mingled' with native plants. The composition of this central area gave great scope in the restoration to create the 'forest lawn' effect with the lawn seeming to glide into the shrubberies. The shapes of the shrubberies, taken exactly from the Nash plan, meander into the lawn, creating irregular islands that overlap and run into each other, like a stage set. The silhouettes give a variety of outline from a dense shining evergreen bush such as Portugal laurel to a delicate thin Laburnum or large native tree. They compliment, rather than compete with the silhouette of the building which rises confidently behind them. The popular Hollyhocks, with their colourful spires, seem to echo the minarets on the roofline.

These central beds would have had the full approval of the designers and gardeners when they were originally created, as the grouping of flowering plants were from then on an essential part of garden design. Repton, if he could have visited the completed garden, may have regarded some of the planting as too 'modern' as he was nervous of new introductions such as the China Rose, although he used lilacs, laburnums, honeysuckles and Portugal laurels which appear in this bed. He would have disliked the fir trees, preferred a straight carriage drive and obviously thought 'Indian buildings ought to have an Indian garden'. Loudon would have agreed with the introduction of more exotic plants in the shrubbery. Snart would have introduced rhododendrons and for Shrives and MacLaren it would be too untidy. Robinson would probably have applauded, although Jekyll would have orchestrated the planting with more careful colour and shape balance.

ABOVE Detail, central part of illustration. The plants include *Helenium autumnale* and *Alcea rosea* which continue to flower into the Autumn.

SPRING

Drifts of flowering bulbs light up the shrubberies and the North Lawn. Early flowers appear on the bare stems of shrubs and trees. New foliage unfurls as the visiting season begins. Herbaceous plants, such as astrantia, crane's bill geranium, Chinese lanterns (Physalis alkekengi), purple loosestrife (Lythrum salicaria) and comfery (Symphytum) are divided as they increase. They form part of the annual plant and seed give-away that revive past traditions in public gardens. Hardy annuals, nasturtium and night-scented stock are sown. Seedlings of foxglove, nigella and honesty are transplanted. March completes the pruning with the more tender hydrangeas, potentillas and fuchsias.

Plan of the restored garden. The beds are given a letter to locate the positions of the plants drawn on the following pages.

SPRING HIGHLIGHTS

The flowering quince; *Chaenomeles speciosa* 'Cardinalis' (not to be confused with the culinary variety) epitomises Springtime, it flowers over a long period, the first flowers ahead of the leaves.

The almond, *Prunus dulcis* is covered in delicate flowers, followed by velvety green fruit containing an edible nut.

The lent lily, or wild daffodil (*Narcissus pseudonarcissus*) is naturalised in grass. In the wild they are now being threatened by more robust cultivars. *Narcissus poeticus* var. *recurvus* (Pheasant's Eye) form groups in the shrubberies.

The *Daphne odora* is a gorgeously scented low growing shrub.

The *Cornus mas* (Cornelian cherry), comfrey, *Kerria japonica*, and the euphorbias are all looking their best.

The white lace cap-like flower globes of *Viburnum opulus* (Guelder rose) compliment the smaller Orange Ball Tree flowers of *Buddleia globosa*.

The drawings of the plants on the following pages are given a letter that corresponds to the different beds in which they appear on the plan. A selection has been made to highlight each season as a guide to the many parts of the garden to encourage exploration throughout the year.

Vinca major (Periwinkle) Beds A, B, P, R, T Flowers from mid February in the Pavilion's garden

Viola odorata (Violet). Beds C, R, T.

Crocus vernus Strewn in the grass in J and S. Flowering from mid February.

Polyanthus Now removed as they were planted as well-meaning colourful and early gap-fillers by the former management team. They would not have appeared in the Regency Garden as too late in date.

Geranium robertianum (Herb Robert). Self seeded. Bed F

Myosotis palustris now **M. scorpiodes** (Forget-me-not) Beds L1, R, V, W Flowers from late February in the Pavilion's garden

Pulmonaria saccharata Beds M, P.

Cercis siliquastrum (Judas tree) Bed A

Rosmarinus officinalis Beds
K, L1 Flowers from late
February.

**Doronicum
austraicum**
(Leopard's Bane).
Beds D, N, P, Q. Easy
to grow and a good
gap-filler after the
fading daffodils.

**Narcissus poeticus var.
recurvus** (Pheasant's Eye)
Beds R, X, Y.

Galanthus nivalis
(Snowdrop). Beds P, Q, V.

Euphorbia myrsinites Beds
D, H, L1, V. A low prostrate
evergreen perennial with
pointed, fleshy grey leaves.

Euphorbia characias (Spurge)
Beds G, H, L2, T, V, W A valuable
herbaceous plant of luxurious
growth, rare in April and May. The
subspecies **E. wulfenii** (as
drawing) has yellowish centres
rather than the usual dark brown.

Astrantia major
(Masterwort) Beds
A, C, L1, T

Aquilegia vulgaris
(Common Columbine) Beds
G, K, P

Geranium sanguineum
(Bloody Cranesbill) Beds P, Q.
Flowers over a long period to
September

Astrantia major (Masterwort)
Beds A, C, L1, T

Coronilla eremus (now
Hippocreptis eremus) Bed N

Daphne mezereum
Beds L3,P

Primula vulgaris
(Primrose) Beds A, B,
H, P, R.

Geranium phaeum (Mourning
Widow) Beds H, L3, P, X

Iberis sempervirens
(Candytuft) Beds K, N, W.

Bellis perennis
(Common Daisy)
Beds N, Y.

Tulipa greigii (Red Riding Hood) Beds L3, N, Q

Bergenia crassifolia (Saxifrage or Elephant's Ears) Beds G, N, R, Y The white flowered variety is a twentieth century hybrid, **x schmidtii 'Silberlicht'**. The large rounded evergreen leaves make a handsome ground cover. The strong outline is also a good contrast to other foliage.

Cheiranthus (Wallflower) Treated as an annual 'filler' although Loudon was to later value them for evergreen autumn / winter bedding

Magnolia stellata Bed C A Specimen tree that was retained although too late by thirty years for the Regency Garden.

Cytisus multiflorus (white Spanish Broom) Bed N

Prunus 'Moerheimii' A small weeping tree of wide spreading habit. A specimen tree that was retained, although too late for the Regency Garden. In the lawn in front of Bed R. See page 112

Tamarix tetrandra
Beds L1, W, X, Y

Allium vulgaris
Beds C, G, H

Iris japonica
Bed K

Syringa x persica (Lilac) Bed L1, M
and **Syringa x chinensis** Bed L1, N
and **Syringa vulgaris** Beds L1, M
and **Syringa vulgaris var. alba** Beds A, C, N, L1

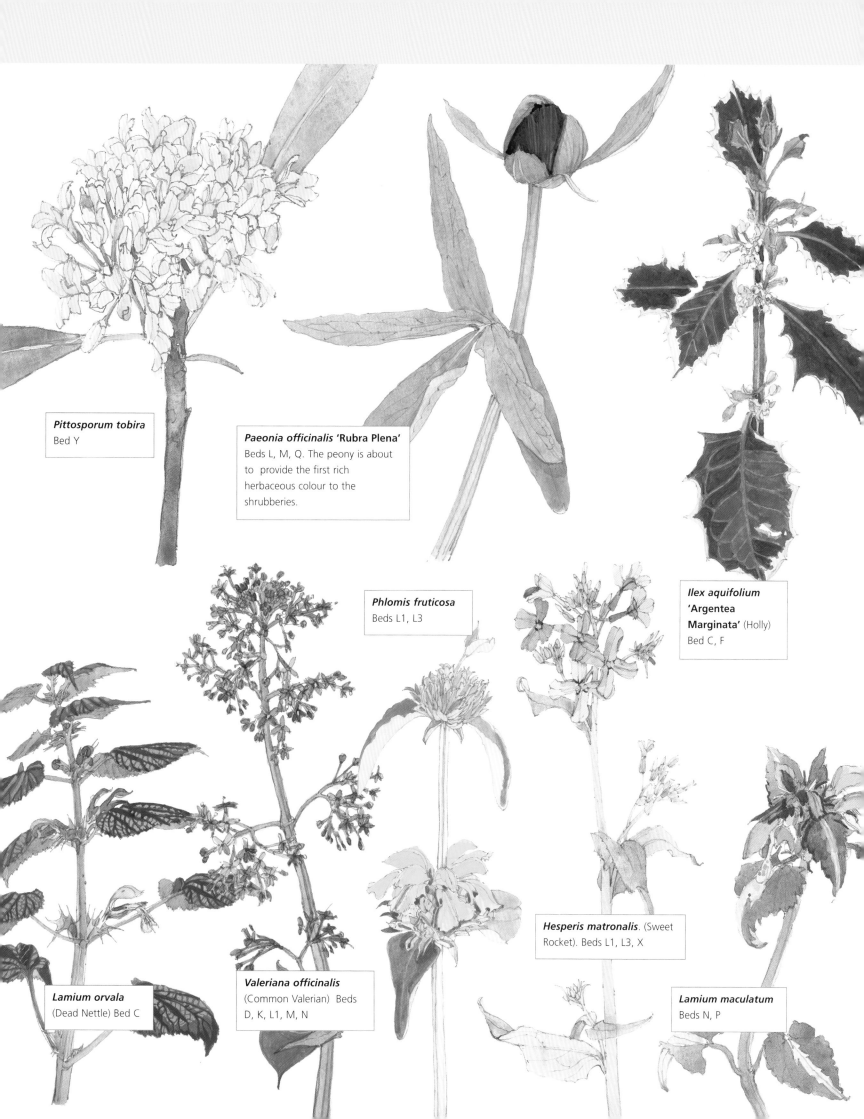

Pittosporum tobira
Bed Y

Paeonia officinalis 'Rubra Plena'
Beds L, M, Q. The peony is about
to provide the first rich
herbaceous colour to the
shrubberies.

Phlomis fruticosa
Beds L1, L3

**Ilex aquifolium
'Argentea
Marginata'** (Holly)
Bed C, F

Hesperis matronalis. (Sweet
Rocket). Beds L1, L3, X

Lamium orvala
(Dead Nettle) Bed C

Valeriana officinalis
(Common Valerian) Beds
D, K, L1, M, N

Lamium maculatum
Beds N, P

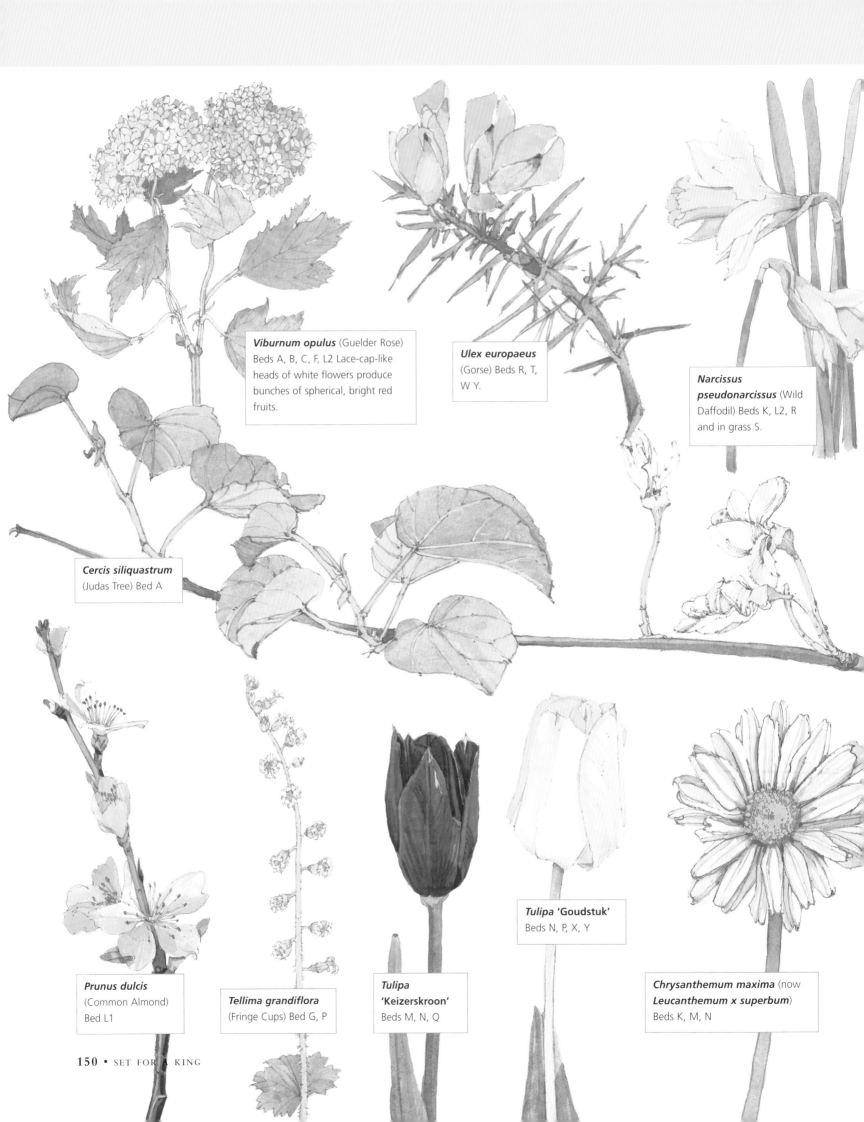

Viburnum opulus (Guelder Rose) Beds A, B, C, F, L2 Lace-cap-like heads of white flowers produce bunches of spherical, bright red fruits.

Ulex europaeus (Gorse) Beds R, T, W Y.

Narcissus pseudonarcissus (Wild Daffodil) Beds K, L2, R and in grass S.

Cercis siliquastrum (Judas Tree) Bed A

Tulipa 'Goudstuk' Beds N, P, X, Y

Prunus dulcis (Common Almond) Bed L1

Tellima grandiflora (Fringe Cups) Bed G, P

Tulipa 'Keizerskroon' Beds M, N, Q

Chrysanthemum maxima (now **Leucanthemum x superbum**) Beds K, M, N

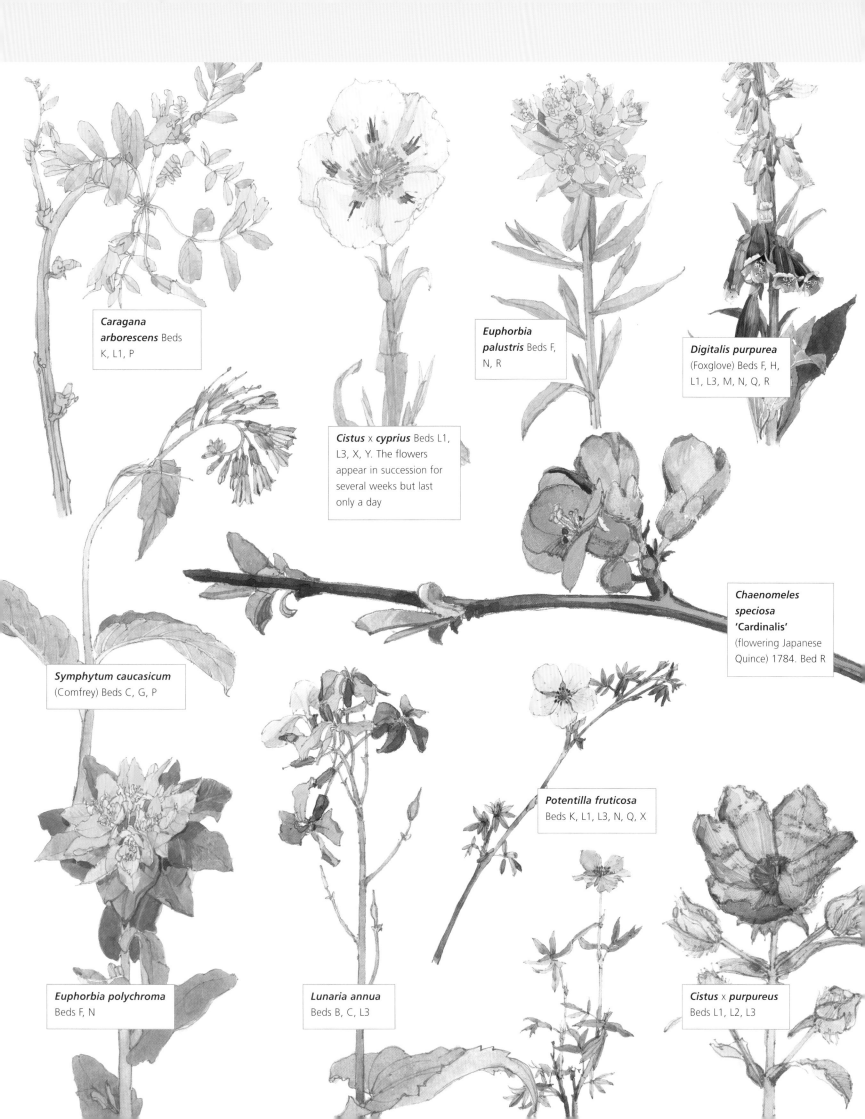

Caragana arborescens Beds K, L1, P

Cistus x **cyprius** Beds L1, L3, X, Y. The flowers appear in succession for several weeks but last only a day

Euphorbia palustris Beds F, N, R

Digitalis purpurea (Foxglove) Beds F, H, L1, L3, M, N, Q, R

Chaenomeles speciosa 'Cardinalis' (flowering Japanese Quince) 1784. Bed R

Symphytum caucasicum (Comfrey) Beds C, G, P

Potentilla fruticosa Beds K, L1, L3, N, Q, X

Euphorbia polychroma Beds F, N

Lunaria annua Beds B, C, L3

Cistus x **purpureus** Beds L1, L2, L3

SUMMER

The garden pulsates with activity and colour. The planting now forms an exciting introduction to the Pavilion. Visitors catch glimpses of the building through the shrubberies. Roses and scented plants are especially appreciated. The lawns, covered with people, are as colourful as the beds. There is a constant party atmosphere, especially if musicians are playing. Hazel sticks (from the personal wood of one of the garden volunteers) are used to support peonies, hollyhocks and Chinese lanterns. As summers become drier, the native plants suffer. The private irrigation system is supplied by underground springs. The roses and herbaceous plants are fed with concentrated chicken manure. No herbicides or pesticides are used, the garden is completely organic; Nature takes its course. Grass is mown frequently as the blades are kept on the highest setting to ensure the lawns do not look artificial. Grass cuttings remain on the surface to restore nutrients.

Plan of the restored garden. The beds are given a letter to locate the positions of the plants drawn on the following pages.

SUMMER HIGHLIGHTS

- Roses, particularly *Rosa* 'Petite Lisette', is a show-stopper near the path with its delicious scent.

- *Philadelphus coronarius* and 'Aureas' (mock orange) also give fragrance to the garden.

- Peonies and poppies give a luxurious atmosphere and the *Hibiscus syriacus* and the Tiger Lily (*Lilium lancifolium*) an exotic foreground.

- *Prunus lusitanica* (Portugal laurel) has fragrant pendant racemes of starry flowers to be followed with cherry-like fruit.

The drawings of the plants on the following pages are given a letter that corresponds to the different beds in which they appear on the plan. A selection has been made to highlight each season as a guide to the many parts of the garden to encourage exploration throughout the year.

Geranium pratense

Mirabilis jalapa

Paeonia officinalis
'Rubra Plena'

***Rosa* 'Petite Lisette'** Beds L3, P, Q. The most popular rose in the garden, partly due to its gorgeous scent, deliberately sited on the entrance way to the Pavilion. Introduced to England in 1817

***Rosa* x *damascena* var. versicolor** Beds L1, P, V

Rosa pimpinellifolia
(Burnet Rose) Beds K, P, X, Y

Rosa 'Duchess of Portland' Bed P

Rosa 'Rose du Roi à Fleurs Pourpres' Bed N

Rosa x gallica 'Conditorum' Bed N

Rosa X centifolia 'Muscosa' Beds L1, Q

Rosa x centifolia 'Muscosa' Beds L1, L2, P, Q

Rosa 'Old Blush China' Bed P (now *Rosa x odorata* Pallida)

Rosa chinensis 'Mutabilis' Bed N (now *Rosa x odorata* Mutabilis)

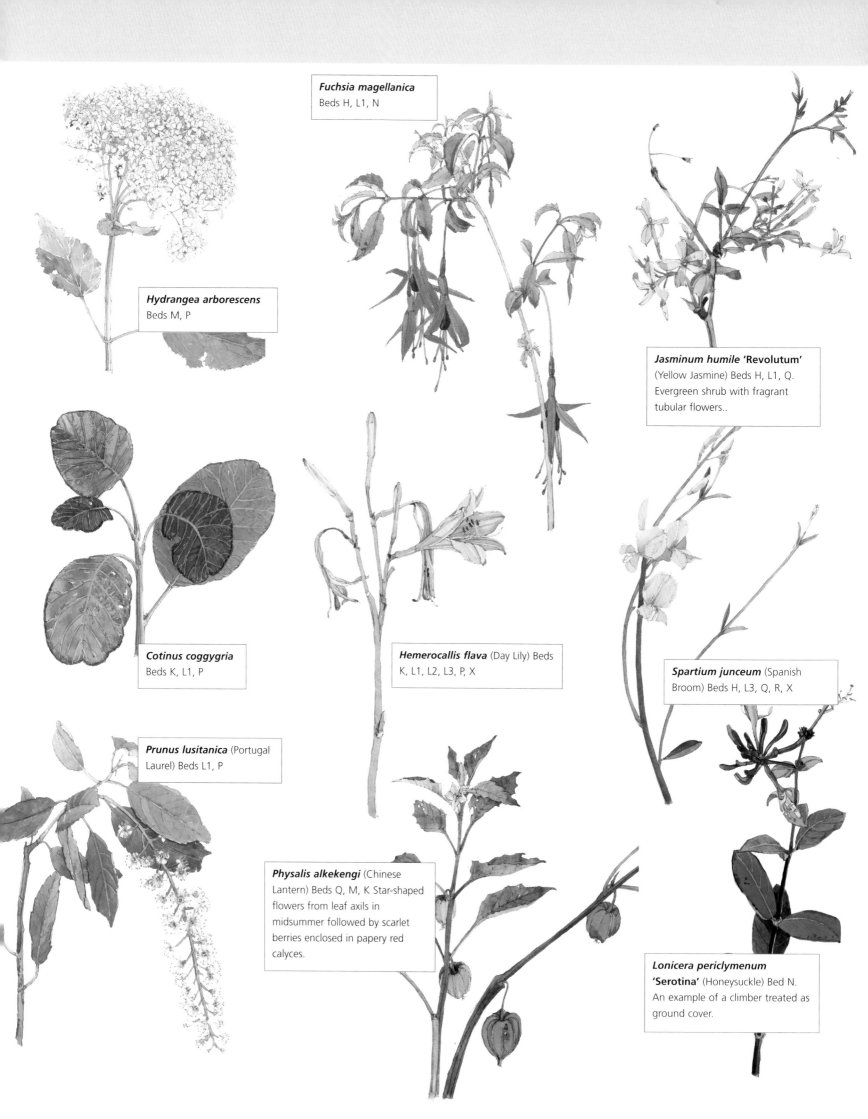

Fuchsia magellanica
Beds H, L1, N

Hydrangea arborescens
Beds M, P

Jasminum humile 'Revolutum'
(Yellow Jasmine) Beds H, L1, Q.
Evergreen shrub with fragrant
tubular flowers..

Cotinus coggygria
Beds K, L1, P

Hemerocallis flava (Day Lily) Beds
K, L1, L2, L3, P, X

Spartium junceum (Spanish
Broom) Beds H, L3, Q, R, X

Prunus lusitanica (Portugal
Laurel) Beds L1, P

Physalis alkekengi (Chinese
Lantern) Beds Q, M, K Star-shaped
flowers from leaf axils in
midsummer followed by scarlet
berries enclosed in papery red
calyces.

**Lonicera periclymenum
'Serotina'** (Honeysuckle) Bed N.
An example of a climber treated as
ground cover.

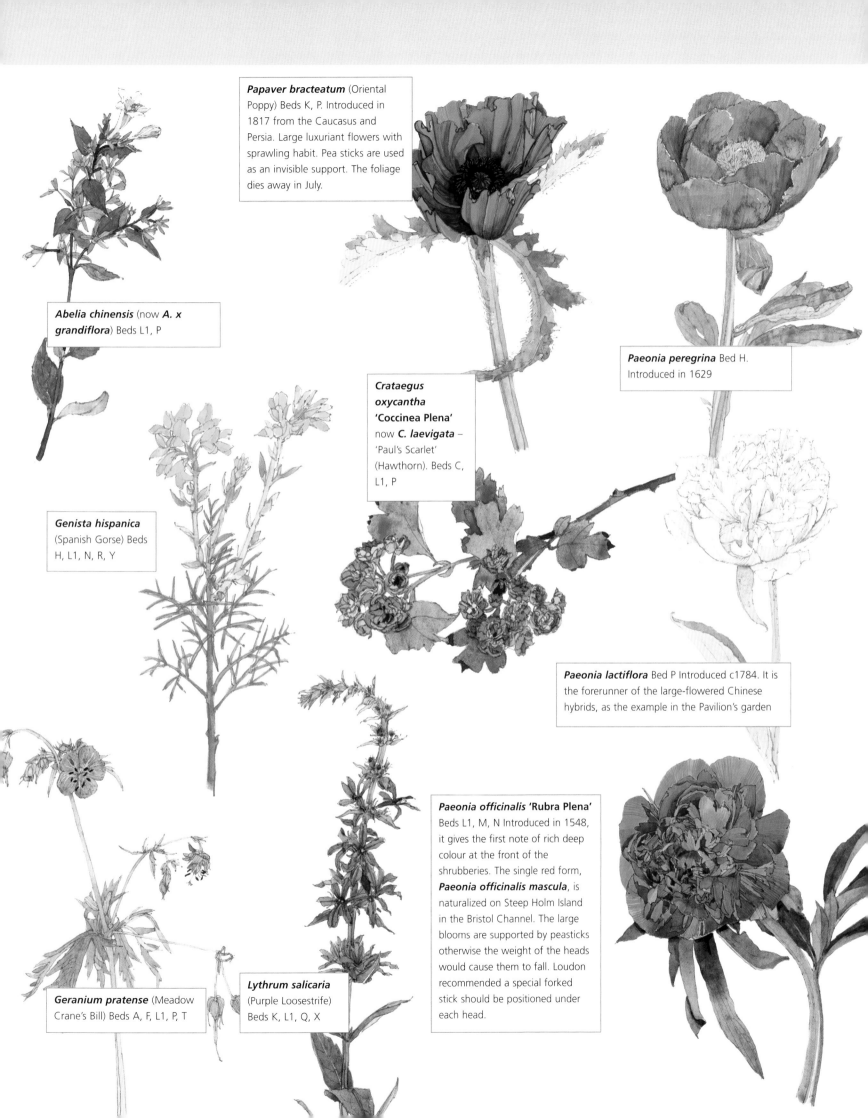

Papaver bracteatum (Oriental Poppy) Beds K, P. Introduced in 1817 from the Caucasus and Persia. Large luxuriant flowers with sprawling habit. Pea sticks are used as an invisible support. The foliage dies away in July.

Abelia chinensis (now **A. x grandiflora**) Beds L1, P

Paeonia peregrina Bed H. Introduced in 1629

Crataegus oxycantha 'Coccinea Plena' now **C. laevigata** – 'Paul's Scarlet' (Hawthorn). Beds C, L1, P

Genista hispanica (Spanish Gorse) Beds H, L1, N, R, Y

Paeonia lactiflora Bed P Introduced c1784. It is the forerunner of the large-flowered Chinese hybrids, as the example in the Pavilion's garden

Paeonia officinalis 'Rubra Plena' Beds L1, M, N Introduced in 1548, it gives the first note of rich deep colour at the front of the shrubberies. The single red form, **Paeonia officinalis mascula**, is naturalized on Steep Holm Island in the Bristol Channel. The large blooms are supported by peasticks otherwise the weight of the heads would cause them to fall. Loudon recommended a special forked stick should be positioned under each head.

Geranium pratense (Meadow Crane's Bill) Beds A, F, L1, P, T

Lythrum salicaria (Purple Loosestrife) Beds K, L1, Q, X

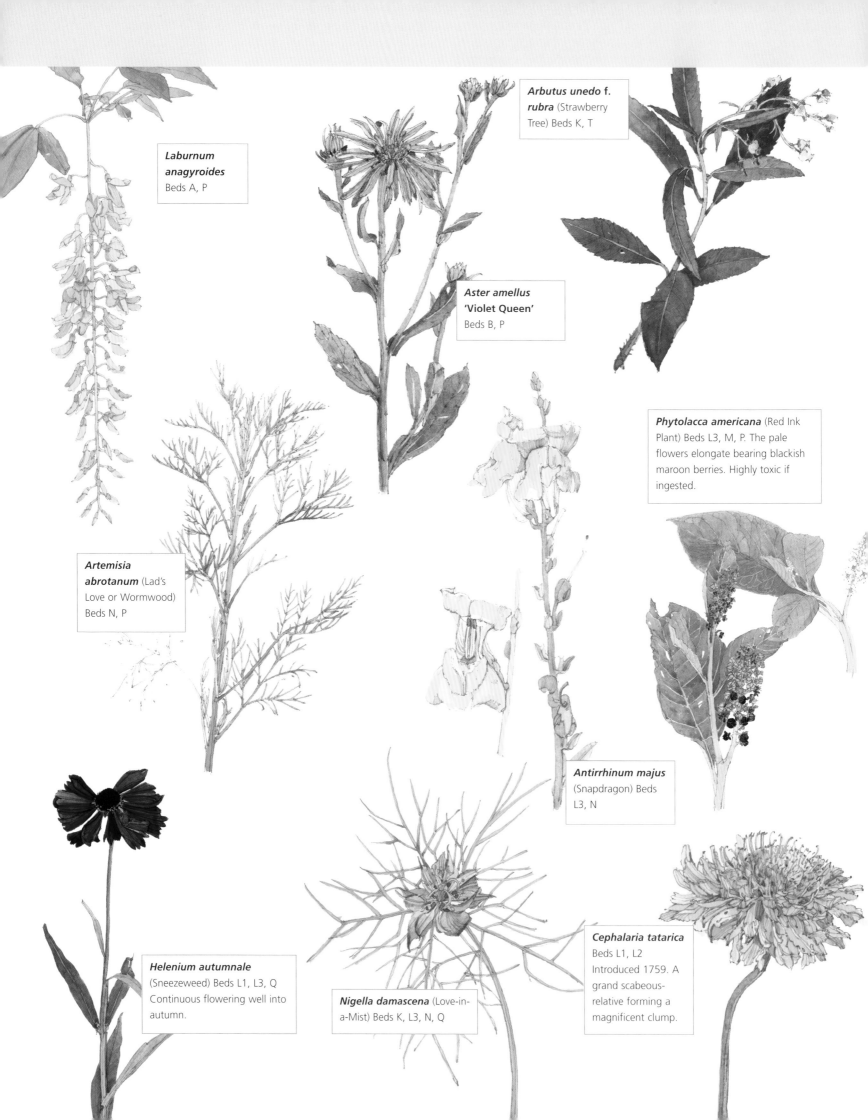

Laburnum anagyroides
Beds A, P

Arbutus unedo f. rubra (Strawberry Tree) Beds K, T

Aster amellus 'Violet Queen'
Beds B, P

Phytolacca americana (Red Ink Plant) Beds L3, M, P. The pale flowers elongate bearing blackish maroon berries. Highly toxic if ingested.

Artemisia abrotanum (Lad's Love or Wormwood) Beds N, P

Antirrhinum majus (Snapdragon) Beds L3, N

Helenium autumnale (Sneezeweed) Beds L1, L3, Q Continuous flowering well into autumn.

Nigella damascena (Love-in-a-Mist) Beds K, L3, N, Q

Cephalaria tatarica Beds L1, L2 Introduced 1759. A grand scabeous-relative forming a magnificent clump.

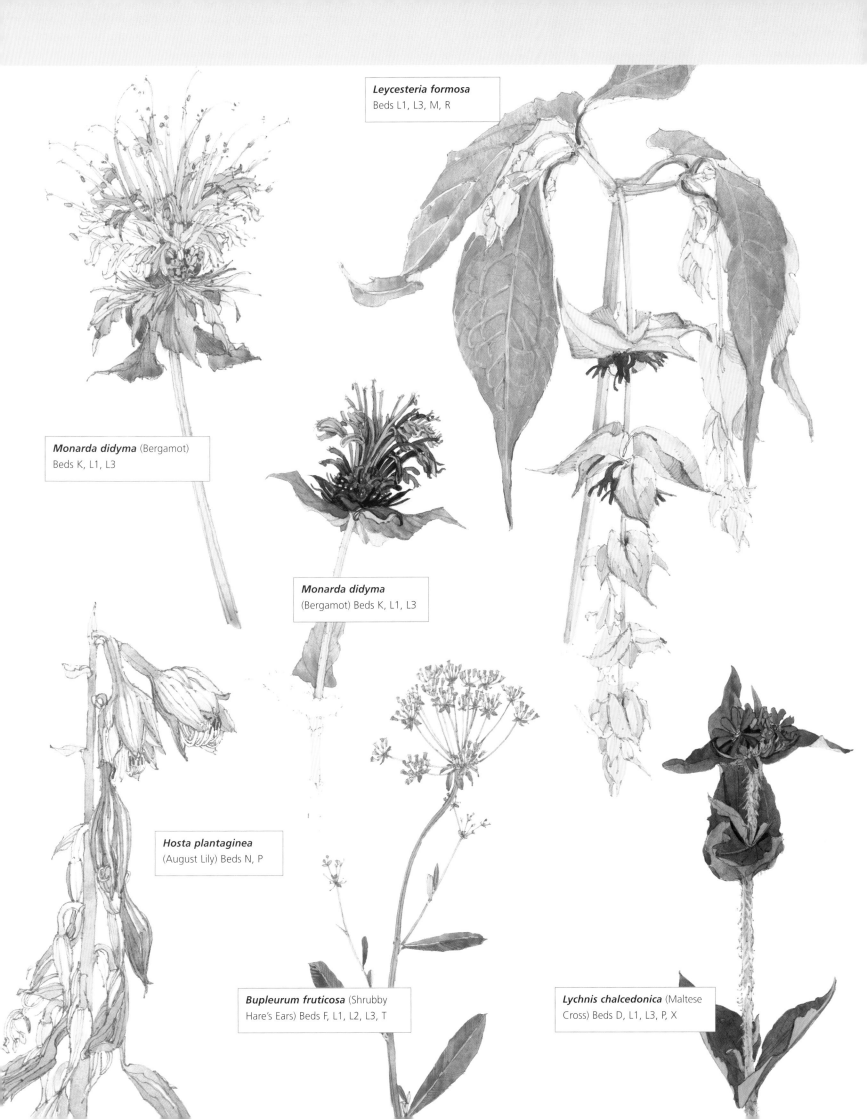

Leycesteria formosa
Beds L1, L3, M, R

Monarda didyma (Bergamot)
Beds K, L1, L3

Monarda didyma
(Bergamot) Beds K, L1, L3

Hosta plantaginea
(August Lily) Beds N, P

Bupleurum fruticosa (Shrubby
Hare's Ears) Beds F, L1, L2, L3, T

Lychnis chalcedonica (Maltese
Cross) Beds D, L1, L3, P, X

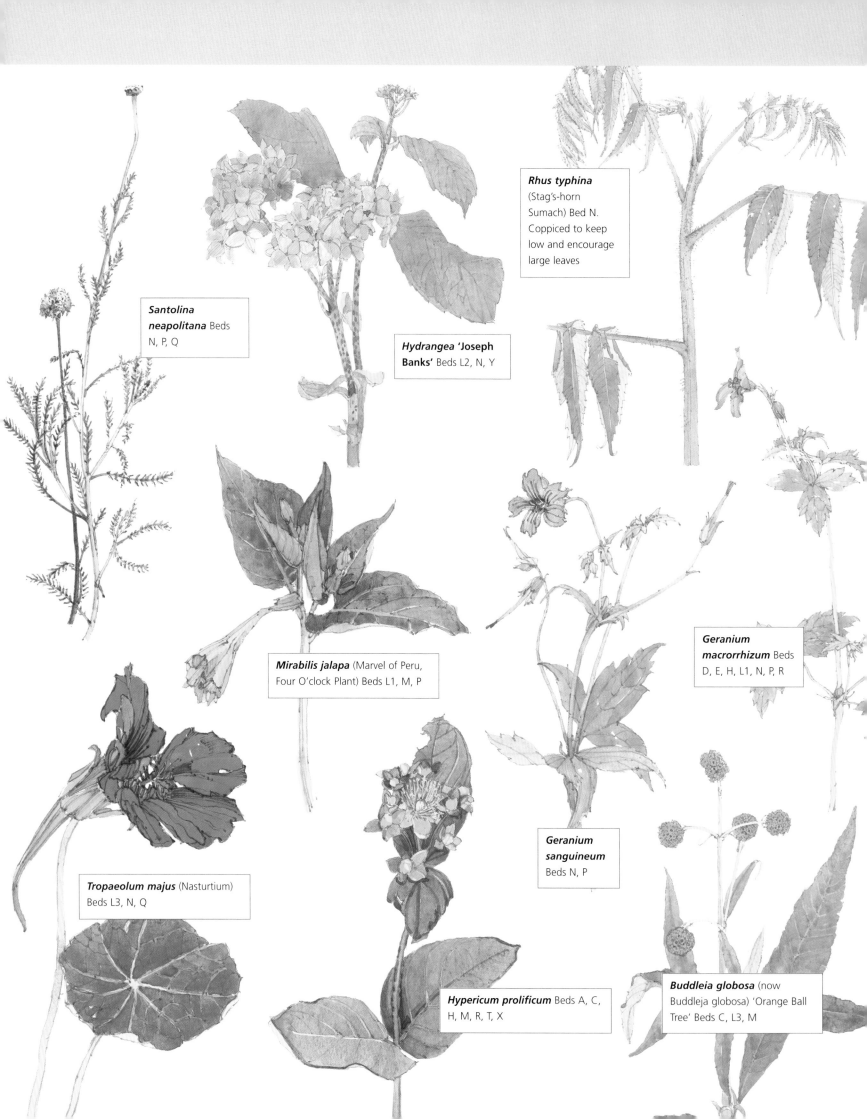

Santolina neapolitana Beds N, P, Q

Rhus typhina (Stag's-horn Sumach) Bed N. Coppiced to keep low and encourage large leaves

Hydrangea 'Joseph Banks' Beds L2, N, Y

Mirabilis jalapa (Marvel of Peru, Four O'clock Plant) Beds L1, M, P

Geranium macrorrhizum Beds D, E, H, L1, N, P, R

Tropaeolum majus (Nasturtium) Beds L3, N, Q

Geranium sanguineum Beds N, P

Hypericum prolificum Beds A, C, H, M, R, T, X

Buddleia globosa (now Buddleja globosa) 'Orange Ball Tree' Beds C, L3, M

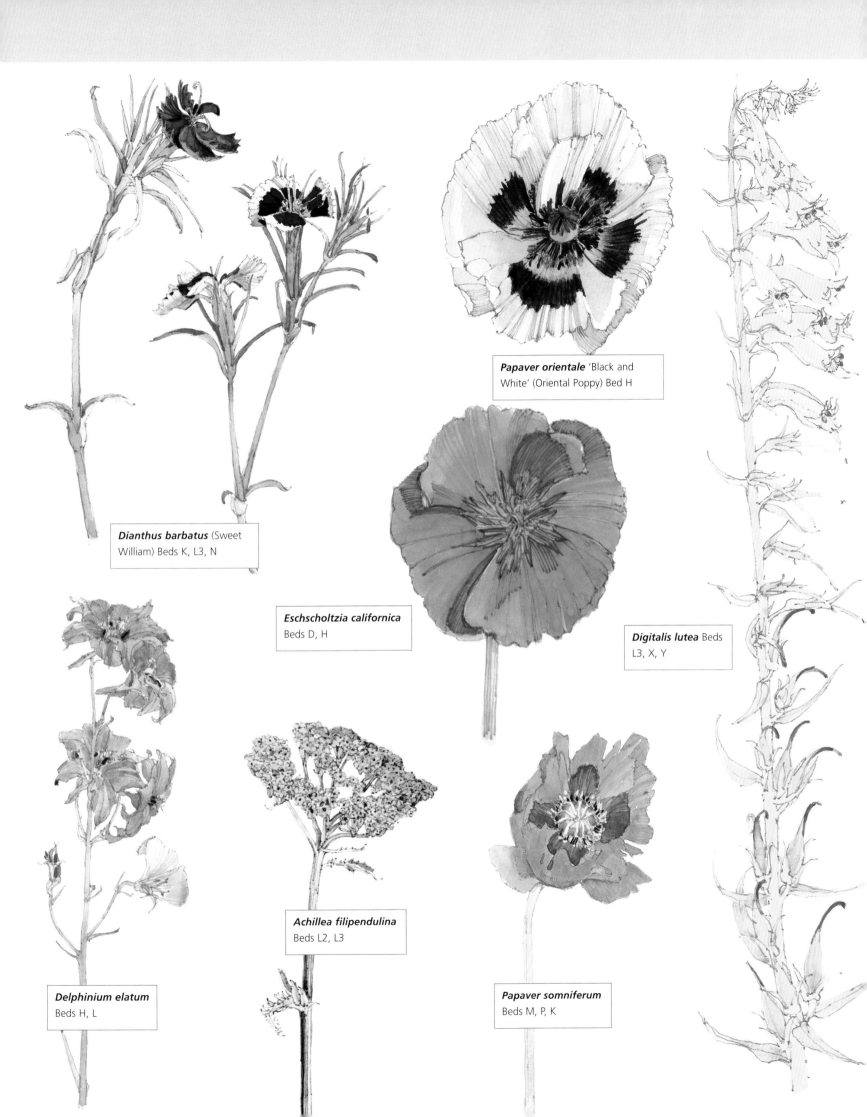

Dianthus barbatus (Sweet William) Beds K, L3, N

Papaver orientale 'Black and White' (Oriental Poppy) Bed H

Eschscholtzia californica Beds D, H

Digitalis lutea Beds L3, X, Y

Delphinium elatum Beds H, L

Achillea filipendulina Beds L2, L3

Papaver somniferum Beds M, P, K

Lavatera olbia
(Mallow) Bed Q

Acanthus spinosus (Bear's Breeches) Beds N, W. An architectural plant of great dignity, represented in classical Corinthian capitals.

Philadelphus coronarius (Mock Orange) Bed P

Hibiscus syriacus 'Woodbridge' Bed P

Alcea rosea (hollyhock) Beds K, L1, L3, N, P, Q

AUTUMN & WINTER

The garden is blousy and mellow, the colours richer as the sun is lower. Hollyhocks are the hit of the season as flowers continue to climb the tall stems. Butterflies and bees make the most of the last nectar and birds feed on seeds and berries. Beds are left to fade naturally as spent foliage and fallen leaves insulate plant crowns from frost, providing habitats for wildlife. The longer the tidying-up process is delayed, the more goodness returns to the plants. It is also easier to clear away in early Spring. Roses are not dead-headed to encourage hips. Leaves swept from paths eventually make good compost. The garden volunteers collect seeds. Bulbs are replenished.

Short days see the garden and the Pavilion lit early with concealed floodlights. The filigree silhouette of trees and shrubs, seed heads, berries and holly give a subtle Christmas magic to the garden. The laurustinus, covered in white blossom, can look like early snow. Pruning (always to retain a natural, not clipped, look) with radical decisions on replacement shrubs or trees to maintain the 'Regency' planting principles and compositions are part of the winter stock-take. Mushroom compost is applied as a mulch, which also inhibits weeds and retains moisture. Evergreens provide variety and structure and Winter sun can suddenly highlight the bare stems of *Cornus alba* in a flash of red.

(A) ***Cornus alba*** Caught in winter sun.

(B & C) ***Iris foetidissima.*** Spring flowers are followed by red seed pods.

(D) ***Koelreuteria paniculata.*** Seed pods

(E) ***Geranium macrorrhizum.*** The leaves turn to crimson in the autumn.

Plan of the restored garden. The beds are given a letter to locate the positions of the plants drawn on the following pages.

AUTUMN & WINTER HIGHLIGHTS

- *Cotinus coggygria*, lives up to its common name 'smoke bush'. The colouring of the leaves and fruiting panicles mature to resemble a smoking fire.

- *Arbutus unedo 'Rubra'* (Strawberry tree) has both curious pendent white flowers and strawberry-like red fruit from the previous Autumn.

- The *Koelreuteria paniculata* (Pride of India) develops amazing salmon-pink fruit capsules.

- *Phytolacca americana* (Red ink plant) bears rich black-maroon berries (highly toxic if ingested).

- *Hydrangea* 'Joseph Banks' fades beautifully as it is not dead-headed.

- *Ruscus aculeatus* (Butcher's broom) has spine-tipped, glossy 'leaves'. Female plants produce brilliant red berries from flattened, leaf-like shoots (cladophylls), worth a close look.

- *Helleborous foetidus* (Stinking hellebore) has bell-shaped pendant green flowers, usually crimson-margined as if gently dipped in ink; the pale green bracts light up a dull day.

- *Iris foetidissima* (Stinking iris) the large seed capsules split open, revealing scarlet or orange berries like large peas in a pod.

- *Pinus sylvestris* (Scots pine) has ripened conical female cones, a process taking over two years. Good for adding to a hot bath for relaxation.

The drawings of the plants on the following pages are given a letter that corresponds to the different beds in which they appear on the plan. A selection has been made to highlight each season as a guide to the many parts of the garden to encourage exploration throughout the year.

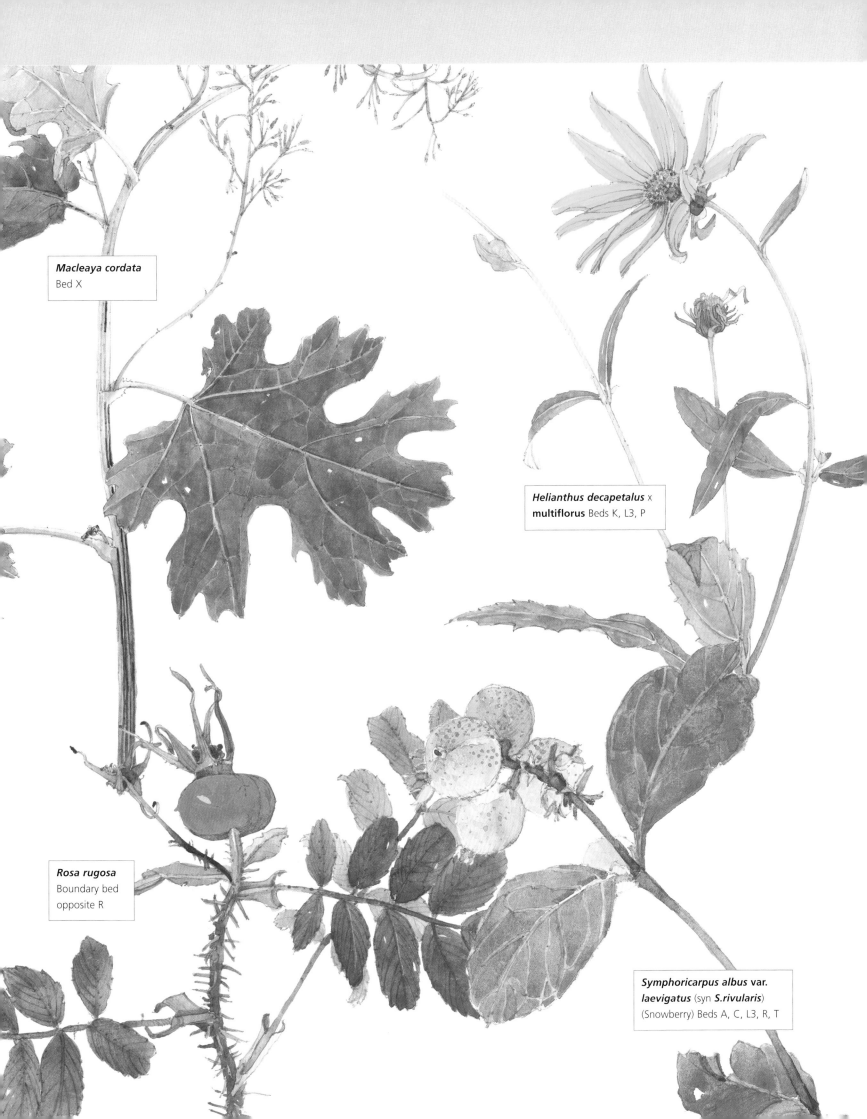

Macleaya cordata
Bed X

Helianthus decapetalus x
multiflorus Beds K, L3, P

Rosa rugosa
Boundary bed
opposite R

Symphoricarpus albus var.
laevigatus (syn **S.rivularis**)
(Snowberry) Beds A, C, L3, R, T

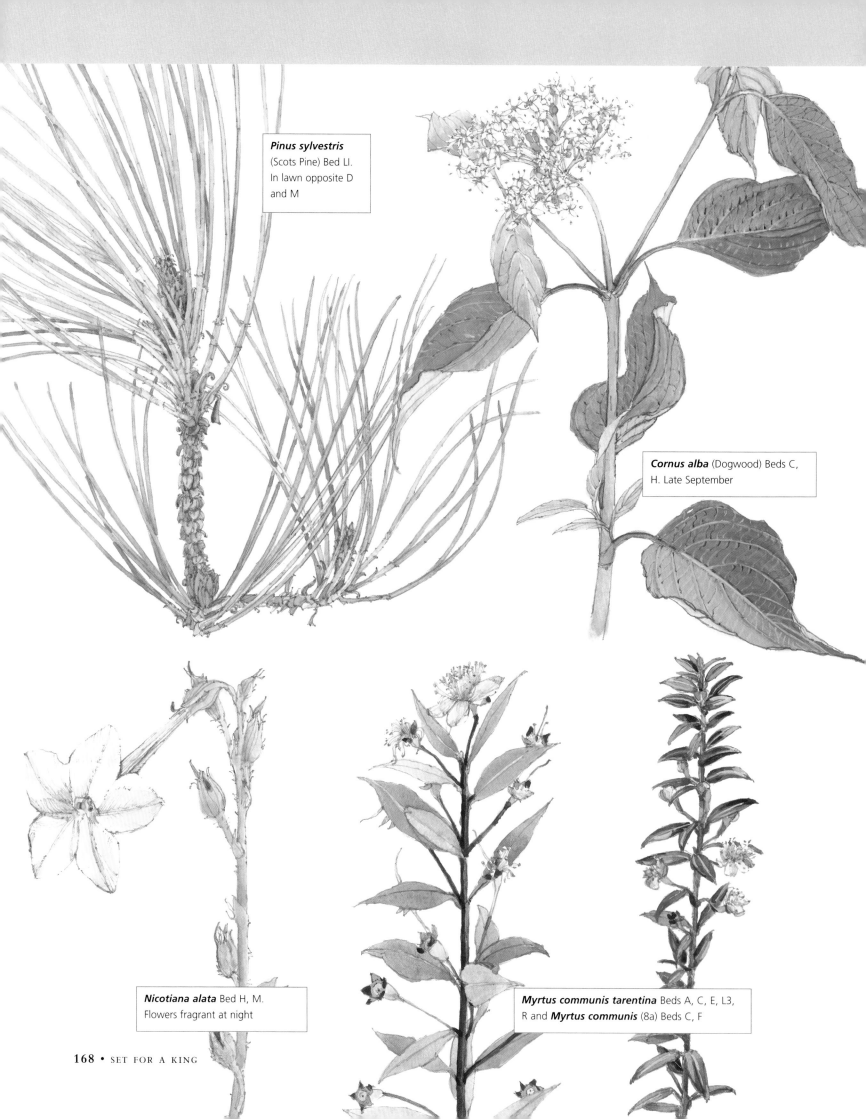

Pinus sylvestris
(Scots Pine) Bed Ll.
In lawn opposite D
and M

Cornus alba (Dogwood) Beds C,
H. Late September

Nicotiana alata Bed H, M.
Flowers fragrant at night

Myrtus communis tarentina Beds A, C, E, L3,
R and **Myrtus communis** (8a) Beds C, F

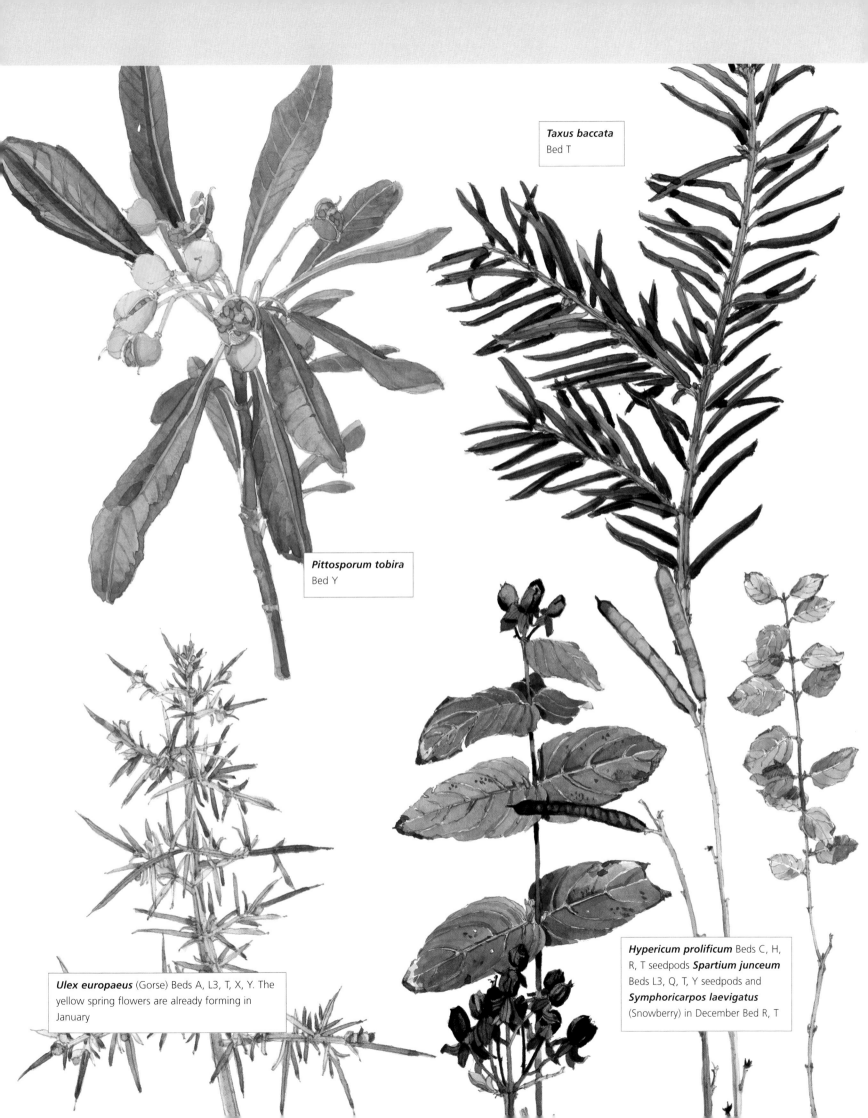

Taxus baccata
Bed T

Pittosporum tobira
Bed Y

Ulex europaeus (Gorse) Beds A, L3, T, X, Y. The
yellow spring flowers are already forming in
January

Hypericum prolificum Beds C, H,
R, T seedpods **Spartium junceum**
Beds L3, Q, T, Y seedpods and
Symphoricarpos laevigatus
(Snowberry) in December Bed R, T

Euphorbia characias Beds G, H, L2, T, V, W

Hedera helix (Ivy) Beds A, C, R, T

Helleborus foetidus (Stinking Hellebore) Beds A, C, M, T The bright apple green flowers, with edges as if dipped in crimson ink, heralds spring in the shrubberies

Ligustrum lucidum (Chinese Privet) Beds B, C, F, T

Ruscus aculeatus
Beds A, B, C, T

Daphne odora
Beds L3, P, X
Wonderful scented
flowers from mid-
February

Viburnum tinus
(Laurustinus) Beds A,
C, H, L1, M, T

Laburnum anagyroides
Seedpods Beds A, P

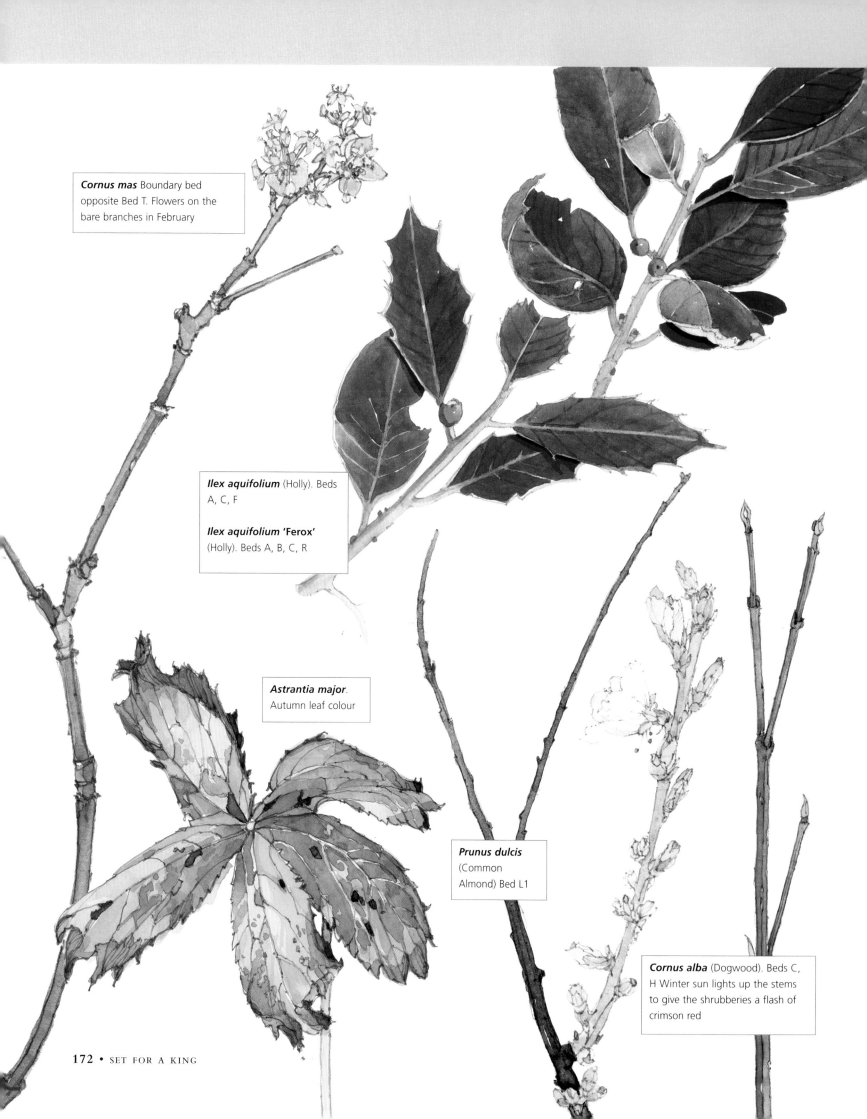

Cornus mas Boundary bed opposite Bed T. Flowers on the bare branches in February

Ilex aquifolium (Holly). Beds A, C, F

Ilex aquifolium 'Ferox' (Holly). Beds A, B, C, R

Astrantia major. Autumn leaf colour

Prunus dulcis (Common Almond) Bed L1

Cornus alba (Dogwood). Beds C, H Winter sun lights up the stems to give the shrubberies a flash of crimson red

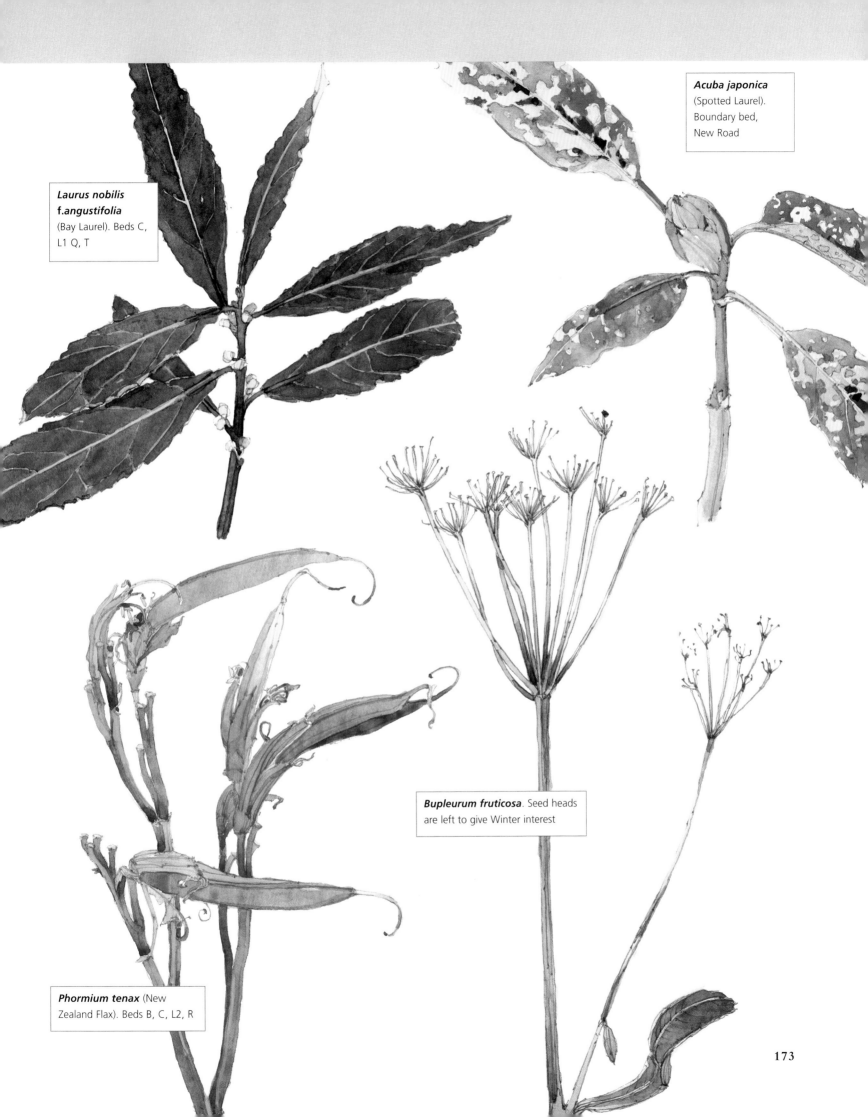

Laurus nobilis f.angustifolia (Bay Laurel). Beds C, L1 Q, T

Acuba japonica (Spotted Laurel). Boundary bed, New Road

Bupleurum fruticosa. Seed heads are left to give Winter interest

Phormium tenax (New Zealand Flax). Beds B, C, L2, R

173

LOOKING AHEAD

'Every time I come into this shrubbery I am more struck with its growth and beauty'.

— JANE AUSTEN, *Mansfield Park*, 1814, VOL.2, CH.IV.

ABOVE Before work started, the shrubbery was checked for recent nest building. The abandoned old nest (most birds do not recycle) with a failed egg, was found to be lined with warm, downy old cigarette butts – a resourceful response to urban living.

BELOW Spring 2005. A mature shrubbery after fifteen years growth requiring serious management. Visitors could not see the entrance to the Pavilion and the evergreens had become out of scale, shading-out the herbaceous plants. All the plant material was composted using a shredder (seen on the right).

BELOW-RIGHT The final fir tree (*Pinus sylvestris*) is removed. The Pavilion is revealed, the planting plan can be restored.

THE GARDEN HAS now matured over twenty years. It will be a challenge to retain the intended appearance of the planting. When should the trees and shrubs be pruned or replaced? The principle of arrested development, essential to the garden's future, will be planned sequentially. Already two laburnums, which had grown too high, have been replaced. In the Spring of 2005 the two native fir trees Pinus Sylvestris in the bed opposite the Museum entrance were removed and replaced and the associated shrubs pruned and coppiced. The 'before' and 'after' pictures show the difference. It is crucial to maintain the intended balance and to preserve the important views across the garden. The security cameras must also be able to operate. We cannot be too precious, the garden is not kept in aspic, it is open every day of the year for everyone to enjoy. The opinion that 'if you can't make love in a garden, or get drunk in it, for God's sake, tarmac it over'[244] could not apply here as those charged with its maintenance are well aware! Unfortunately some changes have had to be made to combat vandalism, such as the replacement of delicate plants with more robust shrubs, although they are still within those specified in the original plant lists.

The garden, which is run on organic principles, welcomes a multitude of insects and birds. It is a haven for wildlife as well as for people. The new awareness and concern for Nature, unimaginable say thirty years ago, has contributed to its continued success. The role of plants in our eco-system and the Green Movement has led us to consider what we can do for plants, rather than what they can do for us. Conservation of native species, wildlife and the role of the garden in providing habitats has led to a new appreciation of the value of a more natural style.[245] In the Pavilion's garden the herbaceous plants and annuals are allowed to remain after flowering which adds subtle autumn interest with their seed pods and changing colours. Some of the shrubs and trees also develop fantastic berries, hips, seed pods and sculptural pine cones.

LEFT A maturing elm tree, wrongly positioned, not conforming to Nash's plan, was in danger of shading out the building and the shrubberies. The root stump was left in the ground to provide a habitat for wildlife.

BELOW The rejuvenated bed ready for the next fifteen years.

LEFT Small replacement fir trees (*Pinus sylvestris*) are planted as near as possible to their previous positions. The blue pipe, an aid to irrigation, will help to establish them over hotter summers.

The Regency Garden is back in fashion. Although the 'oriental' architecture of the Pavilion did not inspire a new style for buildings, the setting had a lasting affect on gardens. The natural style, the wild garden and meadow planting have become an alternative to the 'smart' makeovers of recent years. The clever hard-landscaping, watched by millions on television, often resulted in some 'Victorian' gardens in Brighton being covered in slate chippings with a single shrub, like a grave. Plants are now making a welcome return. The future, with drier summers, may also point in the natural direction as a way to adapt to different conditions. Christopher Lloyd, the gardening guru, in the introduction to his book *Meadows*, writes that 'wild gardening in grass is set to become more fashionable, now that the fine-sward lawn - that featureless expanse of green … is officially under threat from climatic change'.

The Pavilion's garden has become a much valued oasis for visitors and residents, a breathing space, in the centre of the city where, with its Regency backdrop, we can agree with a character from Jane Austen's *Mansfield Park*, 'I shall soon be rested', said Fanny; 'to sit in the shade on a fine day, and look at verdure, is the most perfect refreshment'.[246] The garden will continue to change and develop; we cannot completely replicate the past. Each era will have its own subjective and visible style. In the Pavilion we are still conscious of the pastel colours used in the fifties and the 'Regency stripe', which were well intentioned in their day. Conservation rather than restoration is the way forward. As John Sales, garden advisor to the National Trust has said 'there are things that one would do now that one would not have done then, and vice versa. We are less and less likely to see gardens restored to a single moment in a long history'.[247] Unlike a restored interior, a garden is constantly changing and evolving with the passing of time.

At Brighton there are still reminders in the garden of its long history; the vestiges of the Promenade Grove, a fragment of Weltje's house, perimeter trees planted by Furner and Snart such as a chestnut, poplar and elms. The specimen trees, like the weeping elm; Ulmus glabra 'Horizontalis', near the Dome and the later palms are worked into the layout. MacLaren's pierced wall still forms a boundary and the North and South Gates welcome visitors into the garden. The 1950s café is still a good spot to 'look at verdure' over a cup of tea.[248]

The plants, from all over the world, are a reminder of the debt owed to collectors and gardeners who enabled the incredible range of plant material that we take for granted today to be at our disposal. They also remind us that 'All gardening is pretence. You, the gardener, are trying to per-suade plants to grow in places they have not chosen, in combinations devised to suit yourself'.[249] It is now difficult to imagine any other setting for the Royal Pavilion, itself a hybrid from differ-ent countries, so harmonious and successful is the effect of the building with its garden, as it was originally intended.

The garden has now established its own identity, already it has become the focus of local pride and interest and is used in television programmes and films. The setting is also used as a backdrop for Brighton Festival events. It is a popular gathering place that has become a present day version of the former Promenade Grove. The grounds often resemble Gardeners' Question Time as the volunteers and the head gardener field questions and give advice. The annual plant and seed ex-changes are eagerly awaited events with demand outstripping supply. The popularity and enthusiasm for the Regency Garden increases annually, due to the work of the head gardener and the volun-teers with their commitment to its upkeep and renewal.

LEFT *Ulmus glabra* 'Horizontalis'. (Weeping Wych Elm) c. 1850 has been worked into the Regency garden layout.

Ulmus glabra 'Horizontalis'

LEFT Two exotic birds on the lawn! Throughout the history of the site the setting was embellished with exotic birds, both inside and out. Here they form part of a Brighton Festival fringe event, 2005.

ABOVE The garden volunteers, with the head gardener, Robert Hill-Snook, tending the shruberries in June 2005.

There will be challenges ahead and in the future gardening may have to change if climate predictions are correct. But what is certain is that at Brighton we will all join in with the closing anthem of Leonard Bernstein's musical, *Candide*, 'we will do the best we know … and make our garden grow'.

This unique Regency garden has been recreated for the pleasure and inspiration of everyone. Here we can pause and reflect as Virginia Woolf so eloquently wrote of an eighteenth-century gentleman contemplating his landscaped garden, 'We may also find matter for thought in those eighteenth-century gardens, which were so strangely unlike the house they surrounded. What did the gentleman in knee breeches and brocade think about when he stepped from his exquisitely civilised drawing room into a garden … one may suppose that he thought a great deal about himself, and, removed from the constraint of furniture, rambled in a wilderness among the disorderly recesses of his own mind'.[250]

RIGHT Edward Fox, two drawings, 1850, depicting the newly opened grounds being used for reflection and relaxation.

NOTES

1 William Mason, *The English Garden*, 1783 (quoted on the title page). Mason was a poet gardener who had made a romantic and influential flower garden with irregular island beds at Nuneham Courtenay, Oxfordshire.

2 E. J. Climenson (ed.) *Passages from the diaries of Mrs Philip Lybbe Powys, of Hardwick House, Oxon. 1756-1808,* London, 1899, p.245. The ball was at Wargrave in August 1789.

3 Formerly grand formal gardens, with their vast radiating avenues of trees had also been a good source of timber. Landlords had been encouraged to plant trees after the devastation of the Civil War, especially for ship-building.

4 E. J Climenson (ed), op. cit. 1899 2, p.11. This comment, made in 1756, was surprisingly early. Holkham's landscape, designed by William Kent, had taken over twenty years to create. He was one of the first garden designers to promote informality. He had designed the influential five-acre garden at Carlton House for Frederick, Prince of Wales, in 1734. Brown had learnt his trade from Kent at Stowe, where the famous landscape gardens had been laid out by Kent.

5 Edmund Burke, *A Philosophical Enquiry into the Origin of our ideas of the Sublime and Beautiful*, London, 1773, fourth edition, first published in 1757, p.300.

6 Seeing nature as a series of pictures would have an enormous influence on gardening and the disposition of plants. In *Observations on the Theory and Practice of Landscape Gardening*, 1803, p.117, Repton commented on the shortcomings of using a Claude Glass, 'the finest pictures of Claude … seldom consist of more than one fifth of that field of vision which the eye can with ease behold "without any motion of the head"'. Repton thought that a row of six Claude paintings would be required to take in a view, and to him that 'proves the futility of making pictures our models for natural improvements'. It did not follow that 'the best landscape painter would be the best landscape gardener'.

7 Claude himself had used such a device, in a more serious way, for his landscape painting. The memorable effect of using a Claude Glass was still being referred to in the next century by an American tourist, describing smoke-filled, foggy London, 'When some rays of sun happens to fall on this artificial atmosphere its impure mass assumes immediately a pale orange tint, similar to the effect of Claude Lorraine's glasses – a mild golden hue, quite beautiful'. C. Hibbert (ed.), Louis Simond, *An American in Regency England the Journal of a Tour in 1810-11*, p.33, London, 1968. The later Impressionists, notably Monet, would also respond to the 'pea soup' effects of London smog.

8 William Gilpin's popular book, *Observations on the River Wye and Several Parts of South Wales, Relative Chiefly to Picturesque Beauty*, was published in 1782. Repton had a copy in his library. He launched his career as a landscape gardener in 1788. In a sudden flash of inspiration he circulated a letter to his influential friends asking for commissions. Establishing his reputation was surprisingly easy, as he said, 'One day is much like another – landscape gardening is a good line – no risk of capital – all profit and no loss! A very pretty morning's work'. Humphry Repton's autobiographical *Memoir*, part 2, with editorial comments and notes, chapter XVIII. BL ADD MSS 62112.

9 Humphry Repton, op. cit., 1803, p.126.

10 'There are now few places in which the character of a Garden is preserved near the house … a detached place called the *Flower Garden* has been set apart … at such an inconvenient distance that is seldom visited'. Repton, *Designs for the Pavillon* [sic] *at Brighton*, 1808, p.III.

11 Humphry Repton, *An Enquiry into the Changes in Taste in Landscape Gardening*, London, 1806, p.65.

12 Repton, op. cit., 1808, p.XII.

13 *A Description of Brighthelmstone, a new guide for ladies and gentlemen visiting the place for health and amusements,* published by Crawford's Library, 29 October 1794, p.22.

14 Thomas Mawe and John Abercrombie, Introduction to *The Universal Gardener and Botanist: or a General Dictionary of Gardening and Botany*, London, 1778. The fashion for destroying established avenues to open up views was picked up by the social antennae of Jane Austen, 'there have been two or three fine old trees cut down that grew too near the house, and it opens the prospect amazingly, which makes me think that Repton, or anybody of that sort, would certainly have the avenue at Southerton down'. ('Mr Rushworth' discussing the latest fashions in landscape gardening, *Mansfield Park*, London, 2003, first published 1814, p.53.) Repton himself discusses the pros and cons of the fashion for cutting down avenues warning that fashion could 'reduce all improvements to the whim and caprice of the day'. Repton's point was that unlike transitory fashions such as dress, gardening destroys the work of ages. op cit., 1806, pp.25-27.

15 Two documents in East Sussex Records Office give a short account of this piece of ground describing it as a 'croft whereon a barn formerly stood' (ESRO BRI 86). A second document, ESRO BRI 95, dated 1780, refers to 'a new erected messuage [house]' therefore the house must have been built by 1780.

16 George Croly, *The Personal History of George IV*, London, 1841, p.111.

17 Jane Austen, *Sense and Sensibility*, Penguin Classics, 2003, p. 236. First published 1811.

18 Repton, op.cit., 1803, p.14.

19 *Headlong Hall*, written in 1815, London, 1927, p.30. Sir Patrick O'Prism to Mr Milestone who was a landscape gardener. Mr Milestone was a thinly disguised reference to Repton who had been ridiculed for his pretentious idea of extending an estate by incorporating the client's crest on approaching milestones.

20 'a messe [house] or tenem^t with the Barn Close & Rick Steddle [barn on mushroom shaped stone piers] thereunto belong^g & adjoin^g sit^e near the Castle Tavern'. RA Geo/Deeds/178a

21 RA Geo/Deeds/178

22 RA Geo/33507-08

23 RA Geo/33507.

24 RA Geo/34218.

25 John Trusler, *Practical Husbandry*, 3rd edition, 1790, p.132. Marle is described as 'A general manure, but excellent for dry, sandy, gravely, and light lands: good even for mossy ground and clay. Will make white clover come naturally and happy is the farmer who has a marle-pit in his grounds!'

26 J. C. Loudon, *Observations on the Formation and Management of Useful and Ornamental Plantations; on the Theory and Practice of Landscape Gardening*, London, 1804, p.152.

27 Quoted in Clifford Musgrave, *The Royal Pavilion, An Episode in the Romantic*, 1959, p.19.

28 John van Nost was born at Malines in the Low Countries. He came to England in the 1680s and became the leading supplier of lead garden statuary. His finest works were made for the royal palaces under William and Mary and Queen Anne. After his death in 1728 Nost's yard at Hyde Park Corner was taken over by John Cheere who continued to produce many of the same models. J. T. Smith in his *Streets of London*, published in 1815, remembered as a young man seeing Cheere's figures 'cast in lead as large as life, and frequently painted with an intention to resemble nature … above all that of an African kneeling with a sundial on his head found the most extensive sale'.

29 *A Description of Brighthelmstone*, op. cit., 1794, p.29.

30 William Marshall, *Planting and Rural Ornament*, 1796, second edition, vol.1, pp.278 and 282.

31 J. C. Loudon, *Treatise on Forming, Improving and Managing Country Residences*, 1806, 2 vols., p.482.

32 Ibid. p.468.

33 Walpole comments on Holland's taste the same year as the architect's visit to Paris. Letter to the Countess of Upper Ossory, 17 September 1785 (quoted by D. Stroud in *Henry Holland*, London, 1966, p.67).

34 Repton, *Memoir*, op.cit., chapter XVII.

35 W. S. Lewis (ed.), *Horace Walpole. Selected Letters*, Yale, 1973. Letter to Lady Ossory, 27 September 1778, p.229.

36 Humphry Repton was introduced to John Nash by the owner of Stoke Edith, The Honourable Edward Foley. Stoke Edith was his country house in Herefordshire. Repton later recalled Foley's words in his *Memoir*: "'If you two, whom I consider the cleverest men in England, could agree to *act together* you 'might carry the whole world before you'!". Now this was a bait exactly suited to my aspiring vanity! So I consented to the introduction to Mr Nash!' Repton, *Memoir*, op. cit. chapter XVII.

37 Le Sieur de Neufforge, *Receuil Elementaire d'Architecture*, vol. III, 1757.

38 Repton, *Memoir*, op. cit. chapter XVII.

39 J. C. Loudon, *Treatise on Forming, Improving and Managing Country Residences*, London, 1806, 2 vols. p.382.

40 In 1804 the Prince leased twenty acres from the Stanford Estate on the outskirts of Brighton. The use of the land is not specified in the account. RA Geo/33848. Kennels, a dairy and perhaps a small market garden would all have been appropriate uses.

41 'Account of the works done at Brighton includes 'to valuing the Estate purchased of Mr Weltje and agreeing with Him for the same' - £240.0s.0d. The Weltje referred to was Louis's brother, Christopher. RA GEO/33528-28A.

42 This survival was commented on in a Victorian account of the town: 'Immediately north of the stables were the residence and grounds of Mr Louis Weltjie [sic], Clerk of the Prince's Kitchen. A portion of his brick-faced house still remains, just within the southern entrance of the Pavilion Grounds'. J. Ackerson Erredge, *History of Brighthelmston*, Brighton, 1862, chapter XXVI, p.258. The brick referred to Holland's stone coloured tile facing.

43 Letter from the Dowager Countess of Ilchester to Lady Frampton, 2 February 1816, quoted in H. G. Mundy (ed.), *The Journal of Mary Frampton from the year 1779, until the year 1846*, London, 1908, p.264.

44 RA GEO/33528-28A.

45 H. R. Attree, *Topography of Brighton*, London, 1809, p.7.

46 R. Sickelmore, *Epitome of Brighton*, Brighton, 1815, p.38.

47 A. Aspinall (ed.), *Correspondence of George, Prince of Wales*, 1770-1812, London, 1963-1971 (eight volumes). Letter from the Prince of Wales to his brother, the Duke of York, 3 December 1785, p.204.

48 For a discussion on this phase of the building, see J. Morley, *The Making of the Royal Pavilion*, London, 1984, pp.41-48.

49 That the Prince would be concerned with comfort, as well as style, is confirmed by Sheraton, the furniture designer, who illustrated this room and noted that the sofa had its own heating device so that the long seat could be kept warm! Thomas Sheraton, *Cabinet Makers and Upholsterer's Drawing Book*, 1793, plates XXXI, XXXII.

50 RA Geo/33540.

51 E. J. Climenson (ed.), op. cit., 1899 p.165.

52 RA Geo/33512.

53 RA Geo/33529, April 1802. The document lists the areas to be painted. Louis Barzago 'Agreed with Mr Holland to paint the [listed] works for One Hundred & Fifty Pounds'.

54 Repton, op. cit., 1808, p.II.

55 RA Geo/33540.

56 R. Phillips, *English Watering Places*, Brighton, 1803, p.79.

57 RA Geo/35014.

58 Holland was Brown's son-in-law and executor of his will in which Lapidge was left 1,000 guineas. Dorothy Stroud, *Capability Brown*, London, 1950, p.201.

59 In his own will, Lapidge refers to himself as a surveyor. NA PROB 11/1446

60 *Journal of the Garden History Society*, vol.19, no. 2, autumn 1991. Article by A. Fletcher discusses the grounds at Althorp, p.151.

61 RA Geo/33543.

62 RA Geo/33542.

63 Repton, op.cit., 1806, p.7.

64 Ibid. Repton, p. 4.

65 Le Compte A. de La Garde, *Brighton Scènes Détachées d'un Voyage en Angleterre*, 1834, p.46.

66 NA LS 10/5, p.82.

67 NA LS 10/5, p.39

68 NA LS 10/5, p.137.

69 NA LS 10/5, p.112.

70 NA LS 10/5, p.123.

71 NA LS 10/5, p.203.

72 William Dean's extensive list of plants at Croome illustrates the new fashion for horticulture, plant hunting and the influx of new varieties. Croome, a famous example of Brown's earlier Landscape style, had by 1824 two greenhouses for exotics, 'One for East and West India plants, and the other for Proteas (342 named varieties) and choice Cape plants'. As an example of the thoroughness and one-upmanship of the collection, there were 218 varieties of Euphorbia. *Euphorbia Milliffera* (seventeen of them) were then considered a tender greenhouse subject. Eleven *Lilium Tigrinum* from China were listed. *Croome D'Abitôt, Seat of the Right Honourable Earl of Coventry, to which are annexed an Hortus Croomensus, and Observations on the propogation of exotics*, by William Dean, botanic gardener to the Earl of Coventry. Worcester, 1824.

73 NA LS 10/5, p.54.

74 NA LS 10/5, p.28.

75 Repton, *Fragments on the Theory and Practice of Landscape Gardening*, London, 1816. Fragment XXVIII, Woburn Abbey, p.168.

76 RA Geo/33528.

77 C. Wright, *The Brighton Ambulator*, 1818, p.37.

78 RA Geo/Deeds/178c.

79 RA Geo/33528

80 RA Geo/33531.

81 RA Geo/33528. It was a large sum for fencing, compared to Holland's fee 'for ten journeys myself and three clerks and travelling expenses - £300'. For comparison, the housekeeper of the Royal Pavilion was paid £112 per year in the 1820s.

82 RA Geo/33553.

83 RA Geo/33583.

84 RA Geo/33583.

85 J. C. Loudon, op. cit., 1806. Appendix I, p.704, 'Strictures on Mr Repton's Mode of using Slides and Sketches'.

86 Thomas and William Daniell, *Oriental Scenery*, (six volumes with 144 coloured aquatint plates), published between 1795-1808. Thomas and his nephew William had travelled extensively in India.

87 Repton, op. cit., 1806, p.42.

88 Repton, op. cit., 1808. Introduction p.3.

89 Repton, op. cit., 1816. Footnote Fragment XVII, p.89.

90 Repton, *Memoir*, op. cit., chapter XVII.

91 Ibid.

92 Sir Henry Steuart, Bart *The Planter's Guide*, London 1828, 2nd edition (written 1827), p.10. Steuart was a landscape enthusiast who promoted the idea of creating instant effects with a tree transplanting machine. Steuart cites William Marshall as one of the landscape gardeners who 'gave specimens of transplanting' (p.48), presumably for unsure or disbelieving clients.

93 Ibid. p.309.

94 Ibid. p.318.

95 The Marchioness of Salisbury has returned the garden setting to Hatfield House. It was 'bleak, so flat, so lost, it needed wrapping up, things going on around it, not parkland and gravel coming up to its doors'. The former formal gardens at Hatfield had been replaced with stylised parkland. The idea that houses needed 'things going on around it' was revived by Repton. T. Traegar and P. Kinmonth, *A Gardener's Labyrinth, Portraits of People, Plants and Places*, London, 2003, p.224.

96 John Trusler, *Elements of Modern Gardening*, London, 1800, pp.1-4.

97 Repton, op. cit., 1816. Fragment x from the red book of Stanage Park, p.34.

98 Repton, *Memoir*, op. cit. chapter XVII.

99 Ibid, p.4.

100 Letter to Lord Sheffield 22 December 1805 Pierpoint Morgan Library, New York (LHMS MA 4138).

101 *Humphry Repton, Landscape Gardener*, 1982, p.57, Sainsbury Centre for the Visual Arts. The memorandum quoted is dated 1809. The use of baskets became popular and may have led to the later Victorian fashion for edging beds. This concept was given an amusing interpretation by Loudon's wife in the *Ladies Companion to the Flower Garden*, in 1865, 'Beds are often surrounded with a low frame-work of wire or trellis-work so as to give them the effect of baskets of flowers … very often handles of wire-work are appended to these baskets, over which are trained beautiful climbing plants, such as the Maurandyas'. The Maurandyas are now called Asarinas and are evergreen climbers with scandent stems grown for their tubular flowers.

102 C. Wright, op. cit., 1818, p.38.

103 For a detailed account of Marlborough Row see Heather Wood, 'Number 8 Marlborough Row: A Royal Love Nest Revisited', *Royal Pavilion, Libraries and Museums Review*, July 2000.

104 J. C. Loudon, *Repton's Landscape Gardening and Landscape Architecture*, London, 1840, p.402.

105 Repton, *Memoir*, op. cit. chapter XVII.

106 Ibid. chapter XVII.

107 NA LS 10/7, p.213.

108 NA LS 10/7. p.214.

109 They attacked Repton in print, 'an ingenious professor, who has long practised under the title of "landscape gardener", has suddenly changed his ground and … confessed that his art was never intended to produce landscapes, but some kind of *neat*, *simple*, and *elegant effects*'. Repton was also described as a *walk-maker, shrub planter, turf cleaner or rural perfumer*. Uvedale Price, The Picturesque and the Beautiful, London, 1801, p.88. To which is annexed The Landscape, a didactic poem by R. P. Knight, Esq., p.87.

110 The collection of drawings totalled 273. Nash subsequently built his own castle on the Isle of Wight, which the Prince Regent visited (Aiton sent plants from Kew for the garden).

111 J. Elmes, *Metropolitan Improvements, or London in the Nineteenth Century*, London, 1827, pp.11 and 30.

112 NA LS 9/367.

113 The turf had been cut and brought by barge from Hampton Court. The cost of cutting them and their removal with teams of horses and the barge in June 1812 amounted to £179. 1s. 4d. NA LS 10/7, p.83. This sum included carting gravel from Kensington Gardens. The following year 6,600 turfs costing £45. 18s. were supplied NA LS 10/7, p.85.

114 NA LS 10/9, p.22.

115 NA LS 10/7, p.88.

116 NA LS 10/8, p.221. A measured garden plan was provided by Mr Daniel Todd, who had spent '3 days down there with assistant £7. 7s. 0d.'.

117 NA LS 11/1, p.129.

118 NA LS 11/4, p.64. Their popularity was confirmed four years later when two *Aristolochias* were ordered for Kew.

119 NA LS 10/4, p.21. Aiton's original contract.

120 Repton, op. cit., 1816. Fragment XXIV, p.117.

121 C. Colvin (ed.), *Maria Edgeworth, Letters from England 1813-1844*, Oxford, 1971, p.230. The letter was written by her brother from Badminton in December 1820.

122 Repton, op. cit., 1816. Fragment IX, p.30.

123 J. Austen, *Mansfield Park*, Penguin Classics, London, 1996, p.62 (first published 1814).

124 William Marshall, *Planting and Rural Ornament*, London, 1796, p.282.

125 Ibid. vol. 2, p.335.

126 Ibid. p.412.

127 J. C. Loudon, op. cit., 1806, 2 vols., p.432. Loudon had obviously read William Gilpin's *Remarks on Forest Scenery (Relative Chiefly to Picturesque Beauty)*, published in 1791. Gilpin had popularised, through his publications tours of the countryside, visiting areas of outstanding natural beauty. Through Gilpin forest scenery became influential to garden designers as a new source for studying plant associations and groupings. Although Loudon was enthusiastic of Gilpin's forest scenery, he would later be one of the first to consider the merits of plants in their own right. Planting as a gardener would like rather than a painter.

128 Ibid, p.349.

129 Ibid. p.350.

130 J. C. Loudon, op. cit., 1840, p.8.

131 John Buonarotti Papworth, *Hints on Ornamental Gardening*, 1823, p.94.

132 J. C. Loudon, op. cit., 1806, p.316.

133 NA LS 11/8, p.312.

134 T. Fort, *The Grass is Greener*, London, 2000, p.109.

135 Ibid, p.110.

136 The idea that the middle classes could labour in their own gardens must have met with some snobbish disapproval. As Oscar Wilde's characters observe in his play, *The Importance of Being Earnest* (1894); *Cicely*: When I see a spade I call it a spade. *Gwendolen*: I am glad to say that I have never seen a spade. It is obvious that our social spheres have been widely different.

137 William Watson (ed.), *The Gardener's Assistant*, London, 1937, p.221.

138 C. Hibbert (ed.), Louis Simond, *An American in Regency England. Journal of a Tour in 1810-1811*, London, 1968, p.51.

139 J. B. Papworth, 1823. Op. cit., p.95.

140 NA LS 10/7, pp.217-219.

141 Henry Phillips, *Sylva Florifera*, 2 vols., London, 1823, pp.31-32.

142 Ibid. p.22.

143 Ibid. p.27.

144 Ibid. p.26.

145 NA LS 11/4, p.371.

146 Henry Phillips, op. cit., 1823, p.24.

147 Henry Phillips, *Flora Historica*, 1824, London, p.39.

148 Ibid. p.61.

149 Ibid. p.87.

150 Ibid. p.41.

151 Ibid. p.361.

152 John Nash, *The Royal Pavilion at Brighton, published by the Command of and Dedicated by permission to The King by His Majesty's Dutiful Subject and Servant John Nash* (the large majority of the plates were based on watercolours by Augustus Charles Pugin, father of the more celebrated architect, A. W. N. Pugin). The highly detailed ground plan, its out buildings and grounds shows the building as completed by Nash in about 1821.

153 NA LS 10/7, p.216.

154 NA LS 10/7, pp.216-218.

155 NA LS 10/7, p.216.

156 NA LS 10/7, p.216.

157 NA LS 10/7, p.219.

158 NA LS 10/7, p.221.

159 NA LS 11/1, p.100. Incidentally '4 wks dung of His Majesty's saddle horses' cost only 8s. (1817).

160 John Trusler, op. cit, 1790 chapter XVIII p.133.

161 J. C. Loudon, *An Encyclopaedia of Gardening*, London, 1835 (first published 1822), p.748.

162 R. Bradley (Professor of Botany in the University of Cambridge), *A Survey of the Ancient Husbandry and Gardening Collected from Kato, Columella, Virgil and Others*, London, 1725, p.53.

163 Ibid, p.54.

164 Loudon, op. cit., 1835 p.482.

165 Loudon, op. cit., 1835 p.484.

166 T. Dwight, *Travels in New-England and New-York* (4 volumes), New Haven, 1821, vol.2, p.511, written in 1800. Dwight was president of Yale College, a celebrated preacher, farmer and gardener.

167 NA LS 10/7, p.216 (1814).

168 Loudon, op. cit., 1835 p.748.

169 RA Geo/34026. 458 fir poles estimated at £86. 7s. 8d were sent from Stanmer woods in 1818. The same year the central dome on the Saloon was constructed. Fir poles were used because they were straight and long and could be lashed together with boards, much like a modern day scaffold. Stanmer Park was a short carriage drive from Brighton and was visited by members of the Royal Family when staying with the Prince.

170 NA LS 10/7, p.223.

171 W. Watson (ed) The Gardener's Assistant, London, 1937, p.223. Illus. p. 224.

172 NA LS 11/1, p.127.

173 NA LS 11/1, p.279 (October 1817).

174 C. Wright, op.cit., 1818, p.41.

175 NA LS 11/6, p.127.

176 NA LS 11/1, p.202.

177 NA LS 11/1, p.158.

178 NA LS 11/6, p.128.

179 NA LS 11/1, p.278.

180 NA LS 11/3, p.293.

181 Maria Edgeworth, Letters from England 1813-1844, Clarendon Press, 1971, p. 11. Letter dated 6 April 1813.

182 NA LS 11/6, p.409.

183 NA LS 11/6, p.414.

184 J. C. Loudon, The Greenhouse Companion, 2nd edition, 1825.

185 NA LS 11/4, p.242.

186 'Mr Watier attended by Mr Nixon Clerk of the Works … applied … respecting the opening of the Public Road from His Royal Highness the Prince Regents Pavilion through East Street into the Sea in order to lay down Pipes for supplying the Baths in the Pavilion with Sea Water'. However, permission had to be sought from the Town Commissioners as an Act of Parliament for paving and lighting the town of Brighton prohibited any excavation in its streets. RA GEO/33834, 22 July 1818,

187 Estimate of works to be done at Pavilion in the year 1819 by Nash, 24 March, 1819. RA Geo/33931.

188 William Marshall, Planting and Rural Ornament, London, 1796, p.147.

189 Sir Henry Steuart, The Planter's Guide, 2nd edition 1828. Preface.

190 NA LS 10/7, p.214.

191 NA LS 11/9, p.462.

192 NA LS 11/15, p.352.

193 NA LS 11/15, p.453 (5 January 1831).

194 J. G. Bishop, Brighton Pavilion and its Royal Associations, first published 1875, tenth edition, 1900, p.87.

195 Brighton Herald, September 1923.

196 Georgina, Baroness Bloomfield, Reminiscences of Court and Diplomatic Life, London, 1883, vol.1, pp.42-43.

197 'Notes on Gardens at Brighton' in his Gardening Magazine, 1842, p 347.

198 A. C. Benson, and Viscount Esher (eds.), The Letters of Queen Victoria (8 February 1845), 1908.

199 Ibid., p.36. Letter from Queen Victoria to Lord Melbourne, 3 April 1845.

200 J. C. Loudon, 'Notes on Gardens at Brighton', Gardening Magazine, 1842, pp.112-113, BHC, Brighton Pamphlets, vol. 5, PLO 17

201 Ibid. p. 113.

202 Poster, listing reasons why the Pavilion should be bought. BHC, History of Brighton, Pavilion Folio III.

203 The Brighton Magazine, 28 June 1850. BHC 11SB9 SM1.

204 Recreation Grounds Committee, Head Gardener's Report Book, ESRO. Vol .2.BD/D73/2, 9.2 1885.

205 J. G. Bishop, op. cit., 1900, p.116,.

206 Ibid, p.140.

207 The former stables had been converted into a concert hall in 1867.

208 Proceedings of the Pavilion Committee. Vol. 5, p.423, 23 November 1868.

209 Ibid. Vol. 2, p.440, January 1860.

210 Ibid. Vol.8, p.53, 11 May 1874

211 Ibid. Vol. 8, p.74, 8 June 1874.

212 Ibid. Vol.8, p.342, 5 July 1875.

213 Mrs Loudon, The Ladies' Companion to the Flower-Garden, London 1865 (first published 1841) p.373.

214 Ibid. Preface to 8th Edition, 1865. The book sold over 20,000 copies.

215 Mrs Loudon, The Amateur Gardener's Calendar, p. 340, London, 1857 (2nd edition) First published 1847.

216 Ibid. p. 324.

217 N. Baker (ed), The Lady's Country Companion. Published privately. Bungay 1984. p.353. First published 1845.

218 'Market Gardening under Glass', Gardener's Chronicle, pp. 415-6, April 1893, For further reading on the relationship between industrial development and garden aesthetics, see S. Lanmans article in the Journal of the Garden History Society, Vol .28, No. 2, pp.219-21.

219 Ernest Field, head gardener to Alfred de Rothschild, quoted in P. Hobhouse, Plants in Garden History, p.250, London, 1992.

220 Head Gardener's Report Book, Vol 1, p.67, 11 July ,1883. ESRO, DB/D73/1.

221 Proceedings of the Pavilion Committee, Vol. 11, p17, December 1879.

222 W. Watson (ed), op. cit. 1937, p.12.

223 Ibid. p.11.

224 Over a million Hindu, Muslim and Sikh soldiers fought side by side with British troops in France. After their withdrawal from the Front the hospital facilities at Brighton continued to function for British soldiers.

225 Proceedings of the Pavilion Committee, Vol.29, p.85, 1916.

226 Parks Department Superintendent's Report Book, ESCRO DB/D74/1 May 1919, p.126. In January 1919, 7,000 soldiers awaiting demobilisation, marched on Brighton Town Hall. Work and adequate housing were now seen as immediate necessities for the returned troops. P. Brandon and B. Short, A Regional History of England: the South East from AD 1000, p.360, London, 1990.

227 Brighton Herald, 23 July 1921.

228 Sussex Daily News, 29 July 1922.

229 Talk given by Mr J. Cheale, FRHS, an authority on landscape gardening, reported in the *Brighton Herald* 23,1,1921, it was his report on the state of the trees on the Western Lawns that MacLaren would implement. Joseph Cheal established his family's Lowfield Nurseries at Crawley and had successfully designed many parks, including the nearby Hove Park in 1903.

230 *Brighton Herald*, 17 December 1927.

231 Pavilion and Library and Sub Committee Reports, p 758, 1941.

232 Minutes of the Pavilion and Library Sub-Committee, February 1946.

233 The *Star* newspaper, 1953.

234 *Brighton Herald*, 27 October 1962.

235 *Evening Argus*, 26 October 1962.

236 *Evening Argus*, 12 February 1955.

237 *Brighton Herald*, 7 May 1955.

238 *Sussex Daily News*, 3 May 1955.

239 *Hortus Kewensis, Catalogue of Plants Cultivated in the Royal Botanic Garden at Kew by the late William Aiton*, second edition, enlarged by William Townsend Aiton, Gardener to His Majesty, London, 1810. In the preface Aiton remarks on the fashion for Botany, 'due to the number of plants continually sent home by your Majesty's collectors abroad … and the curious exotics poured into it of late by your subjects anxious to aid that munificent patronage which has rendered Botany a favourite pursuit among all the classes of Your Majesty's People … anxious to emulate his father's industry his son has never ceased to dedicate to the study of Botany the hours of leisure allowed him by his horticultural duties'. In the postscript Aiton acknowledges the help given by Sir Joseph Banks, 'not only for his judicious advice … but above all for the unceasing and unwearied attention … for nearly half a century to the best interests of the Royal Gardens at Kew, by which the increase of the collection, and consequently the value of this Catalogue, have been promoted to an eminent degree'. Mrs Fitzherbert in her retirement bought a villa (1811) on the Thames with a large garden, Sherwood Lodge, Battersea. She was a keen gardener and botanist, according to the *Brighton Gazette*, 24 September 1824, 'Mrs Fitzherbert … is one of the most scientific botanists in the kingdom'. W. H. Wilkins, *Mrs Fitzherbert and George IV*, London, 1905, vol.2, p.135.

240 Jessica Rutherford, the former director of the Royal Pavilion, discovered them in the Lord Steward's accounts for His Majesty's Household in the National Archives at Kew.

241 NA LS 11/4, p.370. In 1820, the year of George IV's coronation, £3. 15s. was paid for beer for Mr Nash's men. In other Royal garden accounts a similar celebratory expenditure occurs.

242 Letter, 14 August 1818. RA/GEO/33654

243 John H. Harvey, *Early Nurserymen*, Phillimore & Co Ltd, 1974, p.89.

244 Quote from Tim Smit, the driving force behind the restored gardens at Heligan and the Eden Project, quoted in Jane Owens and Diarmuid Gavin, *Gardens Through Time*, London, 2004, p.191.

245 The Hon Dr Miriam Rothschild, scientist and naturalist, was instrumental in persuading the Highways Agency to seed the verges of main roads, she had her own mix called 'Farmers' Nightmare', 'I realised with dismay that wild flowers had been drained, bulldozed, weed-killered and fertilized out of the fields'. T. Traeger and P. Kinmonth, *A Gardener's Labyrinth, Portraits of People, Plants and Places*, London, 2003, p.210. Loudon, the previous century realised that the new deep railway embankments then cutting through the country side could be transformed with dramatic tree and shrub planting.

246 Jane Austen, *Mansfield Park*. op. cit., p.218.

247 John Sales, Head of Gardens, National Trust, 1973, writing about the restoration of the Privy Garden, at Hampton Court. op. cit. 245, p.218.

248 The *Evening Argus,* 17 October 1950 reported that it took seven months to build the new tea chalet at an estimated cost of £1,000. It replaced a wooden tea kiosk on the North Lawn. The new 'flagged court' for tables and chairs was described as 'in Continental style'.

249 Robin Lane Fox, 2003. The gardening writer and garden master at New College, Oxford, op. cit. 245, p.98.

250 Virginia Woolf, 'Romance', 1917, repr. in A. McNeillie (ed.), *The Essays of Virginia Woolf*, volume 2 1912-1918, London 1987, pp.73-76. The passage relates to the romantic idea of a return to Nature.

SELECT BIBLIOGRAPHY

PUBLISHED SOURCES

Arnold, Dana (ed.), *The Georgian Villa*, Sutton Publishing, Gloucestershire, 1996.

Aspinall, A. (ed.), *The Correspondence of George, Prince of Wales*, 1770-1812, London 1963-1971 (eight volumes).

Austen, Jane, *Mansfield Park*, London, 2003 (first published 1814).

Austen, Jane, *Sense and Sensibility*, London, 2003 (first published 1811).

Batey, Mavis, *Regency Gardens*, Shire Publications, Buckinghamshire, 1995.

Benson, A. C., and Viscount Esher (eds.), *The Letters of Queen Victoria*, London, 1908 (three volumes).

Bisgrove, Richard, *The English Garden*, London, 1989.

Brandon, P. and Short, B., *The South East From AD 1000*, London, 1990.

Burke, Edmund, *A Philosophical Enquiry into the Origin of our ideas of the Sublime and Beautiful*, London 1773 (first published 1757).

Butler, E. M. (ed.), *A Regency Visitor, The English Tour of Prince Pückler-Muskau, Described in his Letters 1826-1828*, London, 1957.

Campbell-Culver, Maggie, *The Origins of Plants*, London, 2001.

Carter, G. and Goode, P. and Laurie, K., *Humphry Repton Landscape Gardener*, London, 1982.

Climenson, E. J. (ed.), *Passages from the diaries of Mrs Philip Lybbe Powys, of Hardwick House, Oxon. 1756-1808*, London, 1899.

Colvin, Christina (ed.), *Maria Edgeworth, Letters from England, 1813-1844*, London, 1971.

Conway, Hazel, *People's Parks*, Cambridge, 1991.

Croly, George, *The Personal History of George IV*, London 1841.

Dean, William, *Croome D'Abitot, Seat of the Right Honorable Earl of Coventry, to which are annexed an Hortus Croomensis, and Observations on the propagation of exotics*, Worcester, 1824.

De la Garde, Le Comte A., *Brighton, Scènes détachées d'un voyage en Angleterre*, Paris, 1843.

Dewing, David (ed.), *Home and Garden*, exhibition catalogue, London, 2003.

Dinkel, John, *The Royal Pavilion*, Brighton, London, 1983.

Hibbert, C. (ed.), *Louis Simond, An American in Regency England, the Journal of a Tour in 1810-1811*, London, 1968.

Hinze, Virginia, 'The Recreation of John Nash's Regency Gardens at the Royal Pavilion, Brighton', *The Journal of the Garden History Society*, Volume 24: Number 1, Summer 1996.

Hobhouse, Penelope, *Plants in Garden History*, London, 1992.

Hunting, Penelope, *Royal Westminster*, exhibition catalogue, London, 1981.

Hyams, Edward, *Capability Brown & Humphry Repton*, London, 1971.

Jacques, David, *Georgian Gardens, The Reign of Nature*, London, 1982.

'Lancelot Brown (1716-83) and the Landscape Park', in *The Journal of the Garden History Society*, Volume 29: Number 1, Summer 2001.

Lewis, W. S. (ed.), *Horace Walpole, Selected Letters*, Yale, 1973.

Loudon, J. C., *Treatise on Forming, Improving and Managing Country Residences*, London 1806 (2 volumes).

Loudon, J. C., *The Landscape Gardening and Landscape Architecture of the late Humphry Repton, Esq.*, London, 1840.

Loudon, J. C. (Sales, John, and Boniface, P.) *In search of English Gardens, The travels of John Claudius Loudon and his wife Jane*, London, 1988.

Loudon, Jane, *The Amateur Gardener's Calendar*, London, 1857.

Loudon, Jane, *The Ladies' Companion to the Flower Garden*, London, 1865.

Mansbridge, Michael, *John Nash, A Complete Catalogue*, London, 1991.

Marshall, William, *Planting and Rural Ornament*, London, 1796 (two volumes).

Mawe, T., and Abercrombie, J., *The Universal Gardener and Botanist*, London, 1778.

Morley, John, *The Making of The Royal Pavilion, Brighton*, London, 1984.

Mowl, Timothy, *Gentlemen and Players*, Sutton Publishing, Gloucestershire, London, 2000.

Musgrave, Clifford, *Royal Pavilion, An Episode in the Romantic*, London 1959.

Nash, John, *The Royal Pavilion at Brighton*. Published by the Command of and dedicated by permission to the King by His Majesty's dutiful Subject and Servant John Nash (popularly known as Nash's Views), 1826 (published 1827).

Neufforge, Le Sier de, *Receuil E'lementaire d'Architecture*, Paris, 1757 (three volumes).

O'Connell, Sheila (ed.), *London 1753*, exhibition catalogue, British Museum, London, 2003.

Owens, J. and Gavin, D., *Gardens Through Time*, London, 2004.

Papworth, John Buonarotti, *Rural Residences*, London, 1818.

Peacock, Thomas Love, *Headlong Hall*, London, 1927 (first published 1815).

Peacock, Thomas Love, *Melincourt*, London, 1896 (First published 1818).

Phillips, Henry, *Sylva Florifera*, London, 1823.

Phillips, Henry, *Flora Historica*, London, 1824.

Pückler-Muskau, Prince Hermann Ludwig Heinrich von, *Andeutungen über Landschaftsgärtnerei* (Hints on Landscape Gardening), Stuttgart, 1834.

Repton, Humphry, *Sketches and Hints on Landscape Gardening*, London, 1789.

Repton, Humphry, *Observations on the Theory and Practice of Landscape Gardening*, London, 1803.

Repton, Humphry, *An Enquiry into the Changes of Taste in Landscape Gardening*, London, 1806.

Repton, Humphry, *Designs for the Pavillon [sic] at Brighton*, London, 1808.

Repton, Humphry, *Fragments on the Theory and Practice of Landscape Gardening*, London, 1816.

Repton, Humphry, *Memoir* (unpublished draft) Part 2, with editorial comments and notes, 242 folios, British Library Add. MSS. 62112.

Robinson, William, *The Wild Garden*, London, 1894 (first published 1871).

Sitwell, O. and Barton, B., *Brighton*, London, 1935.

Somerset, Anne, *The Life and Times of William IV*, London, 1980.

Steuart, Sir Henry Bart., *The Planter's Guide*, London, 1828.

Stroud, Dorothy, *Capability Brown*, London, 1950.

Stroud, Dorothy, *Humphry Repton*, London, 1962.

Stroud, Dorothy, *Henry Holland*, London, 1966.

Stuart, D. and Sutherland J., *Plants from the Past*, London, 1989 (first published 1987).

Summerson, John, *The Life and Work of John Nash Architect*, London, 1980.

Taigel, A. and Williamson, T., *Parks and Gardens*, London, 1993.

Taylor, Geoffrey, *Some Nineteenth Century Gardeners*, London, 1951.

Temple, Nigel, *John Nash and the Village Picturesque*, Sutton, Gloucestershire, 1979.

The Queen's Gallery, Buckingham Palace. Exhibition catalogue, *Carlton House The Past Glories of George IV's Palace*, London, 1991-2.

Traegar, T. and Kinmonth, P., *A Gardener's Labyrinth, Portraits of People, Plants and Places*, London, 2003.

Trusler, John, *Elements of Modern Gardening or The Art of Laying Out of Pleasure Grounds*, London, 1800.

Trusler, John, *Practical Husbandry or The Art of Farming*, London, 1790.

Watson, William (ed.), *The Gardener's Assistant*, London, 1937, (six volumes).

Woodham-Smith, Cecil, *Queen Victoria, Her Life and Times, 1819-1861*, London, 1972.

BRIGHTON GUIDE BOOKS, NEWSPAPERS AND ARTICLES

Ackerson Erredge, J., *History of Brighthelmstone*, Brighton, 1862.

Bishop, John G., *The Brighton Pavilion and its Royal and Municipal Associations*, Brighton, 1900 (10th edition).

Brighton Gazette 1821-1985.

Brighton Herald 1806-1971.

Crawford's Library, *A Description of Brighthelmstone, a new guide for ladies and gentlemen visiting the place for health and amusements*, Brighton, 1794.

Loudon, J. C., 'Notes on the Gardens at Brighton', *The Gardening Magazine*, 1842.

Phillips, R., *English Watering Places*, Brighton, 1803.

Sickelmore, R., *An Epitome of Brighton, Topographical and Descriptive involving its history from the Earliest to the Present Period*, Brighton, 1815.

Sussex Daily News 1868-1956.

Sussex Weekly Advertiser 1749-c.1900.

Wilkins, W. H., *Mrs Fitzherbert and George IV*, London, 1905 (two volumes).

Wood, Heather, 'Number 8 Marlborough Row: A Royal Love Nest Revisited', *Royal Pavilion, Libraries and Museums Review*, July 2000.

Wright, C., *The Brighton Ambulator*, Brighton, 1818.

INDEX

ACKNOWLEDGEMENTS

I should like to thank the Friends of the Royal Pavilion, Art Gallery and Museums for supporting this publication. The building has been the subject of much study as have its extraordinary interiors and rightly so; they are unique. The garden is a new creation that fostered research into a 'lost' period of garden history. It has made a valuable contribution to the understanding and adaptation of naturalism to gardening. It has returned the final intended setting to the Pavilion so that the garden is now an integral part of the place. It would not have been possible without the garden historians who draw the threads of the past together, the garden designers who transfer the research to the ground and the gardeners who plant and tend the result.

At Brighton we were fortunate that Mavis Batey, then president of the Garden History Society, backed the project, taking up the reins and joining forces with the Sussex Historic Garden Society, to compile detailed research, that became 'The Regency File'. Mrs Batey kindly read through the text and made helpful suggestions. The planting was designed by Virginia Hinze, working with the Landscape Group of East Sussex County Council, who supervised the reconstruction. I thank her for her valued continuing help and commitment to the garden, her relentless attention to the principles governing the planting and for being a guiding force towards its future. Virginia has also made many helpful suggestions and is thanked for checking the nomenclature. The gardeners who do all the work are a small team of volunteers, under the direction of the head gardener, Robert Hill Snook. He is the only full-time gardener, the day-to-day professional eye, who also dispenses tips, advice and knowledge with an enthusiasm that is resilient to the pressures on the garden as a public space.

Brighton & Hove City Council successfully manage the garden after it was established through the assistance of many generous trusts with local and national bodies; The Ian Askew Charitable Trust; The John Coates Charitable Trust; East Sussex County Council; English Heritage; The Esmée Fairbairn Charitable Trust; The Friends of the Royal Pavilion, Art Gallery and Museums; John G MacCarthy and The Historic Gardens Trust (Sussex); The Hove and Brighton Urban Conservation Project; The Ernest Kleinwort Charitable Trust, the Priory Charitable Trust and the Knight Bequest.

We are particularly grateful to Her Majesty Queen Elizabeth II for permission to reproduce pictures and to refer to documents held in the Royal Archives, Windsor Castle. We appreciate the assistance of the staff at the Royal Library and Archives.

For support, help and encouragement with the text, its planning and revision, I thank Andrew Barlow, Keeper of the Royal Pavilion; it has been a shared journey. Maureen Simmonds has shown forbearance and good humour, sifting through documentation and putting all the drafts together. John Bevan has interpreted legal terminology, Allan Watkins and Adam Pollock have provided generous hospitality in London. Jessica Rutherford, Director of The Royal Pavilion (1985-2004) drove the project forward and helped edit the text with Stella Beddoe, the Keeper of Decorative Art at Brighton. The Conservation and Design team at the Royal Pavilion provided support from behind the scenes. Derek Lee, the designer, gave the pages a stylish, professional layout.

Finally I thank 'the book widow', my partner Robin, without whom it could not have happened.

All illustrations are from the collections of the Royal Pavilion, Libraries and Museums (© Brighton & Hove City Council) unless otherwise acknowledged. All the plant drawings and the reconstructed views of the site at different stages are the copyright of Mike Jones.

Photographs, pre-restoration from the Pavilion archives.
Pages 121, 125, 127, 128, 129, 134 Mike Griffin, Director of Parks and Recreation, 1974 to 1991.
During restoration, pages 135, 136, 137 Virginia Hinze.
Page 131 Lanthe Ruthen.
Present day Pages 53, 79, 82, and endpapers James Pike.
Page 129 Andrew Barlow.
All other photography by Derek Lee.

The following abbreviations have been used:
BL: British Library
BHC: Brighton History Centre.
ESRO: East Sussex Record Office.
NA: National Archives (formerly the Public Record Office): The Works Papers, Lord Steward's Papers (LS).
RA: Royal Archives, Windsor Castle: George IV's Accounts.
RPA: Royal Pavilion Archives (Brighton and Hove City Council): Plan Registry: records of works done on the Pavilion Estate (mostly post 1830); Crace Accounts 1802-1822, a typescript of ledger entries from the books of Crace and Sons; acquired by Messrs Cowtan and Sons when they took over the Crace firm in 1899; Proceedings of the Pavilion Committee: minute books from 1850.

friends

OF THE ROYAL PAVILION
ART GALLERY & MUSEUMS

This publication is supported by:

The Friends of the Royal Pavilion, Art Gallery and Museums
Registered charity no. 275242

Patron: HRH The Prince of Wales
Chairman: the Rt Hon. Lord Briggs

For further information on the aims of the Friends and benefits of membership
please contact:

The Friends Organiser
The Royal Pavilion
4/5 pavilion Buildings
Brighton BN1 1EE
Tel. 01273 290900/292789
Fax. 01273 292871
www.royalpavilion.org.uk
www.virtualmuseum.info